The Astrology
of Midlife
and Aging

*

OTHER BOOKS BY THE AUTHOR

Saturn in Transit: Boundaries of Mind, Body, and Soul

Retrograde Planets: Traversing the Inner Landscape

The Astrology of Family Dynamics

Venus and Jupiter: Bridging the Ideal and the Real

Where in the World: Astro*Carto*Graphy and Relocation

THE ASTROLOGY
OF MIDLIFE
AND AGING

✳

Erin Sullivan

JEREMY P. TARCHER/PENGUIN
A MEMBER OF PENGUIN GROUP (USA) INC.
NEW YORK

JEREMY P. TARCHER/PENGUIN
Published by the Penguin Group
www.penguin.com
Penguin Group (USA) Inc., 375 Hudson Street, New York, New York 10014, USA •
Penguin Group (Canada), 10 Alcorn Avenue, Toronto, Ontario M4V 3B2, Canada (a division
of Pearson Penguin Canada Inc.) • Penguin Books Ltd, 80 Strand, London WC2R 0RL,
England • Penguin Ireland, 25 St Stephen's Green, Dublin 2, Ireland (a division of
Penguin Books Ltd) • Penguin Group (Australia), 250 Camberwell Road, Camberwell, Victoria
3124, Australia (a division of Pearson Australia Group Pty Ltd) • Penguin Books India Pvt Ltd,
11 Community Centre, Panchsheel Park, New Delhi–110 017, India • Penguin Group (NZ),
Cnr Airborne and Rosedale Roads, Albany, Auckland 1310, New Zealand (a division
of Pearson New Zealand Ltd.) • Penguin Books (South Africa) (Pty) Ltd,
24 Sturdee Avenue, Rosebank, Johannesburg 2196, South Africa •

Penguin Books Ltd, Registered Offices:
80 Strand, London WC2R 0RL, England

Most Tarcher/Penguin books are available at special quantity discounts for bulk purchase
for sales promotions, premiums, fund-raising, and educational needs. Special books or book
excerpts also can be created to fit specific needs. For details, write Penguin Group (USA) Inc.
Special Markets, 375 Hudson Street, New York, NY 10014.

Library of Congress Cataloging-in-Publication Data

Sullivan, Erin.
The astrology of midlife and aging / Erin Sullivan.
p.   cm.
Includes bibliographical references and index.
ISBN 1-58542-408-0
1. Astrology.   2. Middle age—Miscellanea.   3. Aging—Miscellanea.   I. Title.
BF1729.M52S85   2005   2004062016
133.5—dc22

Printed in the United States of America
1   3   5   7   9   10   8   6   4   2

Book design by Tanya Maiboroda

While the author has made every effort to provide accurate telephone numbers and
Internet addresses at the time of publication, neither the publisher nor the author assumes
any responsibility for errors, or for changes that occur after publication.

To my grandson,
Sascha,
and my granddaughters,
Sienna and Brooklynn,
in whom the mystery of the future resides.

CONTENTS

LIST OF FIGURES

✳

INTRODUCTION
THE GREAT JOURNEY OF LIFE

MEDITATION 17

No man is an Iland, intire of itselfe;
every man is a peece of the continent, a part of the maine;
if a Clod bee washed away by the Sea, Europe is the lesse
as well as if a Promontorie were,
as well as if a Mannor of they friends, or of thine owne were;
Any Mans death diminishes me,
because I am involved in Mankinde;
And therefore never send to know for whom the bell tolls;
It tolls for thee.

—JOHN DONNE

THE CIRCLE OF HUMANITY

We might look back over eons and recognize our own personal self-development. Just as we emerge from the womb, into our infancy, through our developmental years, past adolescence, into our twenties, the Saturn return, the thirties, and the midlife transition, to maturity in the fifties and second Saturn-return phase and on into aging, so does the collective culture emerge and develop.

If we view life as a cycle, or a spiraling sequence of cycles, or a continuum, rather than a linear experience, then the relationship between the individual and the collective becomes quite intimate. Just as a culture evolves, so does an individual. From embryo—total psychic participation with the environment—to birth and through the initial stages of individuation into full ego, or awareness of self, and then the subsequent developmental periods, our phases are remarkably parallel to how we appear to have evolved as a collective world-humanity.

For a book on midlife and aging in our times and for times to come, it is important to draw on some history. Gaining a big-picture outlook helps us gain greater perspective on life's journey. Life is not necessarily, as the philosopher Hobbes said, "nasty, brutish and short," though certainly for those who are in areas of plague, war, drought, and other dire collective conditions, it is just that. For those who are not fated to endure the most horrible aspects of human existence *as a lifestyle*, it is incumbent upon them to find meaning and bring that meaning to their lives. In that way, through each person's individual consciousness, the collective consciousness evolves and is enhanced.

When we are undergoing significant rites of passage, and deeply immersed in our personal subjective world, it is difficult to perceive anything else. If this introspection leads to a greater understanding of the human condition, then it is a good thing. If it simply encourages spiralling into the depths of despair, this is not a good thing. Ultimately, there is nothing that can happen to any one of us that cannot happen to another.

The astrology timing used in the book is "generic": that is, the cycles of becoming and growing older are seen as being locked into the cycles of the ever-changing but rhythmic solar system. Within that ever-changing system, each planet has a regular, predictable cycle of return. The turning points in life are cyclic and ritualistic; if we treat them respectfully, and make the most of the times in which we find ourselves, then we are evolving. Even if it feels difficult and harsh, as long as there is movement and consciousness, it will be right for the times. How our lives as individuals evolve foreshadows how future individuals' lives will evolve. So making it through midlife, into elder status, and thence to old age is for each of us a personal journey, but it is also taken on behalf of our future generations and with the guidance of our ancestors.

Losing touch with our roots, the loss of a sacred foundation based in nature, the disparaging of our ancestors, the decline of emphasis on the family-of-origin as a safe place, and the loss of "place" for the aging and elder population—all these things are a concern because they are all links to the soul of humanity. To approach aging with a sense of honor and purpose means perceiving it as such: an honorable and purposeful task, one that is not over until it is over. There are many stories of successful aging, and because of that, it is important for us to hear them. You do not need to go to lectures or read books on it, but you do need to listen to your own elders in a way that is appropriate to their status as a person.

Historically, it seems that there was a time when we lived with our dead and the not yet born. I am not glamorizing the past nor projecting that it was "better"—but I am saying there are attributes from the past that are appropriate to carry over into new cultural growth; so, as a culture, we need to work toward reinstating our lives as an important and sacred journey.

Every generation bemoans the wreck of the next. And each new generation has to reject, in part, the previous generation as "over." Both of these views are natural, instinctive, and to some degree necessary— but they *are* the extremes. Ultimately, as with any revolution, some of the past is good to keep, and so is much of the future.

Resisting growth can create a rent in consciousness that virtually destroys one's personal link to one's deepest, inner Self, thus divorcing one from the sacred and divine aspect of life. Certainly we have seen this chasm in cultural development grow increasingly vast, even in the last half century. But this is not new, every age has warned about the terrible things that the "new age" will bring. And in turn each age as it apexes says it is the best one yet!

To gain a bit of perspective on this recurring phenomenon: even the ancient Greeks worried about it and fretted over the future. Hesiod, a

Greek agrarian poet who lived in the eighth century BCE, felt that cutting trees, making canoes, and plying the waters was unnatural and would result in all sorts of abominations against natural law. If only he knew—or maybe he *did*, in diachronous time—just how far his descendants would impose themselves upon nature's reserves. So, from writings over 2,700 years ago, we hear the fear of what the future will bring!

Because Hesiod was a farmer, his concerns were *environmental* and *ecological*. Both words stem from Greek origins, but they were not used in common language then as they are now. To experience the anxiety of any age past, all we need to do is read the poets, listen to the music, study the art and architecture, and, through this, understand the archetypal images underlying the culture. Concerns over the split between nature and culture are as old as written history, and only now are we really feeling the effects of desacralization and lack of progress emotionally and spiritually. Hesiod described this decline with a myth that posits that human civilization degenerated through five progressive races of man, beginning with a Golden Age of perfection and culminating, ultimately, in the age in which Hesiod found himself—and in which we still live today—the Iron Age, governed by Mars, god of war.

As our global culture has developed, so have we as individuals—our own small frames of reference, our families—undergone radical rearranging in just the last century, particularly in the last fifty years, and are now rapidly fragmenting into unique formations. All this change has brought about social chaos—which is the genesis of all things. The long-term result will probably be the re-forming of collective groups into new cultural, philosophical, and familial arrangements. The movement of the planets, as seen in a generational system, describes how this is so and how we, as individuals, operate within the big picture.

Coming into midlife and aging in the third millennium is more complex and stressful than even fifty years ago. The choices are both vast and limited. We have the possibility of more options, indeed, but the actual fulfillment of "more" is increasingly difficult for people, especially since the nuclear and its extended family have dramatically changed form in most Western societies.

So, if those of us Baby Boomers who are Pluto in Leo want to have a respectful and a respectable old age, then, as the first wave, we must lead the way. It is our own banner that will lead the next midlife group into their maturity. Indeed, as the Baby Boom generation is now (2005) well over fifty, the next generation, who have Pluto in Virgo, are in their midlife and are already feeling the pinch. If each of us leaves even a small legacy for spiritual and emotional growth, then it will have been a good job well done. If, however, we have left very little in the way of material and spiritual resources, then no job will have been done at all.

THE BIG PICTURE

The two illustrations (figures 1 and 2) in this introduction are images of the big picture, which is related to the immediate present and our own context. Since we cannot move forward completely alone, we are in the company of others. We are in the company of all who have gone before, and those who have not yet been. It is not necessary to grasp these diagrams to dive right into the book, but as you do move through the book, you might look back on them to get an expanded view of your midlife and aging.

The last 2,700 years have seen a remarkable evolutionary leap—technically, intellectually, and socially. However, this quickening of consciousness results now in a time in which a reconnection with natural law is urgent. The movement toward the epoch that is ruled by the sign Aquarius, and out of the twenty-one-hundred-year period of Pisces, marks a turning-point from a way of viewing the world collectively toward a new idealistic yet practical view. These epochal shifts are relative to our development as individuals within the collective *ethos*. As individuals, we cannot move beyond the parenthetical boundaries of the epochal vision.

The Piscean Age (ruled by Neptune, the epoch from circa 500 BCE through 2060 CE) has been a collective "womb" in which the compartmentalized and fragmented concepts of the body-mind-soul of humanity have gestated. The Aquarian epoch will mend the split between nature and culture. The global family—*unus mundus*—is in the last stages of in-

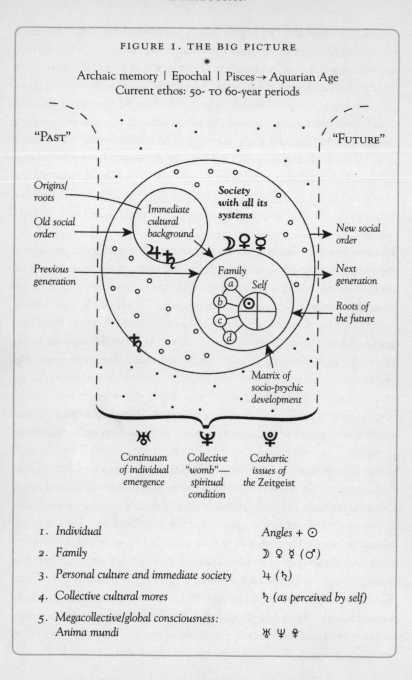

FIGURE I. THE BIG PICTURE
＊
Archaic memory | Epochal | Pisces→ Aquarian Age
Current ethos: 50- TO 60-year periods

"PAST"

"FUTURE"

Origins/
roots

Old social
order

Previous
generation

Immediate
cultural
background

Society
with all its
systems

♃♄

☽♀☿

Family

Self

a

b

c

d

⊙

New social
order

Next
generation

Roots of
the future

Matrix of
socio-psychic
development

♅

♆

♇

Continuum
of individual
emergence

Collective
"womb"—
spiritual
condition

Cathartic
issues of
the Zeitgeist

1. Individual   Angles + ⊙

2. Family   ☽ ♀ ☿ (♂)

3. Personal culture and immediate society   ♃ (♄)

4. Collective cultural mores   ♄ (as perceived by self)

5. Megacollective/global consciousness:
   Anima mundi   ♅ ♆ ♇

cubation, indeed, is in the birth canal. The approaching Aquarian epoch (ruled by Uranus) will demand a participatory relationship between the individual and the collective that is more mutually interdependent.

The maturation of the Aquarian Age will be both an evolution from and a reaction against Piscean monotheistic imagery, wherein someone else died for our sins or a distant, detached, and punitive male god is the one responsible for all earthly and mortal action, and a cultural *ethos* in which the collective is responsible for the individual. Ultimately this has resulted in a gradual fracturing of societies, and alienation of individual persons from not only their culture but also their families. Even more dire, it has alienated the individual from their own sense of self and divinity. Major transitional periods, such as we are experiencing collectively, are fraught with uncertainty, wherein unity is nowhere, and global disintegration threatens. Parallel to the collective disintegration lies the loss of identity of individuals. The liminal phases of epochal transition require a systemic "breakdown" so that a reformation can occur.

The present shift between the two epochs in the early third millennial period is one in which new and experimental ideas proliferate. We are, and will be for decades to come, straddling the epoch of Pisces and the coming epoch of Aquarius. Briefly, the essence of these two ages is:

- Piscean Age: individuals make up the collective; the collective itself is responsible for the individual; all are united under a single godhead.
- Aquarian Age: the collective itself is an organic entity; each individual within it is responsible for the whole of the collective; the divine is not one, but immanent in all things.

Naturally, this great leap will not in itself be complete until the era is fully matured—in about two thousand years! It is a journey of heroic proportions, to be undertaken one by one in the name of all. One must not hold one's breath but must continue to work within the existing systems to push them out beyond the boundaries of convention. This requires listening to a deep inner Self, as well as the *anima mundi*, the world-soul—both of which have innate intelligence.

As Joseph Campbell wrote:

The modern hero, the modern individual who dares to heed the call and seek the mansion of that presence with whom it is our whole destiny to be atoned, cannot, indeed must not, wait for his community to cast off its slough of pride, fear, rationalized avarice, and sanctified misunderstanding. . . . *It is not society that is to guide and save the creative hero, but precisely the reverse.**

Indeed, we have arrived at the time where the individual is responsible for the collective.

Thus, we might look at the big picture in this way (see figure 1):

1. We have an archaic memory, which is the underpinning of all human need for connection to one another—this is *time-out-of-mind*.
2. This in turn is contained within an *epochal signature* (the Ages: Virgo, Leo, Cancer, Gemini, Taurus, Aries, and our own Pisces Age, on through to the arriving Aquarian Age, etc.), which oversees the major images and symbols of the time.
3. Then there is the "current ethos," which is at this stage about fifty to sixty years in duration—the *Zeitgeist*. The *Zeitgeist* moves rapidly, however, and is a shape-shifter.
4. Within those temporal motifs exist the various ethnic cultures in the world.
5. The cultures are further subdivided into sects with social orders, religious beliefs, and historical context.
6. In that structure, we further differentiate into families. Families make up the small clusters within which, at long last, lies:
7. The individual.

Astrologically, and greatly simplified, we might see this depicted as follows (see figure 2):

---

*Joseph Campbell, *The Hero with a Thousand Faces*, 2nd ed. (Princeton, NJ: Princeton University Press, 1968), 391 (my emphasis).

The Zodiac: the circle of heaven, the *anima mundi:* world-soul. It not only defines the Great Year (the 26,000-year cycle of the precession of the equinoxes) but also the earth year, and the single day. In the individual sense, it defines the horoscope.

The Planets: archetypal human agencies seen against the backdrop of the zodiac. The planets are a global picture, seen in the same heavens from all points on earth at different times of day. The planets are rendered individual by *locus* in the horoscope: by degree, sign, and house.

The Houses (*oikos* is Greek for "family" and "house"): the sectors of the heavens as they are divided in accord with the time of day and location of birth, again in relation to the zodiac. They contain and mundify personal, inner experiences. Houses and families give immediate personal relevance to one's outer life. Dane Rudhyar called the houses the "realms of individual experience"; that the houses of an individual's horoscope *personalize* the global astrological/astronomical picture perfectly illustrates the individual's relationship and collusion within the collective consciousness.

FIGURE 2. THE DEVELOPMENT OF THE INDIVIDUAL IN THE HOROSCOPE

Macrocosm
anima mundi
"world soul"
↓
collective unconscious
↓
epochal period
↓
historical context
↓
specific social ethos
↓
Zeitgeist: *spirit of the times*
↓
personal culture/society of family
↓
family
↓
You
Microcosm

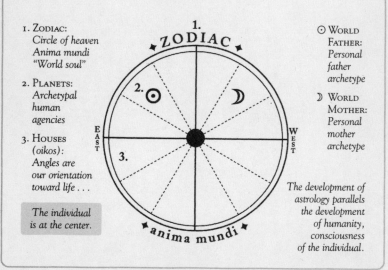

1. ZODIAC:
   *Circle of heaven
   Anima mundi
   "World soul"*

2. PLANETS:
   *Archetypal
   human
   agencies*

3. HOUSES
   (oikos):
   *Angles are
   our orientation
   toward life . . .*

The individual
is at the center.

☉ WORLD
FATHER:
*Personal
father
archetype*

☽ WORLD
MOTHER:
*Personal
mother
archetype*

*The development of
astrology parallels
the development
of humanity,
consciousness
of the individual.*

PART I

A Meeting at the Crossroads

CHAPTER 1

MEETING LIFE HALFWAY

When I had journeyed half of our life's way,
I found myself within a shadowed forest,
for I had lost the path that does not stray.
— DANTE ALIGHIERI, *The Divine Comedy**

THE introduction to *The Divine Comedy* may well be the most popular quotation to introduce any midlife discourse, and for good reason. Dante's words preface arguably the most brilliant and moving journey of a man in midlife who embarks on the universal quest for wisdom—and the divine lover. He invokes the Roman poet Virgil as his muse and traces the journey of the soul from damnation to salvation . . . from darkness to light.

It may seem a bit heavy-handed to use a quotation from Dante to describe the average individual today embarking on the "second half" of

---

*Dante Alighieri, *The Divine Comedy*, trans. Allen Mandelbaum (New York: Doubleday, 1995), Inferno, Canto 1, ll. 1–4.

life, but the archetypal midlife journey is, more often than not, a personal quest of equal numinosity.

Between the ages of thirty-seven and forty-one, in synchrony with the transit of the planet Uranus' opposition to its place in the horoscope, something mysterious takes place within the psyche. Further, Dante says: "I cannot clearly say how I had entered the wood; I was so full of sleep just at the point where I abandoned the true path" (ll 10–13).

The "sleep" with which we are full at the meeting at the crossroads is really the unconscious life that we have within and that is still unlived. Jung said that in this phase of life one is living the "unlived life," assuming correctly that midlife does not begin a time of rapid decay, loss of libido, and inevitable death but rather is a time in which one might recollect one's life and, from that recollection, build upon a profound understanding and conscious action toward the next phase of adulthood.

Obviously, midlife offers a rich array of potentials and opportunities to move forward in life rapidly and explore new paths and territories, with both a past to draw upon as well as a future to create. There are no maps of the territory—except the horoscope—so there are many emotional and psychological as well as circumstantial realms to pioneer within one's own self. With the perspective of life already lived, choices and direction can be much more focused.

Western civilization virtually lost sight of the power of age during the last century, in favor, especially, of the youth-oriented culture that was the post–World War II Baby Boom generation. The postwar generation is the largest and most globally influential generation ever to be born to date, but now as we enter the third millennium, that generation is well into midlife and facing the aging part. That is the part that needs to be brought back into significance if society as a global concern is to continue to civilize and to evolve holistically. To be a whole society, it must contain a full and recognized complement of infants and babies, children, adolescents, adults, midlifers, mature adults, seniors, and elders. And lest we forget, our ancestors.

If we are to have a full and alive society, the midlifer must find meaning and purpose. As with all other phases of life, midlife cannot be stereotyped but will embody archetypal modes. The archetypal experi-

4

ence is a way to describe the universal experience that occurs, but individually there is no model of how to walk "within the shadowed forest."

*

In all my years of working with people, and with various studies of psychology, I have found no perfect way of being; indeed, I have found only *ways of being*, and as many of those as there are people. The creativity that exists in the human psyche is phenomenal, and no aspect of the human condition is boring. Astrology is a moveable feast. It is based in a mobile system (the solar system) that never repeats itself. Because the solar system never repeats planetary patterns *exactly*, it is the perfect exemplar of all systems, including the human "system."

Like the solar system, one is always in motion, circumambulating the focus or core of one's being, and the relationships between our own "parts" or characteristics are in ongoing flux. These parts or psychic components can be likened to the planets, and the planets are never found precisely in the same array in toto. Nor are we.

In this system of planets, the "parts" are archetypal, such as survival instinct, rage, assertion, and passion—a Mars-like attribute—but how this vital life-force is honed and polished depends upon infinite possibilities, which include fate, family, society, culture, the global ethos, and so on. The greatest midlife task is to find within one's own self the most appropriate way to be with one's own self as one crosses the threshold to the second half of life and the parts—such as the Mars part—become increasingly individual and less universal, thus more who one is as a person, and less like the collective, or archetype.

Astrology contains a predictable system, in that it has a beginning—the natal horoscope—and from that origin, or *katarche*, as the Greek astrologers called it, we can time various rites of passage and trends of personal experience. How those turning points, rites, and passages are lived out depends upon myriad factors.

First, there is the epoch in which we live. Second, there are the social conditions and cultural mores in our personal realm. Third, we have to work within the family itself, and its system. Then, there is "me," the center of its own system or universe. (See figure 1.)

5

THE ASTROLOGY OF MIDLIFE AND AGING

The "cult of the individual," introduced by Freud, was further developed by Jung in the work he did on archetypes and the collective unconscious during his own midlife transition. Jung coined the term "individuation" to describe the *opus*, the "work," of the individual to determine who he or she actually is in the midst of all the influences that surround and infuse his or her life. The word *in-divid-u-ation* means "to be against dividing, or to bring unity to divided or separate parts." As a description of life unfolding, and individuals coming into their own, it is a perfect and economical word to describe the intensely personal experience of the individual as he or she sorts and gathers the "parts" of the psyche and becomes fully conscious.

For instance, rather than remaining infantile in our life-force, rage and assertion, we can "civilize" it as we grow. This is fostered by natural development and environmental pressure—family. So, by the age of seven, if we are hungry, we don't scream with infantile fear and rage till our bottle-food comes, but have cultivated increasingly more complex, socialized, *and* individual ways of getting our food.

At midlife, if we find ourselves frustrated, confused, restless, and unfulfilled, then it is time to shift gears into a reorganized system of order. Though one's focus—one's central being—does not change, one's relationship to it can—just as the ever-revolving planets alter their relationship within the solar system around the ever-stable Sun.

The planetary patterns, cycles, and timing used in this book are *generic*. That is, they are the regular, cyclic passages of each planet, beginning with their location in the natal chart—the *katarche*—at birth. This worldview truly describes the quality of the time within a set period of one's life. From the original starting point, the planets reveal the passages and junctures of a lifetime. And this book, in all three sections, describes those movements for an overview of personal development, or individuation.

THE ONE IN THE MANY

As one grows from infancy to old age, one becomes increasingly who one is. But this individuality in which we all take tremendous pride is not achieved alone. Thus, the context in which we become increasingly ourselves is in itself a system. Our personal growth cannot take place outside our family, culture, and global ethos, and even within that, the epochal tone of the era itself.

Becoming ourself, or individuating, is not a work done unconsciously, or only at certain times or ages. Up to a certain point in life, one is an active, ongoing experiment, and at certain stages, more demands are made upon one by one's own deep Self, one's seed of being, to become conscious and decisive about one's way of being. We can all recall "turning-points," times of absolute critical mass with profound psychological and spiritual change, when something has had to give. This book is about particular changes that are defined by the age brackets which the planetary patterns demarcate. I wrote about the rites of passage from birth up to the midlife transition in my book *Saturn in Transit: Boundaries of Mind, Body and Soul*, but this book goes further to delve deeply into midlife and beyond.*

Thus for the purposes of definition, I am concerned here with the timing and delineation of the crossover to midlife, and thence to maturity and into aging.

Choices are present, but only in the restricted context of possibility. In this era of "anything is possible," the work of self-consciousness and individuation is exceptionally complex and slippery. One can choose more actively to become who one is, or one can simply live according to the various rules of epoch, culture, caste, society, and family. The mystery of why some choose to individuate and others do not is simply that—a mystery. Nowadays, at any rate, more people are choosing to go the path of the "lived life" than to wallow in the sad and unfulfilled unlived life.

To my mind, there is no sin in an unexamined life, though the Greek philosopher Socrates said "The unexamined life is not worth living." There may be no sin in living without contemplation, but there is a periodic irruption from the unconscious or the inner Self, which senses that all is not right, life is not as rich and alive as it might be. Not everyone is

*Erin Sullivan, *Saturn in Transit Boundaries of Mind, Body and Soul* (York Beach, ME: Weiser, 2000).

an academic philosopher, but everyone has a philosophy. All people have codes of life and ways of rationalizing their lives, beliefs, and so on.

It is these very codes and beliefs that arise for examination most profoundly at midlife, as we make our way through the mysterious dark wood, having awakened from the long sleep that has brought us there so that we may deepen the quest for personal wisdom and growth.

LIMINALITY AND THE WITNESS

The space between "here" and "there" is a *threshold*. The threshold is a place of sanctity and sanctuary, according to the ancients; the *limen* (Latin for "threshold") is a space guarded by crossroads gods such as Hermes, Hecate, and Janus. The psychological limen is the place in the soul or the psyche in which we find ourselves when we are undergoing a life-change and a transformation. The older Greek word *limn* means "edge," and certainly the edge of the world was guarded by gods and goddesses, elements and supernatural forces. Nothing has changed in this archetypal place, only the manifestations have altered in accord with society.

Thus nothing much seems to have changed in the so-called modern world! We still have little mantras and chants we offer up to unseen deities when things are not as they once were or even as they seem. Together the words *limen* and *limn* have entered our language in common use such as *preliminary, eliminate, limit, limbo, liminal, subliminal,* and, lately, *liminality.*

The term *liminality* validates the state of not being who one once was but not yet who one is about to become. This place-in-between is a sacred location wherein we undergo a mysterious self-insemination, gestation, and eventual birth. We are prodded, urged, and often forced to grow and change. Ultimately, some knowledge on this path of self-development is essential. Faith in the gods is good, but faith in one's own deepest self, which knows who one is about to become, is better. Just as an orange pit knows it is to be an orange tree, not a grapefruit, so does the inner self know who I am to become from what I am.

To be plunged into liminality is characteristic of the midlife entry. The rise of the life unlived is marked first by excitement and anticipation, followed by a sense of loss and grief—and then on to the next phase along the path of individuation.

I have long thought of Uranus as the internal witness, that is, the aspect of the psyche that watches one's behavior. This component or aspect of the soul has no preconceived notions, no morality—no civilization, in fact. It is an objective and observing part of the mind. We encounter the witness often. In the midst of an emotional moment, for instance, or a sudden experience, part of the mind is observing how one is and what one is doing.

In times of crisis, the witness is the airy, rational, and seemingly split-off watcher of one's behavior. Essentially it allows one not only to take active part in one's life but also to observe it. So when we are in the midst of liminality, thresholding, a part of us is watching to see what we do. In that moment of clarity, we can make choices.

The planet Uranus represents the heavens; from that lofty place, we watch ourselves take part in our lives. The subject/object split—the bicamerality—of the mind is active in this witnessing experience. We are objectively observing and subjectively experiencing—simultaneously. Thus, when one has a Uranus transit to one's natal chart, one finds oneself oddly divided, yet capable of incorporating one's observed material into one's subjective self.

Thus, individuation is witnessing oneself in parts and either enfolding those parts into one's wholeness or separating oneself from an undesirable or outmoded part.

The Dweller on the Threshold—Uranus

Uranus is the first planet beyond Saturn's orbit, and the planet that demands individuation. In ancient Greece, Uranus was *Ouranos*, the Heavens themselves—not a god per se but more a realm, a domain, a place. That place was the dome of the sky, the place of the gods and the sacred birds. In the origin myths, Ouranos was the consort of Gaia, our Earth, and they created many children.

The planet Uranus was sighted on March 13, 1781. The Industrial

Revolution at this time changed the way ordinary people lived. The sightings of the modern planets, those beyond the visible boundary of our solar system, have occurred as the collective has achieved a new level of consciousness and innovation.

Uranus's inclusion in the solar system could be said to have precipitated the advent of individualism and the development of what we now call psychology and personal, individual choice. People who once were tied to family, country, and code were liberated to choose paths other than those dictated by birth order. The sighting of Uranus occurred in synchrony with the development of a type of consciousness we now take for granted, even disparage at times. Historically, Uranus has been associated with revolution, mass mutation, and transformation. It follows that as individuals become increasingly conscious, so does the collective, or society itself. Major social and global change only occurs after the individuals within it change—at least one, then another, until exponentially a collective shift occurs.

In natal astrology, as time has moved us on from its discovery, Uranus now is seen as the agency for the seed of the *process* of the development of our individuality. The operative word here is *process*; the ongoing means of becoming, not the outcome of that work. Uranus does not represent our individuality in itself, for that is the complex of DNA, character, environment, *and* horoscope in total.

Conscious individuality and therefore individuation itself are relatively new to humanity. Even just 150 years ago, a full life was often finished by age fifty or fifty-five or, for women in particular, at an even younger age. Now, early in the third millennium, conscious choice, changes in personal direction, and rapid advancement of information has propelled us to a collective threshold, where it is no longer generally acceptable to ignore the inner life and increasingly important to take responsibility for one's psychological and spiritual development.

To be an *individual* means one is measuring oneself against some collective norm. If I say "I am an individual," it means something altogether different from what it did, say, in 1750. In fact, the very word itself has undergone an evolution of meaning from the 1600s to now. Having begun as an impersonal concept of distinguishing some one thing within a group of things, it has become the cult cry of the last couple of decades of the second millennium.

By treating Uranus as the "planet of individuation," we are acknowledging its revolutionary aspect, in that Uranus is a key to evolution, innovation, and continuing creation. And in the natal horoscope, Uranus is a primary agency for the unfolding of Self or, simply, becoming who one is. With this in mind, the Uranus in the horoscope of someone born in 1875 was a very different agent from the Uranus in that of someone born in 1942, or 1999.

The collective psychology and sociology of the human race is changed only by the parts—the individuals—who make it up. The fact that there is a constant sloughing-off and reacquiring of individuals (deaths and births) within the collective means that it is never static, never constant, and always in developmental motion. And the development of personality, selfhood, and so on is not a smooth, predicable action. It is "lumpy," in that as skills are found, tried, and either used or discarded, on the whole, progress appears to be happening, but it consists of fits and starts, direct and retrograde motion. So when we think of the individual in the collective or socialistic group, we can only think of something interactive, each colluding consciously and unconsciously to develop both within and without.

On Being Made Up of Our Future— Promethean Transits

There is a turning point in life at which our future draws us on more actively than our past pushes us forward. Astrologically, this can be described as a Promethean perspective on transits. For example, if Pluto will transit your Sun in six years, even if you do not consciously know that, your psyche does. The constellating power and force that exists already in future time is at work in present time. Preparation for one's so-called future is done in the now. As a result of this phenomenon, a person is a complex of past, present, and future all at once. Being drawn on by the future becomes increasingly a motivation as one moves into midlife, and beyond it.

Midlife is a life-phase, with a distinct rite of passage, and threshold crossing which leads to the age span from around age forty to sixty— roughly, the period from the half-Uranus to the second Saturn return.

That two-decade span has within it many generic cycles and transits that mark turning-points and culminations, leading rather smoothly to the period after the second Saturn return, which marks the next stage of life—elderhood. Since astrology focuses on not only generic cycles but also individual, personal cycles, one sees various generic patterns that are made individual by the natal horoscope's own unique unfolding, and cycles and patterns explicated out from transits, and so on.

So, yes, midlife is a stage that all people enter, pass through, and depart from, but everyone does it differently, according to his or her own inner imperatives, and this is shown clearly by the individual transits, progressions, and so on.

Once the ever-arriving "future" is swallowed by the present, there is a new future—to constellate yet more of who one is becoming, and this creates the tension of the life-force. The elusive consciousness of the future is a great part of the *divine discontent* that lies within the soul; this can become either a neurosis or a stimulus for anticipation of returns on one's life investment—with all the associated risks, unknowns, and hopes and fears.

As I mentioned earlier, the concept of the midlife crisis is relatively new to human consciousness; pre-Uranian societies on the whole did not experience it like modern culture does now. The idea of a meeting at the crossroads of life, at such an advanced age as forty or so, is not altogether a historical thing, though it has played a role in many creative people's lives.

If we consider a life-expectancy and divide it cleanly in half, midlife for the average man or woman in the 1700s was closer to thirty than forty. One's first Saturn return would have been in one's midlife. However, with the changes in health and activity, work, and lifestyle, that median age has grown to incorporate Uranus's half-cycle. Whereas prior to Uranus's sighting the life-expectancy mark for the average individual was a *maximum* of around fifty-eight—the second Saturn-return phase—now, in privileged societies, life-expectancy is extended almost to the Uranus return of eighty-four!

So what is this mysterious experience that is now common currency? Astrology has its way of defining life-cycles and phases of growth and development, and the first quantified indicator of midlife is the transiting Uranus's opposition to itself between the ages of thirty-eight and forty-five, depending on the natal position/sign of Uranus.

People born in the 1930s, 1940s, and 1950s have the half-Uranus earlier, between ages thirty-eight and forty-one, while those born in 1900–1920, and again in the 1960s, 1970s, and 1980s have it at the later age, between forty-one and forty-five.

This is because Uranus has an eccentric orbit, which means those with Uranus in Scorpio, Sagittarius, and Capricorn have their half-Uranus at the later age, in the early forties, while those with Uranus in Taurus, Gemini, and Cancer have their half-Uranus earlier in life, in their late thirties, or at forty in the case of Cancer. All the other signs fall in the median age of forty-two.

To put it simply, when transiting Uranus reaches its first opposition to itself is when we approach the threshold of midlife. That initial opposition is very likely to be followed by two more passages over the subsequent eighteen-month period, during Uranus's annual retrograde cycles. And there are numerous rearrangements of the other transits during that eighteen-month to two-year period that offer much information about what it is that is most at issue.*

Carl Jung thought it was a great mystery why some people fell apart at the seams at midlife, and others did not. He pondered this phenomenon before his own thoroughly classic—thus fulfilled—midlife transition. Jung himself had a profound midlife experience, filled with numinous visionary experiences; an anima "possession" that trans-

*See Erin Sullivan, *Retrograde Planets: Traversing the Inner Landscape* (York Beach, ME: Weiser Books, 2000).

lated into a muse; a *volte-face* and thorough examination of his previous patterns and beliefs; his loss of reverence and affiliation with his mentor, Freud; and his work on the archetypes—one of the most stable and profound concepts he ever developed. Out of his midlife came masses of creative work and some of his best work, after all was said and done.

There appear to be two extremes:

1. Total collapse of previous beliefs, perceptions, and action, which results in the individual scrambling to correct the situation and revert to the past and maintain his or her status quo, sometimes even reverting to old ways of being.
2. An awakening to potential and conscious desire to change patterns and move toward a new level of life experience, which results in a major perceptual shift, along with acquiring new skills and interests in life.

Between those two polarities lie typical experiences of midlife and the half-Uranus cycle. The most common experience is described as a time in which all previous ways of being simply stop being comfortable or useful. Individuals find themselves looking inward if they have never done so while on the other hand looking outward for increasing meaning in action.

Ultimately, the crossing of the threshold into full-blown midlife is chaotic and requires a great deal of work. Being thrust not only out of one's comfort zone of the "past" but also catapulted toward an unknown future is unnerving, even to the most sophisticated people. In fact such persons' midlife can be the most dramatic, due to the number of options and opportunities made available to educated, adventurous, traveled, innovative people. More life experience results in more alternatives, which, in turn, create the possibility for too many "unborn" potentials that arise in midlife!

The groundwork for conscious midlifing was established by the Pluto in Leo generation. They were the first in modern times to decide that the previous generations' simplistic "red sports car and affair with the twenty-year-old" was *not* quite elevated enough for their taste. Hence they rolled out the therapies, created the workshops, and wrote the books—and turned midlife into a cool, if still earth-shattering, thing.*

This is good. That the Pluto in Leos took it upon themselves collectively to mine this hidden resource is quite appropriate. For Leo is the sign of the Self, and Pluto is the planet of existential experience. Thus, they not only had their midlife crises but capitalized on it too.

This is not to say that midlife crisis and the transition toward maturity did not occur prior to 1939. Indeed, all biographies of creative and progressive individuals through history tell of a time in midlife when the historical person underwent what appears to be a classic crisis, and reevaluation of life, love, and work. Jung, Freud, Byron, Marie Curie, Churchill, Gandhi, Joseph Campbell, Marie Louise Von Franz, June Singer, Mother Teresa—all their life stories include a meeting with the opposite and a "dark night of the soul." The fact that they underwent those inner/outer shifts is precisely why we know about these people to this day. There have been many creative people who do not survive their midlife crises and either crash or die—the *puer* and *puella* types, in Jungian psychology, are the exemplars of those who simply cannot, and ultimately will not, cross the threshold of midlife.

The idea of an inner life and magical interior experiences did not begin with Freud, but certainly modern psychoanalysis did. From the ancient Greek plays, the tragedies and the comedies, we know that ancient human beings began to interiorize their previously god-based external psychology over 2,500 years ago. However, Freud was the innovator of the idea that the inner life, the *psyche*—the Greek word for "soul"—was the impetus underlying all behavior. What Freud did *not* do was think that anyone over the age of fifty still had something to do—psychologically, that is. Freud depended almost wholly on the personal history of a patient; he advised analysts against taking on patients over the age of fifty

---

*Pluto in Leo generation: Pluto entered Leo on August 4, 1938, and moved out of Leo in October 1956, when it entered Virgo. See figure 6, on page 124 for a Pluto generational overview. Throughout most of this time period, the planet Neptune was in Libra, which creates a cultural ethos of idealistic and youth-oriented values. This generation also experienced, by and large, an acceleration of opportunities and privilege—at least in most of the "Westernized world." By the turn of the third millennium, however, this changed drastically.

because he believed that the "elasticity," or the capacity for great mental changes to occur, decreased or even ceased after that age. Certainly after Freud reached that age, his own elasticity appeared to arrest, but even so, his originating idea has remained profoundly seminal for contemporary attitudes to aging. That is, he was a man of his time and has since been transcended by time.

So it was left to Jung to continue the legacy of the unconscious to which Freud had opened the door. Appropriately so, as each generation must take the wisdom and the torch of the previous one and carry it further, illuminating the future.

Jung found in his own personal life that at fifty, growth, rather than stopping, increased in intensity and interiority. The midlife and post-midlife individual began a process Jung called individuation; and only after midlife could one truly begin the remarkable work of becoming who one is. Interestingly, Jung paid very little attention to one's childhood and origins, thinking that if a child exhibited neurotic traits or disturbance, it bore looking at the parents' psychology!

Jung's interest in the problems of adult development originated with his own midlife crisis when he was thirty-eight. Jung dove headlong into his own midlife, and surfaced first with his work *Symbols of Transformation*.* Facing an inner life that at times threatened his own sanity, he explored regions of the unconscious as intrepidly as any pioneer heading to the edge of the earth, or to the inmost reaches of the soul. His grappling with the midlife forces was profound and rich, leaving us with a new way of approaching twentieth-century psychology.

Jung was thirty-seven when his descent into his own psyche began. He was married and had children and a good practice—both clinically and privately. However, "something happened" in the years 1913—1915. Jung had natal Uranus at 14° Leo. His ascendant was between 2° and 4° Aquarius. In 1913, Uranus transited his ascendant at 4° Aquarius, and by 1914, he was in the midst of his first Uranus opposition! So midlife began for Jung at the half-Uranus, as it does for all of us. And in

*Carl Gustav Jung, *Symbols of Transformation*, vol. 5. Bollingen Series XX (Princeton, NJ: Princeton University Press, 1956).

his case, it was at the age of thirty-eight. In the autumn of 1913, he had a prophetic dream about the Great War (yet to arrive), and that precipitated his immersion into the unconscious and the archetypal realm.

In his memoirs, he says of this period: "I was frequently so wrought up that I had to do certain yoga exercises in order to hold my emotions in check. But since it was my purpose to know what was going on within myself, I would do these exercises only until I had calmed myself enough to resume my work with the unconscious."*

In his essay "The Stages of Life," he says:

But we cannot live the afternoon of life according to the programme of life's morning; for what was great in the morning will be little at evening, and what in the morning was true will at evening have become a lie. I have given psychological treatment to too many people of advancing years, and have looked too often into the secret chambers of their souls, not to be moved by this fundamental truth.†

Keep in mind that Jung's exploration into his own midlife began in 1913, and he wrote "The Stages of Life" in 1930, and though his expression of the concepts is quaint, the essence of the ideas is archetypal, and immutable. "The very frequent [i.e., classic] neurotic disturbances of [midlife] adult years all have one thing in common: they want to carry the psychology of the youthful phase over the threshold of the so-called years of discretion" (para. 776).

We have benefited from a more recent psychological shift by openly acknowledging the necessity for rites of passage in adulthood. About that, there is no question! However, the Pluto in Leo generation's midlife is not a prototype of every generation's midlife but an extreme exemplar from which a template for all life's transitions can be cast.

---

*Carl Gustav Jung, Memories, Dreams, Reflections (New York: Random House, 1965), p. 177.
†The Structure and Dynamics of the Psyche, in Collected Works, vol. 8, Bollingen Series XX. (Princeton, NJ: Princeton University Press, 1960), para. 784.
   "The Stages of Life" was published in Modern Man in Search of a Soul (New York: W. S. Dell and Cary F. Baynes, 1933).

Often astrologers will meet a client the first time during his or her midlife—the numbers of half-Uranus people that telephone or email for a consultation are noteworthy. The job of the astrologer is to put the client's life in perspective and to aid the client in making important decisions by outlining their timing through transits and various other symbolic planetary movements as those refer to their natal chart.

The cycles and returns of all planets are important, but the most significant transits at midlife are the Uranus opposition to itself, and Saturn's opposition to itself at mid-midlife.

The issues that arise at midlife are tailored to each individual's growth needs. Various choices or options arise. Thus the options of people with Pluto in Virgo or Libra or Scorpio or Sagittarius and on through the zodiac will be in accord with the times, and also with their own future needs.

At midlife and adolescence one is most conscious of one's mortality as a critical phase of maturation. The adolescent is often careless and longing for death, as the poems and stories and behavior of adolescents reveal. This is a poetic state, an important phase of self-discovery, when a young person first explores his or her inner reaches. Adolescent "immortality" is a state in which both anxiety and elation propel the adolescent to test his or her powers and defy the laws of life—most often this experience is metaphorical, but it also can be dangerously literal.

In contrast, the midlife person becomes conscious of mortality through life experience, not fantasy: through losses of friends and elders in the family, and clear messages that the body begins to relay. And so the work begins for the maturing individual.

Midlife—all life, in fact—is a process, it is not an event. Thus, the work involved in midlife is an ongoing and imaginative operation, marking a time when the quickening of conscious individuation occurs more profoundly and in more rapid sequence than at other times in a life. There are several quickening periods in life—the ages of two, twelve, twenty-one, thirty, forty, fifty-eight, seventy-two, eighty-four, and so on. For unique personal and individual timing, astrology and its transits to your natal chart will illuminate specific periods of quickening in your personal individuation process, and in that way will put the experience of <NOW> in brackets of history (the past) and possibility (the future).

CHAPTER 2

THREE STAGES OF THE MIDLIFE TRANSITION

IN ASTROLOGY, the midlife transition presents some distinct features. These aspects of midlife are not clocked in quantitative ways, nor are they in perfect sequence, but they are characteristic of the twenty-year transition toward the next crossover age—after the second Saturn return (ages fifty-eight to fifty-nine).

The second Saturn return is an astrological timing point, as is the Uranus opposition. Although the solar system itself and each of its planets have precise cycles and patterns, that are predictable and quantifiable ad infinitum, we do not. Just because a planet makes a transit does not mean that like a clock one ticks over into that next second, minute, or hour of planetary experience. It happens, yes, and is frequent, definitely, but it is rare to experience a major generic cyclic transit as an event. Such a transit inaugurates a process; it does not trigger an event per se.

Astrology is a brilliant metaphor for the human system, as it is a brilliant metaphor that aligns its reality with such other systems as the stock market, the political climate, and the chaos of weather patterns. But people, like weather, are unique to their own moment in time, location, and prevailing climate, and thus are not predictable. They are *likely* to do a certain thing, or *inclined* to act out a thing, or even *fated* to do so, but astrology can offer the time frame—in this instance—of transitional experiences as they occur in a generic pattern.

After more than thirty years of study, teaching, consulting and theorizing, I have come to see my work with astrology as "whole system astrology." Nothing is isolated. The solar system—hence we in ourselves—is completely interdependent. No one element is separate from its whole organization. We integrate and are integrated within the system synchronously. Something I have learned is astrology is *not* everything, but is a brilliant exemplar of the motion and continuum of life, a perpetually changing but familiar pattern. It is not the only system to depict this harmony, but it is the system I resonate with as a primary focus. Within the motion and harmonics of the astrological system lies the key to a unified theory.

The stories I use, in all my books, of both clients and well-known creative people are there because they are exemplary manifestations of human will coupled with cosmic design. I tell these stories to illustrate how vast and various are our choices—many of them unconscious, instinctive, or fated—in the clockwork of our systems. Like an apple seed that knows it is to be an apple, and not an orange, the psyche, the human seed, knows who it is to be but expresses versions and shapes during its evolution from birth to death.

Apple seeds *will* become apple trees and bear fruit, but they need care and nurturing to do so. The seed itself has an archetypal design, and that design can be corrupted by weather, animals, blight, and so on. But it can also be enhanced and brought to perfect fruition with care—pruning, trimming, and picking the fruit at its point of perfection. As with all of nature, such caring is needed too, and as the tree grows, so shall the fruit form.

Thus, I will outline many characteristic facets of midlife and, later in the book, the process of aging, but for each individual they are *not* as precisely timed as are the interpretive sections in the book. If you or your client, or your mother or friend, have not undergone the "required" changes, attitudes, or situations at the precise moment of Saturn opposite Saturn at age forty-four to forty-five, you or they have not necessarily "blown it" or missed something. Many factors would feed into such a divergence, not all of them negative.

We are not clocks, I repeat, yet there is indeed a precise date at which astrological midlife begins: the day the planet Uranus first transits opposite to the place it is in the birth chart. Depending on who you are, your background, your family, your cultural imperative, your DNA/genome structure, your place in the global ethos, and myriad more facets of the external world, you will experience this phenomenon of exact transit of Uranus in a way that is specific to your seed-need—your Self, in other words.

I have an immense respect for people and their singular individuality. That is why I have spent so many years studying astrology and the human experience. I am constantly amazed and impressed with the power of the human spirit and its *nemesis*—its "righteousness," according to the Greek meaning. That is why I attract a certain type of person as a student or a client. And *nemesis* is what we meet on the path of individuation—a very specific and personal experience or realization that irrevocably moves us forward to meet our future selves.

I would no more typecast a person by an astrology term or cycle than I would have tried to force my children to be me instead of them. I am fascinated by the creativity in the soul, the eternal ingenuity of the mind, and the strange and inexplicable interventions of fate. I believe wholly in both fate and free will. I do not see, as many do, a split between the two but feel them to be inextricably entwined—a both/and kind of thing. Our life is not found in either a particle or a wave—perhaps in a "wavicle"?

There is too much "You are destined to be in difficult relationships because you have Pluto conjunct your south node in the seventh house." This is so old, so *over* in the third millennium, that it is frightening to think that it is still being swallowed wholesale by hapless "clients" or web browsers. This is dangerous astrology—not because of the obvious moral or ethical reasons, or that it is scary stuff and is negative input into a seeker's soul, but simply because it is *wrong*.

There, I've said it—that kind of astrology is wrong. Everyone is destined to have some kind of difficult relationship in the course of life, because relationships are difficult, and often we are biologically and psychoactively attracted to sexy people who stimulate our "danger zones"; and relationships are multileveled; and it is unlikely that there is one person who has not had a challenging friendship, parent, sister, or colleague.

And we are not perfect; thus our relationships are not perfect. Ideally, we learn from our experiences of pain and difficulty, and move on to less threatening relationships. If someone is repeating, over and over, a "bad" relationship *pattern*, then they need to analyze this, not blame the north node or some other esoteric thing but get to that dark and scary place within themselves that requires this test.

Now, this is what Pluto conjunct the south node in the seventh house *could* mean: seek the darkest side of yourself from within, and see how it might be projected out and thus a part of the negative partnering pattern; see how you might even be excited by the more steamy, brutal aspect of intimacy! One's natal horoscope is one's own, but in the course of life and relating, one must come to terms with one's own role in life's experiences.

In writing the interpretive material, there is a soul struggle within: how can I say something that is as true individually as it is universally? Well, it is hard; in fact it is near impossible. So I have come to rely on the truth that lies in what I call whole system astrology, because it helps people to realize that they are part of a vast complex in which a web of interactive systems are at work. And, astrology is the closest to measuring—delineating—that which we explicate from the system.

With all this in mind, let's look at some of the phases and transitional experiences along with some of the terms and conditions that we all undergo, but are personally translated into our own individual experience.

MIDLIFE STAGES

Separation, liminality, integration. Only three, you might ask? Well, these three phases do not come nicely sequestered and consecutive. It is likely that one has aspects to one's natal chart occurring simultaneously with the half-Uranus cycle. (I call the Uranus opposite Uranus the "half-Uranus," for obvious reasons.) Nonetheless, if one is experiencing transiting Pluto conjunct the Ascendant over an eighteen-month to two-year period, and also Saturn conjunct natal Venus, and then the half-Uranus intrudes into this already loaded condition, we could hardly say that the half-Uranus is "doing" everything associated with the midlife crossover.

What we might say, however, is that the individual in this hypothetical example is experiencing the half-Uranus—the person's universal formal entry into midlife—in context with the powerful personal requirement of dropping all facade, burning off the dross of personality (Pluto to the Ascendant), while seriously reevaluating priorities in relationships and personal worth (Saturn transiting natal Venus).

Too, the three midlife stages are not always distinct, in that one can feel both split or separated and liminal simultaneously. Too, the entire life is one of integration, so there are periods in which one feels simultaneously liminal *and* integrative—this can be on a monthly basis or an hourly basis—but, as with all captive cycles, there is a longterm "plan" in process, and over time, all three stages will be undergone. Having reached, myself, the "integration" phase according to the astrological cycle, I actually feel that integration occurring on a purely instinctive, natural level. I still at times feel a bit liminal, but it is specific to me— my life issues or work—not to my stages of age and growth according to the midlife timing.

There are definite stages that need attention, and the common tendency for people is to put off, procrastinate, and delay at the threshold of these stages. The struggle at the threshold of change is part of the archetypal "heroic journey"; we all have some reason to stay just another minute, hour, year at the threshold of age or adventure. Again, this is "normal"; when it becomes neurotic or pathological, then we can say a stage is being ignored, and the hero is ignoring the call, and thus misses out on some of the wealth and riches to be gained by taking that courageous step across the threshold.

So with that caveat, here follow the primary phases of midlife.

I. SEPARATION—FROM THE SELF

A profound sense of interruption occurs in the psyche. The sense of separation from what is known might be totally interior, but equally it might be instigated by an external event. This phase of onset of midlife is a "shock." This experience can irrupt overnight or creep up slowly, encroaching on one's confidence and giving one the sense of disintegrating and vanishing from previous ways of being.

Murray Stein, the author of *In Midlife*, says: "At midlife there is a crossing-over from one psychological identity to another. The self goes through a transformation."*

The most common description I have heard is as follows: "Suddenly, everything was different. I felt restless, unfulfilled, dull, exhausted, fed up, that my life had been marking time, that I had not done what I was supposed to do, but I don't know what that is!" Okay, we might feel that in the middle of a Tuesday afternoon, too. But it passes. This won't pass. This demands attention and focus. The half-Uranus concurs with these statements; indeed, you *are* restless, unfulfilled, dull, exhausted, and so on.

What is it that one is actually separating from? One's spouse? One's job? One's heretofore passions? From the "bad" society in which one lives? Perhaps, but those are symptoms, not the cause. The cause is present in the symbol of Uranus. You are separating from yourself. Your deep Self has said, "You have lived thus for this many years, and that is fine, but now you must separate from that ego-persona and get to the work of maturing toward who you are to become." That one needs, *must* change shape at midlife does not negate the entire past or invalidate one's whole life to date.

Again, Stein says:

By the time that midlife comes, a person has usually settled into familiar psychological patterns and is ensconced in work and family. And then, suddenly, a crisis: you wake up one day and you are unexpectedly out of gas; the atmosphere of personal ownership

*Murray Stein, *In Midlife: A Jungian Perspective* (Dallas, TX: Spring Publications 1983), p. 3.

stinks, the sweet milk of achievement is sour; the old patterns of coping and acting pinch now. . . . Where did it go?" (p. 4).

It is not that what you have done with your life or who you appear to be is bad or wrong or that you have wasted time (well, you probably have, but that isn't what I mean here). The separation is from *who you used to be*. Full stop. This does not readily become who you are now, or who you are to become. The stage of separation can be a month, it can be two years, it can last the whole midlife period—depending on your horoscope, you, and the world you have lived within for the previous thirty-eight to forty-two years.

However, for the sake of formula, the initial phase of separation consists of the period between the first half-Uranus through the Saturn opposite Saturn at age forty-five.

Meanwhile, separation in the astrological sense is activated by the transit of Uranus to your natal Uranus. Thus all facets of your nature that are expressed in your whole being as both Self and Persona seem diminished and ineffectual. At the very least, one is called to face an unknown future.

One of the most powerful features of Uranus is "witnessing." Uranus is the heavens—not a god, not a deity, but a *place*. A place high up from which earthly activity is observed. You will find yourself *watching* yourself, witnessing your own behavior and experience from a lofty vantage point. Uranus transits have the effect of allowing the objective mind to clarify subjective experiences. In a sense, you are thrust into a place where you are objectively experiencing your subjective life. This is why there is so much self-absorption and internal self-referencing in the first stage of midlife.

It is essential to your development to allow this distancing, observing, and clarifying of your personal self—your needs, actions, habits, and individual characteristics. The psyche is demanding that you do so. Dreams will come that compel you to see yourself as someone in conflict or someone who has to deal with something or someone who has died or gone "under." The conflict is healthy, and the resolution of that conflict is essential. Indeed, all of life is a resolution of conflict, and the higher ground is won by interacting with that inner dialogue.

It is easy to understand and sympathize with people who literally split off, become "different," and are described by their cronies as behaving "uncharacteristically." Inconstant feelings and actions are part of the separation process. The genuine sense of conflict that arises can refine your maturing character and thus your choices for the future.

It is impossible, absolutely not possible, to be out of character—though people say they are or that other people are. One can *not* be uncharacteristic. Even if, for example, you never lose your temper, you are always serene by nature, and your personality is imbued with the peaceable kingdom itself—if, when you blow up, you say "I wasn't myself." I would answer, "Well, then, who on earth were you?"

For example, Rupert has turned forty. He begins to express moods, feelings, wants, needs, or behavior that he's never before shown. We say, "Oh, he isn't himself, something's "got into him," and "Well, he'll come to his senses soon enough." In fact, what is happening to Rupert is he *has* come to his senses. His senses are telling him that he's ignored them long enough, and he continues to ignore them at his peril.

Ideally, if we could all have a paid leave for rites of passage of this nature, the world might be a less alarming place. Rupert has spent twenty of his forty years striving for recognition in the field of law. In an ideal world, he has achieved it and is offered a judgeship. His ego and persona are thrilled to pieces, and he is rightfully honored by this distinction. What his *deeper Self* is doing is another story. His deeper Self, though not contradicting his appointment, is questioning the soulful underlying meaning. That is, it has become more important to Rupert not *what* he does but *why* he's doing it.

MOTIVE—THE "UNLIVED LIFE"

Rupert is midlifing. He's well into his half-Uranus phase, and as his process of individuation is quickening, he feels a sense of uncertainty, whereas prior to this he never has. (Rupert has no planets in water signs.) Rupert is having moods and feelings. He's sad. There is no "reason" to be sad. He's supposed to be happy. Or so his conscious mind thinks. In reality, Rupert isn't sad because his life is a drag and people don't like him, or his wife is leaving, or he's a failure and hasn't lived up to his potential. He's sad because he has never experienced feelings in a "feminine" way before. He left that up to the projections; that is, his mother, wife, and volatile teenage daughter.

Now Rupert is crying at the drop of a hat. He becomes embarrassed. He thinks he must be having a breakdown. At his wife's (the contrasexual projection or anima) encouragement, he goes to an analyst. He discovers he's not alone, that all over the world men are reading Robert Bly's *Iron John*, *The Fire in the Belly* by Sam Keen, and *The Power of Myth* by Joseph Campbell.

He becomes more conscious of his inner life, his Self, his interior motivations. He obsesses. There has been nothing immoral or greedy about his brilliant rise in his legal career. He does his work because he loves it, he loves justice, and he loves to win; he donates time *pro bono* to the homeless, the insane, and adolescents. He is Sagittarius with a Gemini Moon, and he has a seventh-house Jupiter in Aries opposite to Saturn/Neptune rising in Libra. A born litigator and barrister! But he's midlifing.

In his early stage of separation, Rupert is frightened. He doesn't want to lose his edge. And he's right, he shouldn't have to lose his edge. He shouldn't have to lose anything. He needs to gain something, however, and it isn't to be gained by promotions or causes, or winning. It is to be gained by allowing his interior, "unlived life" to emerge. Rupert is growing up, again. When he realizes that millions of men are also experiencing something odd, he feels a bit better; misery loves company. But when he goes to a drumming group, he finds himself a bit alienated. The men in the men's group are not experiencing what he's experiencing. Rupert feels left out, weird, weak.

Over time, a year or so, Rupert begins to feel a sense of liberation and comfort. He's managed to deal with his free-floating anxiety, his fury at routine, his disgust at the legal system, and his diminished sexual interest. He turns down the judgeship. Instinctively, jokingly, he says: "Catch me at fifty, when I am with 'fair round belly, good capon lin'd.' "*

He again feels excited by work, he's managed to undergo a private dis-

*William Shakespeare, *As You Like It*, II. vii.

integration of old persona and ego, and he is no longer frightened of his new-found feelings or needs for reassurance. But he still doesn't know what the hell is going on. He knows now he's having a midlife crisis, but he had no idea it would be like this! He thought it would be "over soon." Well, Rupert still has time to spend riding the high seas of liminality. The crisis has turned into a manageable lifestyle, and he's not as traumatized.

He has questioned his motives for law, his practice, his suite of partners, and he has faced the big question about turning down the bench in favor of the barrister's docket.

2. LIMINALITY—ON THE HIGH SEAS OF TRANSITION

Liminality is a sacred precinct, a place in which one is protected by the gods who watch over journeyers and wayfarers. The gods of the *limn* are Hermes and Hecate. Hermes is the only god of the Olympians who is allowed to pass to and fro across the threshold of the living and the dead. In this guise he is the soul guide, the psychopompos. His function is to take the souls to the netherworld, where they await rebirth in a new physical form (destined by the Moirai, the triple Fates).

Hecate is the goddess of the dark, the underworld, and she is seen in the prophetic face of the last phase of the moon. She has two hounds to comfort her, and the three-headed dog, Cerberus, who guards the gates to Hades. She stands at crossroads, awaiting the journeyer, and guides the righteous across, or lures the unfortunate to her nest below.

These might sound like pretty doleful characters—hardly individuals one wants to invite willy-nilly into one's life. But at this stage they are the kindly ones, who will serve and protect you in your threshold position. These are the god and goddess of the *limn*, and they guide us subliminally to our deepest recesses, and require that we do magical acts to appease them. By paying attention to portents, augurs, ciphers, and signs, we make our way through the mysterious transitional place.

Both of these mythic characters are witnesses to all threshold crossings, and they enliven liminality by offering symbols, signs, and sudden insights. Hermes is our astrological Mercury, and as the psychopompos his role as intermediary between the living and the dead assists the midlifer in to-ing and fro-ing between the conscious ego/persona and the unconscious Self. If you think of the "underworld" as your unknown self, the seed-self within, and your conscious mind as the living, working, quotidian self, then you are understanding the function of your inner mediator.

Hermes is multifaceted and androgynous in spirit. His capacity to impart understanding through symbols and oracles needs to be respected. The casting of I Ching coins, the spreading of Tarot cards, the setting of horoscopes—all the various oracular tools that we employ in our search for meaning and truth—are all ruled by Hermes/Mercury. People become quite religious-minded in states of helpless ego-less-ness!

They become open again, willing to learn and to find new and exciting ways of thinking and solving problems; they find ways of interpreting their visions, imaginings, and synchronicities. Synchronicity becomes commonplace during liminal transitions, and thus heightens one's awareness of the metaphysical elements in the world around. These are all hermeneutic (Hermes) activities—interpreting the meaning of signs and symbols.

Hermes himself is a liminal figure and is known for shape-shifting. As a trickster, he plays a role in making fun of his charges and creating strange and mysterious "accidents," or "little fates," that seem incredibly alive and numinous. This facet of the shaman's role is vital. To seek help from the god who most closely resembles the "problem" and propitiate that god—this is shamanism. Hermes is our inner fool, who finds meaning in humor, or in accidental happenings. It is ideal if the midlifer can find pleasure, enjoyment, and humor in the tricksterish things that happen to him and her on the road. To laugh at oneself is to find the greatest humor of all.

Part of midlife is about the return of the child. Hermes is a figure associated with the psychological aspects of the *puer aeternus* and *puella aeterna*, or the eternal boy and girl. At some stage one has to come to terms with getting older, but that doesn't mean one cannot remain eternally youthful in character and being. A playfulness of spirit is beautiful, and not to be lost in the winds of age and time. Possibly Hermes is the silly one who gets the early midlifer to act up, be childlike, and emulate the youth culture of his or her day.

The liminal aspect of midlife is vital, in fact is a sacred space. In rites of passage from one stage of life to another, tribal peoples have definite rituals to acknowledge and assist the transitioning individual. In *Transitions*, William Bridges says: "Without quite knowing why, people in the middle of transition tend to find ways of being alone and away from all the familiar distractions. Perhaps it is a long weekend away in a borrowed cabin on a lake, or perhaps it is a few days alone in a city hotel."* Indeed, it is vital to take time out, time to wander, and time to ponder, and to give permission to yourself to simply be—as someone once put it, "a human being, not a human doing."

If we try to resolve our liminality experiences purely on an intellectual level, we make ourselves anxious and upset. Sometimes people do crack under the pressures of the world they have created and found themselves in. In this case, they have found that the only way out of whatever they were in was to abdicate completely. That is an extreme, but it is not always a bad way out! We find fault with our "uselessness." The conscious mind is limited—incredibly limited—to stay sane and productive. In the liminal mind, however, anything goes.

Ultimately, the liminal phase is sporadic, but there are strong waves of it initially, in the midst, and at the transition out of midlife. The most important factor is to have conscious awareness that one is actually going through this, not to understand it. *The unconscious Self gets in touch with you, not you with it.* That is the "rule" of the unconscious. It is *just* that—unconscious!

No Name, No Face

The one law of the liminal person is illustrated clearly in the *Odyssey*, the Homeric epic of Odysseus's return from the battles of Troy to his hearth fire in Ithaka.

In a brief and truncated way, I'll tell here the story of an ancient sea journey—a midlife journey, in fact. The Greek warrior hero Odysseus

*William Bridges, *Transitions: Making Sense of Life's Changes* (Reading, MA: Addison-Wesley Publishing Company, 1980), p. 113.

leaves the battlefield of Troy and embarks for his home, Ithaka, on the west side of the Peloponnese. There waits his patient, faithful wife, Penelope, whom he hasn't seen for the duration of the ten-year epic war between the Greeks and the Trojans. He encounters many delays, some by choice and some not.

When he arrives at the cave of the Cyclops Polyphemos, he decides to kill him because he has been eating and terrorizing far too many people. So wily Odysseus gets the Cyclops drunk, and blinds his single eye with a hot pole from the fire. Polyphemos leaps about in pain and rage, screaming "Help me, help me, I am blinded." His neighbors call back to him: "Who has blinded you, who has hurt you?"

The Cyclops calls down to Odysseus, who by now is hastily retreating down the cliff to his waiting ship, "What is your name, who has done this to me?"

Odysseus replies, "I am *oudeis*, I am No-body." (The Greek word for *nobody* is a pun on his name.) So the Cyclops calls to his neighbors: "Nobody has blinded me!" So the neighbors go about their business, not taking any more notice.

However, Odysseus falls victim to *hubris*, and, as he leaps into his ship with his men and crew, calls back up to the odious Polyphemos: "If ever mortal man inquire how you were put to shame and blinded, tell him Odysseus, raider of cities, took your eye: Laërtês' son, whose home's on Ithaka!"*

With that statement, he has blown it. He has defied the primary etiquette of liminality, of transience, of being on the sea journey—and that is not to have a name, an ego, or an identity. The one rule that is essential for support from the "travel gods" is to remain unnamed, thus without ego/identity! From that moment on, Odysseus is plagued by endless trials and danger, deaths and torturous travel. Poseidon is the father of the Cyclops, and he wreaks his revenge the minute he knows who has blinded his son. Had Odysseus remained incognito, he might have got home sooner. Eventually, Odysseus does reach Ithaka, but after

---

The Odyssey, trans. Robert Fitzgerald (New York: Anchor Books, 1963), ll. 504–507. The entire story of Odysseus and the Cyclopes is found at ll. 105–525.

ten years, not just a week or so of pleasant sailing around the cerulean Aegean Sea!

The point of this story is to assure midlifers that they, too, are on a sea journey, and dependent upon the gods within, and the intuitive function of the psyche, to carry them on into the next stage of life. Without identity, without name, without ego.

The ego must soften and adjust to the burgeoning Self. The ego is the marvelous container of the Self, and with the ego we can do many things. And in midlife, the Self insists on more "room" and growth. Ego is important, but it is important also not to overstep one's bounds when in the midst of a stage of ego-less-ness; it is a time to say "I am nobody, I am not who I was, nor am I yet who I shall be."

It is interesting that in the story *Ten Thousand Leagues Under the Sea*, the skipper's name is Captain Nemo (Latin for "nobody"). It seems that sea journeys are meant to be taken by the faithful only, those who believe the gods will help and support them, regardless of who they are or, more significantly, who they think they are. The motto is: Do not pretend to know who you are; rather *allow* who you are to emerge.

This poem by the Greek poet C. P. Cavafy lauds the Odyssean journey as something to be savored—to be prolonged, even! Certainly, there are wonderful things to be had on the sea journey of midlife, and those are to be treasured, nurtured, and taken into old age.

Ithaka
As you set out for Ithaka
hope the voyage is a long one,
full of adventure, full of discovery.
Laistrygonians and Cyclops,
angry Poseidon—don't be afraid of them:
you'll never find things like that on your way
as long as you keep your thought raised high,
as long as rare excitement
stirs your spirit and your body.
Laistrygonians and Cyclops,
wild Poseidon—you won't encounter them

unless you bring them along inside your soul,
unless your soul sets them up on front of you.

Hope the voyage is a long one.
May there be many a summer morning when,
with what pleasure, what joy,
you come into harbors seen for the first time;
may you stop at Phoenician trading stations
to buy fine things,
mother of pearl and coral, amber and ebony,
sensual perfume of every kind—
as many sensual perfumes as you can
and may you visit many Egyptian cities
to gather stores of knowledge from their scholars.

Keep Ithaka always in your mind.
Arriving there is what you are destined for.
But, do not hurry the journey at all.
Better if it lasts for years,
so you are old by the time you reach the island,
wealthy with all you have gained on the way,
not expecting Ithaka to make you rich.

Ithaka gave you the marvelous journey.
Without her you would not have set out.
She has nothing left to give you now.
And if you find her poor, Ithaka won't have fooled you.
Wise as you will have become, so full of experience,
you will have understood by then what these Ithakas mean.

—C. P. CAVAFY*

*In C. P. Cavafy, *Collected Poems*, rev. ed., trans. by Edmund Keeley and Philip Sherrard and ed. George Savidis (Princeton, NJ: Princeton University Press, 1992), p. 36. Permission to reprint granted to the author.

3. INTEGRATION—INCORPORATION, CONSOLIDATION, RECLAMATION

In one's mid-fifties, literally at fifty-four to fifty-five, several generic planetary aspects form, initiating the consolidation of the midlife toward the crossover at sixty, when Saturn returns for the second time.

The integrative experience that one has from about age fifty-five onward is a relief to many. One is finally over the loss of physical youth and has entered into one's "new" face, figure, and stature. The mid-fifties is still a time of coming to terms, however, and many options arise for men and women.

For those who have lifetime vocations or careers, this phase is one in which possibilities for growth, expansion, promotion, and prestige arrive. For those who have the urge to do something different, this too is feasible at this phase.

From a time of separation, where we find ourselves in a "dark wood," or certainly in a state of mind that is confusing and disorienting at the outset, and thence to a liminal space wherein we seek and test out new ways of experiencing ourselves and our lives, we arrive at a place of relative comfort and new empowerment.

This is an empowerment phase of midlife, a period in which we incorporate our new worldview, and our energy returns, in a more steady, calm, and mature way. Ideally, if one has left behind the things that are not possible and thrown oneself into life as an experience and not a striving, then the mid- to late fifties are deeply gratifying.

For men, this is often a time of renewed ambition and direction— their work and focus returns, as they offload youthful fantasies of immortality and the attitude that "anything is possible." For women, the biological transformation of menopause is finished. Like men, they experience increased ambition and focus on goals. For many women, the menopause is a serious emotional and physical struggle; more women suffer from the natural effects of menopause than not. Though our contemporary society is more open about the natural changes that both men and women undergo in their transition through midlife to aging, they continue to be somewhat hidden.

The men's climacteric is a natural process of physical and psychological change. Men often fear losing sexual potency and drive. And for a while, many do struggle with loss of affect and feeling. Sexual dysfunction, or impotency, can be biological if there if disease present, such as diabetes or prostate problems. If sexual dysfunction is not physical but psychological, a man must evaluate the source. Most men are in fact not sexually dysfunctional but need to reassess sex and its reality.

Because men's and women's biological imperatives—for procreation—cease to be aligned at midlife, the tendency is for one or the other to blame the other person. There is no fault here; nature is playing a part in our roles as men and women.

In procreation, women are selective and highly complex in nature, with limited eggs, limited reproductive cycles, and a limit to the number of children they can bear. Men do not have this restriction. The complex biology of a woman is mirrored in her psychology. Psychosexual differences in men and women become more divergent at midlife, and rather than bringing them together, separate them further.

Generally, women have spent time caring, nurturing, and supporting on an emotional level. A woman is likely to work at a job or career as well. Her workload is massive, and she becomes well trained in multitasking. It is no wonder, then, that with the majority of her middle years (twenty through fifty) having been spent in juggling layers and tiers of "work," her "change of life" is toward freedom, liberation, and emancipation from emotional cycles.

Women are ruled by their bodies and psyches in their mothering roles; even in these days of choice, when women may not bear children if they choose not to, they are still locked into the lunar cycles in their lives. Now that PMS (humorously referred to as pre-monstral) has become socially acceptable and menstruation products are sold on television, we are superconscious of female biology; nonetheless, it is not often acknowledged as an important feature in psychology or aging.

SEX, DRUGS, AND POSTPONING THE INEVITABLE

Sex drugs, such as Viagra, are not new to humanity. There have been aphrodisiacs since the beginning of time, whether it was rhinoceros horn or Amazonian plants. Sex has been important to all people, all cultures, through all time. But in contemporary society, one feels a sense of panic around both men and women when it comes to the middle years, when aging is apparent.

Aphrodite (the root of *aphrodisiac*) is a goddess who demands her due, and during the midlife she creates havoc between the genders. Men tend to think they have to be sexually at the ready all the time, as they were in youth. This is fallacious, because this is a time when a man needs to find his soul and his feelings. If men continue on with thinking that sexual dysfunction is a "bad thing," then they are missing the point. Indeed, I once told a close friend of mine that his "problem" was a matter not of his part but of his heart.

As men grow into their late fifties and into their sixties, their sexuality will bloom again in a new way. The biological imperative is still reproductive, but their feelings and emotions are far more at the forefront than when they were younger. This is part of a man's midlife and aging process: coming to terms with the fact that, as a man, his sexuality was a major part of his identity (even if secretly), but it is not now. His feeling nature is rising, and his emotional needs are more demanding; whereas it is a woman's thinking function and her ambition level that is ascending.

In the separation state, and during "middlescence," men and women do grow apart—it takes a deep, solid commitment and a truly healthy relationship to sustain a marriage through the massive changes of midlife. Because the sexual imperative in both men and women is so vastly different, staying together in a marriage requires total revisioning and rescripting of the marriage.

Men may seek out a potency drug, and women have choices too. With the advent of hormone replacement therapy (HRT), as well as natural remedies, women can choose to reinforce their estrogen/progesterone balance and literally avoid the more disturbing and disruptive symptoms of menopause. There are strong opinions here, as with Viagra, but there are options—which have opened the doors for certain menopausal and postmenopausal women to function well and without discomfort, depression, or osteoporosis.

The use of HRT is still in the experimental stages, as it has not been in use for more than a generation and a half, in various forms. There are natural methods, using plants, roots, and seeds, but the drugs are taken by millions of women worldwide.* Supplementing or enhancing a woman's physical functioning with natural or chemical hormones also keeps her "juicy"—her skin supple, her body limber, her bones stronger and denser, and her sexuality relatively unaffected by her biological aging.

Choices for style of aging are vast and varied, but age we will. Once one comes to terms with the facts of life, then the real work can begin.

Gender, Gender, Gender

Gay men and women experience their midlife and aging process precisely the same way as heterosexual individuals, yet with quite dissimilar social and psychosexual imperatives. When you have two men in relationship, you have just that—two men. Double the male archetype, and you have two hunters, two natural men, in a social and emotional commitment, or looking for it anyway. With lesbians, you have the feminine archetype squared, as well, thus a vastly different dynamic in midlife and aging.

How does this affect them in their relating and sexuality? Well, it seems that the hunter instinct in men causes havoc in their social bonding anyway, thus, their committed relationships are predicated in a male way—which brings many gay men a tremendous sadness and resistance to age. The majority of gay men at midlife and older find they are not as attractive to each other—their bodies have been foremost in their relationships, whereas now they, like all men, need more emotion and nurturing in relationships. No longer is the cruise as satisfying or the one-off quite as fulfilling. Gay men want love, and partnership and long-lasting companionship, in their late midlife and sixties.

This means they have to undergo considerable transformation in re-

*See Germaine Greer, *The Change* (London: Penguin Books, 1992).

lating, and come to terms—as do heterosexual men—with the shift in the "hunt." Heterosexual men often find themselves wanting younger women; this is no different from a gay man wanting a youth as a lover. The bond of the male midlifer is shared by both gay and hetero men— both have come to a time when their bodies are no longer the lure but their heart and soul are crying out for friendship, intimacy, and sex.

By nature, gay women are less inclined to multiple partners, but not exclusively so. Their primary motivation to sex and relating is the relationship *itself*. There is no big difference in the psychology of a woman based on sexual preferences. They still are the "gatherers" and, as such, two women together are primarily about relating. Women who are "victims" are no safer in a lesbian relationship than in a heterosexual relationship; there are plenty of lesbians with pathological needs as well! Ultimately, relationships have precisely the same dynamics, regardless of who is having them. More often than not, however, lesbians do not measure each other primarily by sexual standards; their relationships are more often based in a soulful, emotional origin and are nurtured and fostered by feelings of safety, containment, and communication.

Gay people, regardless of the social climate, have had to ask themselves serious questions and endure long periods of anguish that heterosexual people have not. Thus, to be vastly generalized, there is a lot of psychological "content" in their relationships. But men being men, and women being women, the generalization stops there . . . human beings need love and care. They need to give love and care as well.

And in this stage—the final stage of midlife—the primary urge arises in all human beings for emotional safety—and how that safety is found is highly individual. Some women consciously choose complete independence from intimacy with men—they may have been "relationshiped out" and are thrilled to find themselves in themselves! They have given and cared and nurtured, and now they don't have that sense of responsibility; either their kids have grown, or they never did have them; they have been married and remarried, and taken lovers, and at the age of fifty-five truly do not have the same needs that drove them to their earlier relationships.

SOLITUDE, NOT LONELINESS

Having spoken with many single women about their choices, I have observed that many still have desires for partnering, for love, and even for sex, but what they *do not have* is the energy or desire to "work" at a relationship. Women are very aware of the fact that they have lived longer than they will live, and they perform exceptionally well within the context of solitude. Especially if a woman has a rich history of relating, involving her own children and/or her partners', she is more prepared to "go it alone" than a man ever is. Often the desire to "work" on a relationship doesn't renew itself after menopause but in fact disappears entirely. If a good marriage is part of a woman's life, then both she and her husband will undergo their individual changes with compassion and love toward each other and head into the sunset together.

Not only are women more self-sustaining by nature but they are more socially comfortable and integrated than their male counterparts. However, generally speaking, society finds single women uncomfortable still, and thus a mature, single woman has to find ways of being creative and self-sustaining, and not dependent upon a couple-oriented society.*

Often this is a high point in a woman's life. She is free now of the lunar emotional cycle and has formed a good relationship with her inner "contrasexual element"—her *animus*—and integrates the feminine creative with the masculine imperative quite well.

This can be a man's high point, as well, but first he must make friends with his *anima*—his own contrasexual element within. This is the man's task as he approaches his late fifties and sixties. Generally speaking, men do not thrive alone as well as women do. This is not simply a social issue; it is biologically and psychologically embedded, too. He is driven to find a mate, a partner, one who will care for him and indulge his needs and "do" for him. Unless he is willing to do the same for a woman, he is going to have a difficult time finding a woman of his own level of life experience and age.

*See Stephanie Dowrick, *Intimacy and Solitude: Balancing Closeness and Independence* (London: Women's Press, 1992).

Women who have relied primarily on external image will dally at the threshold of age, dying their hair and having every possible upgrade, including face-lifts, lip/eye tattooing, implants, liposuction, dermabrasion, and botox shots—you name it, it can be done! The problem with that aspect of postponing the inevitable is that it arrives all at once. There is no gradual softening, and blurring of features and skin tone. There is nothing wrong with a tuck, but if there is no "tuck within," then it does nothing to help either a man or a woman come to terms with the maturation process and may, in fact, delay it in ways that are unhealthy. Anything in extreme becomes unattractive at a "certain age," and I still recall, in my mid-thirties, at my health spa, being fascinated by an aged woman, probably in her seventies, with a fatless body, good bone structure, and a good physique, and naturally *very* saggy skin. She also had breasts that perked and stayed in place—even lying down in the sauna! I was both fascinated and saddened by the vision.

COMING INTO ONE'S OWN

When we say someone has "come into his or her own," we really mean that they have arrived at a certain age and time in life when they exude a sense of deep contentment. There are periods of "one's own" that are apparent in several phases of life, when everything seems to come together and create a deep sense of personal wholeness. In the last stage of midlife, around ages fifty-five through fifty-nine, there is the opportunity for one of these "coming into one's own" phases, which, if taken on as a life-intention, will endure through the next couple of decades—for some, the rest of their lives.

Many people find this latter phase of midlife a relief. It marks the end of child rearing, husband/wife sponsoring, other obligations that are not as satisfying, and brings many emancipating experiences. Very often the liberation that is felt at the end of the two decades of midlife is deeply internal, personal, and highly individual. There are no rules for midlifing!

People tend to trust their instincts and listen to their inner voice more attentively because they have had to let go of so much, and reconcile so much, that they have come to a more relaxed attitude toward their lives. This does not mean that all people over fifty-seven are released from neurosis or angst, but it does mean that they have had the opportunities to do more work both on the inherent and acquired habitual discomforts. By the age of sixty, resolutions for personal growth and change will present themselves, but it is vital that a quickening of individuation take place at the time one feels it's most needed, in order to move through the process of maturation according to one's own inner timing.

CHAPTER 3

THE SIGNIFICANCE OF SATURN AND URANUS IN THE MIDLIFE TRANSITION

The transitions of life's second half offer a special kind of opportunity to break with the social conditioning that has carried us successfully this far and [onward] to do something really new and different.

—WILLIAM BRIDGES, *Transitions**

T HE two planets that are most consistently lively in a psychoactive fashion during the midlife transition are Saturn and Uranus. Prior to the sighting of Uranus in 1781, Saturn was the ruler of the sign of Aquarius, and, as with all the signs with modern rulers, the ancient ruler is not only still effective but also acts as a highly significant agent in the sign's behavior or manifestation.

Saturn and Uranus embody antithetical properties and have strongly polarized characteristics:

---

*William Bridges, *Transitions: Making Sense of Life's Changes* (Reading, MA: Addison-Wesley Publishing Company, 1980), p. 52.

1. *Saturn* embodies the positive agency of homeostasis and urges us to stay the same, to automatically correct any influence toward change, transformation, or upheaval. Saturn's agency, thus, is to maintain earthy, practical needs, even at the risk of calcification or depression. If Saturn is not honored in life, then it can bring a sense of soulless conventionality and psychological and physical stuckness to bear on the soul.

2. *Uranus* is the planetary medium that impels us toward change and acts as the inner agency for experimentation, growth, evolution, and individuation. And Uranus is our inner witness, watching for opportunities to change habitual behaviors, disrupt the status quo, and stir up any stagnant pool. If Uranus is not honored, then anxiety and manic behavior can irrupt, forcing one to "wake up" to what is required.

As you might suspect, if we were made up only of Saturn and Uranus as planetary agents for life-forces, we would not survive the stress of the conflict! In fact, the conflict of Saturn and Uranus is older than time, and heralds the archetypal struggle of heaven and earth that is present in all forms of creative struggle, whether that is sociopolitical, interpersonal, or within one's own self.

IN THE BEGINNING . . .

Mythologically, Uranus is the eponymous planet of the ancient Greek god who represented the heavens as, in fact, a *place*. Ouranos was never worshipped as a god, nor are there any shrines, emblems, or evidence of temples and the usual indicators of an individual entity. That Ouranos was *the sky*, and not *a sky god*, gives him a very special place in myth— not as a singular entity but as a realm of experience. This is very significant in considering the astrology of Uranus and the interpretation of its qualities both as a natal planet and in transit.

Ouranos came into being because Gaia—Mother Earth—created him herself to comfort her and be her consort. After she birthed many other earth and nature divinities on her own (or with the aid of Eros, according to the oldest myth) she grew lonely and wanted a mate. So she created Ouranos, the heavens, to surround her and keep her constant company, and he enveloped the earth in all his aetheric power. Their union produced many offspring, such as the Cyclopes and Titans.

Then, Gaia found herself pregnant with new offspring, the Heka-tonchires, or "hundred-handed ones." They were multiple and mon-strous but, being a mother, Gaia loved them anyway. Ouranos did not. He was horrified at their monstrosity, their imperfect and fearful traits, and prevented her from birthing them. Naturally, Gaia grew uncomfort-able and angry, and she employed the youngest of the Titans, their son Kronos, in an act that would change the course of mythic history.

She presented Kronos—Saturn—with a scythe made of adamant (obsidian)—a clear, hard, crystalline sickle—and told him to reach up, "as Ouranos lay round Gaia, longing for love," and castrate him.* Which he did—forever separating the archetypal parents, as well as launching a new mythology.

*

We can view this myth variously, but it is clear that with the ensuing battle of the Titans and the collapse of the unified male/female, and the polarization of "above and below," a new archetype issued into life. The separation of heaven and earth, of male and female, the split of the ar-chetypal parents into separate quarters, remains a strong and influential component in our collective and individual psyches.

We can view the "above/below" polarity in many ways. Not only does it symbolize the manifestation of conscious and unconscious be-havior but it also represents the first inklings of dual perception—that there is something "outside oneself" or even deep within ourself that is in opposition or conflict.

Jung thought mediation of conflict was the stuff of life; that inner conflict resolution was the reply to the universal challenge toward wholeness. This is a powerful concept, and more often than not resolu-tion of inner conflict results in conscious peace of mind for individuals.

*Hesiod and Theognis, *Theogony*, trans. Dorothea Wender (London: Penguin Classics, 1973), p. 28, ln. 176.

The function of Saturn and Uranus, the mythic father–son conflict, as we experience it in midlife, is about resolution of conflict and the need for change, even if it involves a violent or disruptive act. As a psychic complex, or a dichotomy, Saturn can act as the severing and swallowing function of our creative ideas. We might be so worried about our own creativity that it never actually is given birth but is "castrated" before any idea, concept, action, or experiment is enacted. In contrast to this suppression, if Uranus has the upper hand, so to speak, then we can be too outrageous, too eccentric, and simply unable to get our point across or find an acceptable median for behavior or communication.

The urge for creative experimentation and individuation at midlife can be stuffed back down inside the psychic womb, just as Ouranos stuffed the Hekatonchires back into the womb of Gaia. It would then take an "adamant" personal attitude toward ones' own self to birth the inner urge for creative change.

Howard Sasportas, in *The Twelve Houses*, says:

Uranus' house may show where we rashly disrespect the limits of our human-ness. Presuming we can automatically transcend the restrictions of the physical body or "rise above" the instinctual components of our nature, we commit the sin of *hubris* and invite punishment to fall on us.*

Saturn is the planet that held domain over the entire solar system until 1781 CE, the period of both the French and American revolutions, inaugurating the Industrial Revolution and involving the whole of Western civilization as it was then. Prior to that era, social life existed within the bounds of family and cultural limitations. In synchrony with the advent of the "new planet," sighted by the astronomer William Herschel, there followed decades of phenomenal innovation and discovery. The flourishing of science, technology, philosophy, literature, music, social opportunities, and change in virtually every aspect of human life, exploded Western civilization toward liberation, freedom, and choice.

*Howard Sasportas, *The Twelve Houses* (London: Aquarian Press, 1895), p. 266.

45

Uranus has become the standard-bearer now in astrology for such terms as *liberation, freedom, choice, individuality, uniqueness, innovation, challenge,* and *breaking out of old ways* and *challenging the status quo.* Saturn was and remains the criterion in astrology for the *opposite* of those values— indeed, is often relegated to a kind of "prison guard" realm. So it may seem curious that I equate the overthrow of Ouranos/Uranus by Kronos/Saturn with liberation and freedom, according to the rote astrological definition of each planet—and call that act the beginning of a new way of being.

The planets Saturn and Uranus, as "celestial sacred" symbols, are both heavenly in position (in the sky), but they are quite different in meaning. As I mentioned earlier, Saturn is to do with the *realm* of the world and its forms, while Uranus is to do with the *ideal* of the world and its forms. To propitiate both is the trick. How to acknowledge the perfection of the Ideal, while humanly existing in the realm of the Real?* Essentially, we are required, periodically, to give birth to ourselves as if we were a new idea, a new culture, a new mythology, just as mythic gods overthrew the old guard to begin a new regime.

Naturally, there is an underbelly—a shadow—of the Uranian attribute that also refers back to the origin myth: if we don't trust our ability to render a creation or idea into form (Saturn), we abandon it, abort it, before it can be given birth. Or we "refuse" its birth, *swallowing* our creative issue as Kronos/Saturn did with his own offspring. In other words we refuse birth of the creation due to its imperfection—just like Ouranos and the Hekatonchires.

In her book *Creation Myths,* Jungian analyst Marie-Louise Von Franz says about crossing the threshold from the Ideal possible to the Real thing:

PEOPLE SOMETIMES RESIST BECOMING CREATIVE BECAUSE ONE'S WOULD-BE CREATIVENESS IS ALWAYS SO MUCH MORE IMPRESSIVE AND IMPORTANT THAN THE LITTLE EGG ONE LAYS IN THE END WHEN BIRTH TAKES PLACE![†]

---

*See Erin Sullivan, *Venus and Jupiter: Bridging the Ideal and the Real* (London: CPA Press, 1996).
†Marie-Louise Von Franz, *Patterns of Creativity Mirrored in Creation Myths* (Dallas, TX: Spring, 1972), p. 85.

It is during such times of high innovation and creativity as adolescence, midlife, and the threshold of old age that we have difficulty in trusting our own creative powers.

One might think that the principles of *Uranus* overpowering *Saturn* would be the "new way," but rather the opposite is what happens in our inner life. *It is in this paradox that the astrological and therefore psychological struggle for identity lies*.

As psychic components, both Saturn and Uranus are needed for wholeness. For innovation to become manifest, it requires the adamant sickle of old Kronos—the discipline of matter over mind. The *eidolon* itself, or imagined thing, is simply the archetype of Uranus, while the Idea takes actual form with the effort and adamant labor of Saturn. A harmonious equilibrium between both is the substance of progress and evolution and, in turn, the development of consciousness.

At the midlife threshold, we arrive at a crossroads, at which stand both the god of change and the god of stasis. These gods, represented by Uranus/change and Saturn/stasis, begin a dance toward the future.

It is at this very threshold—the doorway between youth and old age—that we meet many facets of ourselves that have remained dormant or sleeping, awaiting this moment of development for their proper time. At this threshold, as I said earlier, this liminal place, we are *not who we used to be but are not yet who we are to become*. For most extraverted people of this era, this experience of liminal living is a most uncomfortable and, at times, deeply distressing place.

RITES OF PASSAGE

Every transition in life demands recognition and respect. Whether it is birth, adolescence, marriage, midlife, old age, or death, all have rituals and sacred associations that all people in all times have observed. Every culture observes its human conditions differently, but the human condition remains constant. How we approach our own individual transitions is bound up with our culture.

If we find culture to be disrespectful or, worse, ignorant of the value of ritual and sacred passage, then we find ourselves lost in a wasteland, isolated and anxious for understanding. Often, a psychotherapist or an astrologer will be the first to announce to a person in transition that he or she is okay, is not mad but rather in transit.

Since time began, humanity has sought sacred space and sacred time to honor rites of passage and demarcate stages or spaces in life's journey. All thresholds have their gods and their icons. Whether or not we acknowledge them consciously or ritually is quite beside the point. They exist.

Humanity has a sense of the sacred imbued in its collective psyche, and has given us our religions and places that are called sacred, whether they be church, mosque, synagogue, temple, mountain, tree, or valley. A sacred space is called a *temenos*, a place wherein the divine is honored, if not actually immanent. In his book *The Sacred and the Profane*, Mircea Eliade says:

> A ritual function falls to the threshold of the human habitation, and it is for this reason that the threshold is [an object of] great importance. Numerous rites accompany passing the domestic threshold—a bow, a prostration, a pious touch of the hand, and so on. The threshold has its guardians—gods and spirits who forbid entrance both to human enemies and to demons and the powers of pestilence. The threshold, the door *show* the solution of continuity in space immediately and concretely; hence their great religious importance for they are symbols and at the same time vehicles of *passage* from the one space to the other.*

What is of greater importance to an individual person than acknowledgment of his or her threshold crossing? And what greater thresholds are crossed than the significant passages into the distinct ages in which our lives all are bound? Every sacred space has a numinous quality to it, and we can feel that when we enter a *temenos*. We look for signs, symbols, and other forms of indicators for our safe passage, or respectful acknowledgment when we transition into and through a sacred space.

*Mircea Eliade, *The Sacred and the Profane: The Nature of Religion*, trans. Willard Trask. (New York: Harcourt Brace Jovanovich, 1959), p. 25.

Again, Eliade says about this phenomenon:

In such cases the *sign*, fraught with religious meaning, introduces an absolute element and puts an end to relativity and confusion. . . . A sign is asked, to put an end to the tension and anxiety caused by relativity and disorientation—in short, to *reveal an absolute point of support*. (p. 27)

Astrology, ancient and contemporary, has been always a point of reference, and one that transcends the human intellect. "The higher regions inaccessible to man, the sidereal zones, acquire the momentousness of the transcendent, of absolute reality, of eternity" (p. 118). Celestial "signs" and symbols hold archetypal truths, which far outreach the mind and intellect, and in this way the astrological timing, cycles, and imagery serve as guideposts and acknowledgment that we as humans are taking part in eternal and sacred passages in our lives.

Again, Eliade:

Driven from religious life in the strict sense, the *celestial sacred* remains active through symbolism. A religious symbol conveys its message even if it is no longer *consciously understood* in every part. For a symbol speaks to the whole human being and not only to the intelligence. (p. 129; emphasis in original)

The loss of sacrality and the disenchantment of our world from the realm of archetypal rites has resulted in mass neurosis and medications rather than acceptance of certain times in which we do not know "who we are or whence we go." To some degree, the astrological cycles and symbols can relieve that neurosis and reenchant for us the world—in which we are not only sane but also conscious.

In the midst of a capsizing ego comes an opportunity. All transitional states are guided by gods; all myths from all time tell us that a person in transition, a journeyer or sojourner, is protected by the gods. The one stipulation in that guardianship and guidance is anathema to Western culture, American culture in specific. The Odyssean caveat to a safe crossing is: Go *without an ego*. "I am" becomes an impairment, not a container.

Obviously, to be practical, one must have some face to maintain, and one can do so even while acknowledging the state of liminality or thresholding that is being experienced. Thus, the "loss of ego" doesn't mean a psychotic break but a ritual recognition that one is *in medias res*—in the middle of things—and thus in a state of high innovation and re-creation of self. With this understanding, the crossover from youth to midlife and thence the crossover from midlife to aging can be done with a modicum of grace and a sense of purpose to it.

Throughout this book, in both the midlife and aging parts, I give descriptions of the times and the ages that the planets, from Saturn through Pluto, demarcate these turning points in life and growth. At any moment in any of these phases we are offered by our own deep Self, our own immanence, the opportunity to stop growing or to move onward to the next phase. Giving birth to one's own self is part of maturing, and that kind of rebirth or renaissance is the stuff of heroism.

The two primary planets of midlife and aging are symbolic of the realms we experience, the idealism of the idea and the realism of the real. Both are vital to birth.

*

Fortunately, at this writing, 2004 CE, there is a bit of psychological history to midlifing as well as the inherent magical and symbolic meaning. And several good books on and about midlife and aging can be found in the reading list at the end of this book. Because the post–World War II generation, the Pluto in Leo people, explored the advent of midlife thoroughly, and in various ways, it is hoped that the following generations will evolve new ways of transitioning through the midphase of life and toward aging, with yet more options. The timing will always remain the same, but the enactment ever changes.

I suspect no generation after Pluto in Leo will reap so much emotional and material reward from a single generic life passage! In so many ways, the Pluto in Leo generation remythologized our popular culture, bringing to light the timelessness of rites of passage as they are lived out, again and again, in contemporary times. Throughout this book, I return repeatedly to this idea, clarifying how breakthrough can be the result of breakdown.

Here follows a list of ages and the astrological indicators of adult development, from the meeting at the crossroads in midlife through the arrival at sixty and elderhood.

TRANSITING MIDLIFE: ASPECT TABLE

AGE	GENERIC ASPECTS
38–44	Uranus 180° Uranus: Uranus in Aries, Taurus, Gemini, and Cancer, and have the half-Uranus at 38–39; Leo, Virgo, Libra, and Scorpio at 42–44; Sagittarius, Capricorn, Aquarius, and Pisces right around the median age of 42
38	Moon's nodes return for the second time
40	Saturn 120° Saturn
42	Neptune 90° Neptune (first time)
44–45	Saturn 180° Saturn
44–46	Uranus 150° Uranus
47	Inversion (180°) Moon's nodes
48	Jupiter returns for the fourth time
50	Saturn 120° Saturn
52	Saturn 90° Saturn
54	Second secondary progressed Lunar return; Saturn 60° Saturn
55–56	Uranus 120° Uranus; Neptune 120° Neptune
57	Moon's nodes return for third time
59–60	Second Saturn return; Jupiter returns for the fifth time at 60; secondary progressed Moon and Sun repeat their phase at birth (natal lunation phase is repeated in secondary progressions)

Note: Pluto has such an eccentric orbit and inclination to the ecliptic that its own cycles to itself occur at vastly different ages. Pluto is in Taurus for thirty-two years, while it is only in Scorpio for twelve. Thus, for the middle signs, Pluto in Leo and Aquarius, the transit is for twenty to twenty-one years. Thus, the Pluto in Leo generation receives the Pluto square Pluto in midlife.

The Pluto in Leo, Virgo, Libra, and Scorpio generations have transiting Pluto square to their natal Pluto in earlier (midlife) stages of life, while people with Pluto in Sagittarius and all signs following have the Pluto square Pluto at increasingly elder ages. As Pluto transits signs from Capricorn on, the square varies from age fifty (Pluto in Sagittarius) to age ninety-three (Pluto in Taurus).

Thus we see the "generational imperative" change from one generation to the next, in an increasing age factor. (See chapter 6.)

CHAPTER 4

URANUS BY SIGN AS MIDLIFE PURPOSE INDICATOR

DREAM OR FANTASY?

Because we are exploring the half-Uranus cycle as the gateway to midlife's transition, the sign that Uranus is in natally contains characteristics of the opposite sign as its "unlived life." When any planet in transit comes to the opposition point to itself in the natal chart, a half-cycle is noted. As with all half-cycles, it simulates the lunation cycle as a "full planet phase," which allows for the fullness of the experience of that planet to emerge and reflect back the messages and lessons learned. That is, the opposition, or the "half-cycle," is an illumination from the transiting planet and its manifestation of intent, as it reflects back to the natal planet its "secret intent."

The fullness of any experience always is in reflection of the things "not had"; if we long for chocolate cake, it is because we haven't had it in a while. Similarly, if we long for something we haven't had for a while, or *ever* had perhaps, often it is something that actually does lie within the realm of possibility, and, more important, within one's own Self.

This potential "thing" that could happen *must* lie within the seed of self, or it won't be possible. Facing reality is important here, and so is facing the myriad contexts in which we live out our dreams. If you have never studied the piano, then it is unlikely that you will become a concert pianist in midlife. However, if you have always longed to play the piano and learn music, it is certainly something that can be done in midlife and enjoyed.

So the half-Uranus is the beginning of a time of high potential to carry out a life dream you have always carried within, as time and circumstances have arrived now to live it. So, if you have nurtured a dream to get a degree or take up a new trade or travel to foreign places, but so far life has not presented you with the environment or context to fulfill those dreams, and at midlife you find yourself in a new life situation (for example, the children have moved on, your partner is supportive, or you are on your own), then it is entirely possible.

Distinguishing between *fantasy* and *dream* is important in midlife. Fantasy serves a meaningful function for us—the psyche needs time off, playtime, and fantasies are very healthy for that. They are often not rendered into reality, however; for example, *wanting* to play the piano—not knowing how does *not* prevent the psyche from exploring what that would be like. So an elaborate fantasy might be built around playing a complex and beloved piece of music at the piano, doing it brilliantly, and basking in the applause at the Metropolitan in New York or the Royal Albert Hall in London. No harm done.

But a dream, ah, that is different. Dreams are often linked to a real potential. Dreams are always good to nurture, while fantasies are to be indulged in. A dream comes true if both Saturn and Uranus are working at optimum. Saturn will remind you what you cannot do, and Uranus will prod you to explore, to experiment, and to define what it is your genius or daemon is dragging you toward. Between the two agencies, you can harness your creative potential and live it out realistically.

The half-Uranus is a time of awakening to the unlived life and the time to assess your assets and liabilities objectively. Being able to witness yourself and your own true limits and boundaries, while simultaneously appreciating that which is really possible to fulfill, is the task assigned at the crossroads. Mediating the gods of "stop" and "go" can generate a very fruitful quest.

Saturn's job is to let you know what your limits and boundaries are, and in that safe, contained place, you can become successful. You might say to yourself "I can do anything I want, within limits."

So when your natal Uranus is opposed by transiting Uranus, it is sending you a message that all the unique traits and characteristics that you embody but have not yet brought to life are calling out for realization.

It is obvious that the midlife can bring far too many "unlived" aspects of your life to the fore—hence the panic and angst that are frequently associated with midlife crisis. The creative aspect of divine discontent comes most alive at the threshold of midlife, and thence periodically throughout the entire transition.

I have associated Saturn with divine discontent, but it is a quality of Uranus as well.* The two planets walk hand in hand on this journey, and, as mentioned before, Saturn is the planet that defines our limits, while Uranus is the planet that offers all possibility. Being grumpy and miserable is *not* necessarily divine discontent, it might simply be being grumpy and miserable. However, the mood, the tenor, and numinosity associated with divine discontent is a prod from the unconscious toward greater creativity, to find the means to exploit your talent.

In chapter 5, you will find the house-to-house interpretation for Uranus opposite Uranus.

INDIVIDUATION AT MIDLIFE
THROUGH THE SIGNS

Aries

Uranus in Aries meets itself halfway from the sign of Libra. The individuation process from Aries to Libra, as a sign function, primarily brings up the polarity of self and others. With natal Uranus in Aries, the prime motivating force of your individuation "seed" ultimately is toward absolute and utter psychological independence. Should you achieve

---

*Erin Sullivan, *Saturn in Transit: Boundaries of Mind, Body and Soul* (York Beach, ME: Weiser, 2000).

your Uranus return at age eighty-four, you will know this to be true, and in the meanwhile, periodically in your life, you know this to be true. The meeting at midlife is about capitulation to your opposite, where you submit or yield to the opposite intention of your individuation seed. Ultimately, your first half of life is all about You, and the second half, or the "unlived life," is about you and how you are with others. By experiencing yourself as a model of all people, your level of sensitivity and compassion is forced to grow at the midlife crossover.

Taurus

Uranus in Taurus meets itself halfway from the sign of Scorpio. The individuation process from Taurus to Scorpio addresses issues that are related to trust. Holding fast to your security in any way brings up your fears of losing your identity and self in a relationship. The function of Taurus is to maintain the status quo as a healthy and positive holistic balance in mind and body, so that all the important features of security—which include pragmatic things such as home, friends, money, and love—are naturally seen as significant necessities to your identity. At the crossroads of midlife, however, there is a meeting of the opposite, which is about finding security in more intangible ways—psychological security, security in the world at large, and a growing sense of your own self-value as it emerges as a "real" quality, not just an inner resource.

Gemini

Uranus in Gemini meets itself halfway from the sign of Sagittarius. The individuation process from Gemini to Sagittarius is about ideas, attitudes, opinions, communication, and all things of the mental zone. Freedom of thought, speech, and individual identity are primary needs with Uranus in Gemini, but it becomes less personal and increasingly more collectively focused after the midlife crossover. Ultimately, as the half-Uranus occurs, the purpose of one's life becomes bigger, has expansive ideas, greater freedom of movement, and an increase in cultural and social change.

Cancer

Uranus in Cancer meets itself halfway in the sign of Capricorn, and both those signs are primarily motivated from a territorial viewpoint. Cancer as the natal sign shows that you were born to find alternatives to the prevailing cultural norm regarding family, property, territorialism, safety, and emotional security. Often the path of individuation for you becomes divided between enmeshment with family and culture or massive changes made by you to alter the status of family and culture. It is an either/or imperative—either return to family or re-create the concept of family.

This generation was the first to really have choice in family organization, and because of the "sexual revolution" and the advent of convenient and easy birth control, many of this generation of women chose to not have children of their own.

Ultimately, the intent in the individuation process for Uranus in Cancer is to become bigger than a nuclear family, to take on the family of humanity in some important way. Capricorn is the sign that has to do with social status and authority and authenticity—and the midlife process involves the entire structure of the concept of family.

Leo

Uranus in Leo has its crossover experience when Uranus transits Aquarius. Since Leo is the archetypal sign of the heart and the child, there are many indications that the first "half" of life is spent playfully and without concern for the collective, but suddenly there is a calling at midlife to nurture the world-soul. The polarity of Leo and Aquarius embodies the syzygy of individualism and collectivity. That is, you and the group. Within the social and tribal collective we exist as an individual, but it is only in the context of *others* that we can define our individuality. The conflict that exists at midlife for the Uranus in Leo is primarily one of finding one's own self within a supportive group, and to begin a process of humanitarian individuation.

Virgo

Midlife occurs when Uranus enters Pisces and the polarity between serving or suffering on behalf of the world rises to critical mass. Since the most recent Uranus in Virgo group has a majority of individuals who have the Uranus/Pluto conjunction (1966–1967), the quality of their midlife is amplified by this nuclear aspect. Uranus in Virgo is about individuation through the process of being useful, serviceable, helpful, and on call for those who suffer. Now, when the half-Uranus cycle occurs, there comes a sacrifice to be made that will serve each individual psyche toward its ultimate intent—to sacrifice something deeply personal to the demand of the global ethos. Through inventiveness and "progress," the culture arrives at a time of maximum sacrifice, and in that environment, the Uranus in Virgo generation comes of age. Finding a life purpose through organization and reculturalization will bring the essence of Uranus in Virgo's ultimate intent in life.

Libra

Uranus in Aries is the advent of midlife for those who were born with it in the sign of Libra. As each sign represents an evolution from the previous and a preparation for the next, it follows that the intent of Uranus in Libra is to find a balance between the individual and the collective. Now this has been said before with the other signs, because Uranus itself represents the concept of the "one in the many"; however, it is especially significant for Libra/Aries. The restoration of the individual rights and prerogatives of each person in balance with a new social order is the key to this individuation process. The first half of life is spent coming to terms with relationships in an intensely personal fashion, while the crossover experience into midlife induces the psychic demand to find ways for *all* individuals to have a sense of equality, belonging, and influence in the world.

Scorpio

When Uranus enters Taurus, and opposes the natal Uranus of those who have it in Scorpio, the shock of "real world" practicality awakens a new impetus for personal growth. Uranus in Scorpio has already spent half its life in a state of mystical and transformative experience, and at midlife must transmute the esoteric intangibles into manifest form. Uranus in Scorpio urges the individual to explore his or her uniqueness and individual self in ways that are often dark and mysterious. The path to self and wholeness involves incorporating the shadow self and, in midlife, acknowledging the purpose of the shadow. This will take the form of dealing with collective shadow material and working with it to integrate the darker aspects of society and the world and ultimately, to perform a kind of magical transformation for the future. The inner resources of Uranus in Scorpio are profound, drawing on an ancestral level of information. But the impulse to truly embody the "work of the ancestors," either through good works, teachings, or commerce, becomes essential to one's sense of inner purpose.

Sagittarius

Uranus in Sagittarius is all about global unity and consciousness, and little about individual success or self-interest. The "unlived life," therefore, will lead the Uranus in Sagittarius person toward more specific areas of interest and work. The tendency to depersonalize very personal issues is part of this planet/sign relationship, and the proclivity to mythologize, psychologize, and even astrologize deeply personal and emotional experiences is so high that a kind of impersonal detachment is part of the first half of life. There is an element of the puer/puella in this axis of Sagittarius/Gemini, in that the identity is bound up with freedom concepts. The reality of freedom, however, changes at midlife; the actual meaning of freedom alters. Thus, the crossover experience at midlife may be a shock because what once represented freedom becomes yet another trap. It is an intellectual sense of emancipation that this sign wants, not a lonely, isolated, unattached life. This is because the demand from the psyche toward wholeness calls to the globalized, impersonal attitude to get more specific and personal. Being lofty and philosophical, the test is to bring the high-level beliefs into individual life. In this way, the calling to true humanitarian and global consciousness is more effective—when it is not simply a theory but an act of volition.

Capricorn

The half-Uranus at midlife for people with Uranus in Capricorn calls them to a deeper level of feeling. Having spent half a life trying to find individuality in social forms, the release at the crossover experience is toward true human feelings, emotions, passions, and sensations. Being inherently inclined to individuate through social order, Uranus in Capricorn is difficult indeed. But the midlife brings up all those unexperienced emotional zones to be fully engaged in. The struggle between what others want and think is the right thing to do and what this individual really needs for himself or herself to advance and evolve means that two very different forces meet head on. In this illuminating time, if the person has indeed "bought into" the status quo, he or she might rebel against that and create a new type of rulership based on self and family only. If the deep Self has been suppressed in favor of the family myths, then the separation between the person and the family—even just psychologically—will bring a deep sense of relief and freedom.

Aquarius

Uranus in Leo comes around to oppose the natal Uranus around the ages of forty-two to forty-four, the latest age bracket of generational midlife. This seems appropriate, since the signs of Leo and Aquarius are signs that embody "youthfulness" or puer/puella characteristics. That the midlife crossover event occurs later than the others simply adds to the level of change that occurs. The unlived life is about losing one's self and self-identity in the collective, and the crossover event is likely to be about asserting one's own ego and self more vigorously.

Pisces

Uranus's transit of Virgo marks the halfway point in the life of those who were born with Uranus in Pisces. The sacrifices made by the individual who has Uranus in Pisces can be so overwhelming by midlife that a descent into the personal unconscious can arise. Indeed, the last generation of individuals born with Uranus in Pisces (1920–1927) underwent serious collective losses and sacrifices in the form of global war and collapsing economy. They went on to create a new society, but with many personal sacrifices en route to this new dream of a world. Since Uranus entered Pisces in 2003 and remains there through 2010, another generation of individuals arise who also may undergo types of individual sacrifice on behalf of the collective. The midlife crossover experience when Uranus enters Virgo is all about coming back to the self, and the body, and the wholeness of one's individuality. This is not an easy task for a sign (Pisces) that, by its very nature, is one of universal unity. The midlife shock can be coming out of a dream world (or a sacrificial state) and into the real world, where the dreams and sacrifices need to be made real and manifest.

CHAPTER 5

The Half-Uranus House:
The Unlived Life

The Midlife Transition

The advent of midlife, the half-Uranus cycle, in itself speaks volumes about what one is experiencing as the "crossover episode."

One could spend days interpreting the horoscope of a midlifing client simply using the transit of Uranus and the hemispheric experience, as well as the planetary transit pattern inversion that occurs at that juncture in his or her life. In the next chapters I will explore the inversion of transit pattern at the half-Uranus.

With transits, time + distance/space = experience, because each planet has its own time cycles. For instance, Uranus takes seven years to transit a whole sign of the zodiac, thirty degrees, but that seven years is qualified by the space/distance it covers in a natal chart. For example, if Uranus is transiting the sign of Aquarius, and the chart has Aquarius on the ascendant, say 12°, then Uranus will spend part of its seven years in Aquarius in that chart transiting the twelfth house, and the rest of that seven years in the first house. The distance and time is the same for the

FIGURE 3. PATTERNS OF THE HALF-URANUS

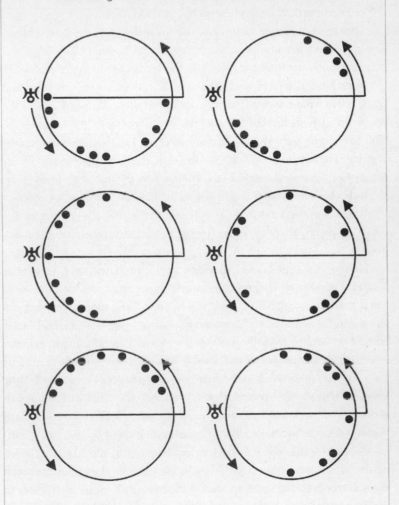

This illustration of the half-Uranus describes the point of origin of Uranus—that is, its natal place—and the arrow describes its subsequent transit around the horoscope wheel to its opposition. The "dots" are planetary positions or patterns that are possible in individual charts that further describe the more "personal" aspects that Uranus can make to the chart for the "first half" of life, followed by the resulting "opposite" aspects post-midlife.

planet cycle, but the space is different because of the personalization of the horoscope. That is, it is possible for a house in a horoscope to span 60° or even just 12°, depending on the latitude of birth.

Thus the experience of the time and the space is unique to that chart. The space, in this instance, is the house, or the "realm of individual experience," as Dane Rudhyar called the twelve houses of the horoscope.*

Natal Uranus, its sign, and its placement by hemisphere, quadrant, and house tell us what it is that is so very significant about a person's midlife *develop-ment*, which literally means "the act of opening," or "unfolding," akin to opening the envelope of one's outer life to discover what message is inside. The very seed of individuality lies in the symbol of Uranus. By its natal place, and its relationship to other planets by aspect, we know even more about what it is that makes one individual distinct from another.

We also understand more deeply what it is that lies within an individual's psyche that demands ongoing development and periodic revolution.

Uranus has a quality of tribalism, which it shares with the planet Jupiter. The primary difference between Jupiterian and Uranian tribalism is that Jupiter is about coded beliefs, ethics, and morality, which are culture and epoch specific. Uranus is also about beliefs, ethics, and social mores but more universally applied. For example: Jupiter might refer to a person's ethnic origins or ancestral links, which are directly related to the personal realm, even to the family realm; whereas Uranus will show a bigger relationship—the relationship an individual has with his or her generational hopes and desires; the collective ideology and mandate that lies encoded within each seven-year grouping of people.†

Because Uranus is the modern ruler of Aquarius, and Aquarius is the natural sign ruler of the eleventh house, there are all the ramifications of those symbols in the natal Uranus. Underlying all Uranian features is the element of air, which is a "relating" element, involving the experience of groups, organizations, and collectives that are socially based; and

*Dane Rudhyar, *The Astrological Houses: The Spectrum of Individual Experience* (Garden City, NY: Doubleday, 1972).
†Refer to page 75 ff. for the explanation of natal Uranus in each sign, and see the diagram on page 63.

Uranus is the planet that generates a distant, objective, and nonpersonal view of the world around us—it is the "heavenly" perspective; and finally, Uranus is about finding ways to lead others to new ways of thinking and acting, hence its "revolutionary" tone, and Promethean urge to move far beyond accepted thinking and introduce innovative concepts.

Uranus has been called a "transpersonal" planet, but in reality it is a profoundly personal planet, because the planetary array—the entire pattern of one's psychic contents—in the natal chart must work through the planet Uranus to find a unique, complex personality. So begins the serious work of individuation.

For instance, if we are of a specific race and tribal affiliation (Jupiter) and we are beholden to the laws and codes of that tribe (Saturn), then where is our individuality to express itself in direct relation to those important "containers"? Pre-Uranian society, as history informs us, found no bridge between the culture and personal choice. Of course there are individual people among those societies who performed Promethean acts and opened doors to the future, unheedful of the Saturnian bounds of their epoch, society, and family. But these are always the exceptions to the rule, when there are people who transcend the bounds of epoch, culture, and society. In themselves, those Uranian people existed—as Uranus did—long before Uranus was sighted.

So the principles of Uranus—innovation, freedom of thought, revolutionary acts/ideas, explorations beyond the known boundaries, heresies, and so on—clearly existed before the discovery of Uranus, thence to become global options after it. Eventually original and innovative ideas are fully integrated into the collective psyche, but usually not until some form of revolution occurs. Now all people have a Uranian option to break free from the paradigms that form their smaller worlds and to make choices based on individual needs, interests, and discoveries.

Paradoxically, when we are at our most rebellious and insistent on our uniqueness and individuality, it is in direct mirroring that we can make these distinctions between "me" and "all the others" who populate our world and society. That is the function of Uranus. It is just that paradox inherent in the agency of Uranus that we can say we are "different from" *whatever*, but we are different *only* in relation to being "part of" that same *whatever*. Someone who feels (or is) outside the realm of social law is only such in relation to the selfsame laws.

In part, this is why radicals or innovators have a difficult time—their adherence to the role of outsider or heretic is only defined by the thing they are radicalizing or heretical toward. How annoying for them! The problem that always faces the radical or heretic is the time when his or her Promethean offering becomes the status quo, and their rebellion is thus redundant.

One doesn't have to be radical or ingenious to feel an outsider or a misfit. It is inherent in the human condition that we each are outside the realm of others. Remember in the myth of the castration, where Ouranos was split off and divorced from Gaia forever? That image is the underlying archetype for the outsider, the misfit, the observer.

Ouranos/Uranus is not involved in personal, emotional, or earthly decisions. It does not have to do with "staying the same" or adhering to the status quo. It is above all that—beyond the seamy, steamy earth functions, and thus not of the realm of human-made laws, rules, dogma, religious organization, or general approval.

All that is up to other planets, not Uranus, who remains as superior in its view of earthly action as it did so very long ago. Uranus is an elitist; it is a planet by which one assumes one is superinteresting and unique in comparison to all others. This elitist shroud in which Uranus cloaks itself can be genuinely true to an ideal, or it can be ruthlessly and self-destructively outside the realm of possibility.

We all know people who are quite probably geniuses. But intellectual genius (Latin for "spirit" or "guiding spirit") is not *in itself* useful in a mundane, quotidian way. Often individuals who have intellectual genius do *not* have a social genius. Hence Uranian people are nonconformist—even quite mad—or slightly autistic and socially disorganized; certainly Uranus is our own personal eccentricity, thus our own stance "away from the center." This does *not* diminish a mad person's contribution to innovation or advancement, but often they are not an emotionally, socially, or relationally oriented person. Too, it allows one to accept one's own difference-by-comparison—something much more agreeable to one after forty!

THE HOUSES: MEETING YOUR OPPOSITE AT MIDLIFE

1. First House Midlife Transit/Natal Seventh House: Me, Myself, and I

Natal Uranus in the seventh house means that the half-Uranus midlife trigger arises in the first house. The first house, in simplistic terms, is "self," while the seventh is "others." The midlife individuation *begins* with yourself—which might sound odd, since so many astrology books define Uranus in the seventh house natally as "independent, self-directed, uncommitted, transient in relationships," and the like.

Ultimately, Uranus in the seventh house is a "freedom/closeness" issue. There is the need to be in partnership or a committed alliance in order to fully understand oneself, but at the same time there is a restlessness in the heart and soul of Uranian seventh house people that can drive them from one relationship to another, or into "impossible" relationships, or toward unavailable partners who act out the individual's need to "be alone."

In the exploration lies the seed of individuation, which will emerge at the half-Uranus transit in the first house, and a real sense of individuality and selfness comes about. No longer is one's identity bound up wholly with another person or partner or relationship.

Since the Uranian seventh house person's dictum is "freedom from others," when Uranus transits the first house, there emerges a stronger understanding of one's limits and capabilities in relationships, and now one can go about simply living without either constantly diving into relationships or continually avoiding them. While the need to see the self in the mirror of relationship is human, an obsessive need to be either alone *or* partnered is based in self-fear.

The midlife Uranus transit occurring in the first house will bring one face to face with one's own heretofore unreflected self-image, bringing with it some brilliant solutions to relationship issues. By midlife, often one has sorted out many frailties and strengths in relating, but now it is mandatory to explore new feelings of independence and self-awareness diligently.

This time is about finding a sense of true, inner, personal security. For instance, if you have been in a marriage or partnership that has outlived its health and vigor and has become "dead," and you have remained in it for reasons of emotional security or finances or "because of the children," then you might find yourself with some strange courage to leave that relationship. Conversely, if you have been trotting along quite happily in an unpartnered state, running from commitment, you may finally meet your match!

If you have put your own individuation process on the back burner in favor of supporting the development of your partner's (thus projecting your own Uranus onto your partner), then you are more than likely to find this unworkable now. No longer will you be able to take a back seat or wait your turn to be heard. Your rebellion takes a very personal turn. You'll need to cast off restrictions and burdens that others bring to you—keeping in mind that you have played a significant role in this problem.

For the first time in your life, you may be able to perceive that you have avoided your own growth out of fear and insecurity, and now have the age, wisdom, and courage to analyze this objectively. This stands for those who have hidden in the bosom of relationships as well as those who have fled from them habitually!

2. Second House Midlife Transit/Natal Eighth House: Coming to Your Senses

The place of Uranus in the eighth house is another "family" indicator—but it is the family as an ancestral league, from which you derive various traits that you share with the laterally extended family, such as uncles, cousins, aunts, and so on. Meeting up with relatives at midlife is always fascinating, and you might well contact family whom you have either never seen or have not seen for years.

However, the primary motivation underlying the half-Uranus phase from the second house to the eighth house is about self-worth and money! People with Uranus in the eighth house have an unusual relationship with finances and other people's money. This placement can indicate a loss of investment or legacy from the family inheritance, among a myriad other things.

At the least, Uranus in the natal eighth can mean that one has a sense of anxiety, even fear, about money and/or love being removed, lost, dying, or taking away personal freedom. I have a client whose eighth house Uranus actually did present a disinheritance from the father in the midlife transit from the second house; the same woman also left a bad marriage, in which she had lost her own nest egg to her husband's bad judgment and bankruptcy! This woman learned a very hard lesson, and over the subsequent ten years after her half-Uranus, she became financially independent and also happily in relationship with herself.

Many fears and childhood trauma can come to resolution when Uranus moves to its opposition from the second to the eighth house—true freedom, true self-worth, and true personal value become the impetus to create life anew. Unlocking all the personal resources that lie embedded in one's self and soul is what is required during this phase of life. Sometimes it precipitates a shock, as with the woman I just mentioned; at other times it is a windfall of conscious awareness of what one is *really* worth and where one's genius lies in creating a sense of personal worth.

A new relationship with security is created as well. For instance, if you have spent your life to date being careless or uninvolved with money and your personal finances, you will develop a fascination with savings, retirement funds, land, and all the things money can bring—the most important of those being freedom.

Since a cry for freedom is inherent in a Uranus transit, it is really a matter of what freedom means to *you*. Since the investment of time, love, and money primarily has been merged with others in your life to date, it is time to explore an independent relationship to those important assets.

The dichotomy between the life-force and the existential consciousness of the inevitability of death—which Freud called the eros/thanatos duality—becomes a sharp reality for this transit. A kind of carelessness or even overadventurousness can flip to become cautiousness and steadiness in behavior. The meeting of opposites, in this case, can manifest as a sudden awareness of mortality. You may have lived as if you might never die or, conversely, risked your life in a "death-defying" lifestyle, but this midlife will bring you to your senses, literally.

Your senses become heightened, and your love of life can become the prime motivator now, not the wild and reckless urges of youth. Changing your lifestyle for something that is more original to you, though it might be conventional to others, is not surprising, since the carefree attitude of your youth up to now is now coming up for serious questioning.

3. Third House Midlife Transit/Natal Ninth House: Ideas, Ideas, Ideas

Uranus transiting the third house, in opposition to a ninth house position, marks a radical change in one's mental energy and interests. Having Uranus in the ninth house immediately suggests an iconoclastic attitude toward any and all dogma. A strong resistance to all forms of fixed ideology is instinctive. It is a highly innovative and often intellectual position for Uranus, and quests for truth and knowledge constantly occur. The primary problem that can present with Uranus in the ninth house is dilettantism. Even brilliant thinking needs to be based in a daily reality.

The lifelong search for Truth and Wisdom may end up just being that—a lifelong search. This in itself is not bad and, indeed, is certainly a valid path of existence, but the conflict that arises when elitist Uranus faces its own dogma is profound. The third house is what I call a "fact-based house," and the ninth house is the "theoretical arena of the mind." Both houses are polarized at the core of what all spiritual paths call Truth. We are not normally privy to absolute truth; the fact that what is true changes constantly is quite in tune with the mutable houses of Mercury and Jupiter. If there is a core truth and a universal constant, still it is orbited by bodies of concepts and constructs.

Within the imagery of Uranus lie both abstractions and systems. If the god-image of the ninth house is Uranian, then it is "all encompassing," yet there is a system to the revolution of the planets, the organisms of the world, and the multiversal cosmos. In fact, the Greek word *cosmos* means "order."

The dissolution of arrogance and self-importance that can be part of the Uranian ninth house may well launch a midlifer back to basics. Education becomes very important, and if all signals allow, then one might literally go back to school, take up a new training, or advance ideas in a logical and mature way, for example, by writing, teaching, or traveling the world in search of more knowledge.

Certainly one's family and background arise in this third house transit too. If there have been ideological or family splits and siblings have been "lost," you might remeet and find a new relationship with them. Uncovering each story in the family might be part of your maturing education, as well, and the changes your siblings and family undergo will affect your thinking patterns too.

Opportunities to correct "bad habits" or conceptual problems— literally, thinking problems—that inhibit your openness to new ideas arrive with Uranus transiting the third house. Certainly experimenting with ideas, movement, and change are viable, but, as with all Uranian transits, it is best to explore within your own construct and situation as it exists before leaping into new areas without some healthy caution.

4. Fourth House Midlife Transit/Natal Tenth House Homeward Bound

The midlife transition that is "launched" when Uranus is transiting the fourth house accents the home/career dilemma. It may be that you discover a new kind of freedom associated with family, home, and roots and that the ideas of personal security are in need of attention and revising. Having Uranus in the tenth house natally means finding your individuality and power of personal inventiveness in the arena of career and public relations, all of which may now mean something entirely different.

More often than not, Uranus in the tenth house is impatient with the status quo and moves on continuously, either to new jobs or careers, or veers radically, according to spontaneous urges for change in life focus. Certainly, there is an aptitude for unusual or very individualistic types of work and social attitudes.

Midlife may well mean "meeting your opposite," by suddenly realizing that there is more to life than constant revolution and social and career change and that individuation now depends on creating a new and stimulating life based on more safe and contained lifestyles.

When Uranus actually crosses the IC and into the fourth house, there can be an explosion of energy that releases forgotten, suppressed, or latent traits and personal gifts. The family dynamic is housed here, and thus, a tenth house Uranian is likely to have barrelled through his or her first half of life, now to suddenly discover a whole new range of abilities and talents that are embedded in the family dynasty. Many people will do things such as search out their roots, move to a wholly new location, change jobs, and begin to travel for pleasure and learning.

In addition, as this is a midlife transitional transit, it is associated with family changes, such as children either entering adolescence or actually leaving home. One's parents become more significant, either as elders or, depending on circumstances, losing a parent during this period. Certainly one's individuation process is bound into the structures of the family psyche, and thus it behooves one to act consciously if there are problems in the family or in marriage.

Howard Sasportas says of Uranus transiting the fourth house: "The fourth house shows the influence of our family of origin on us, our early childhood conditioning and our inborn predisposition. From these factors, we form 'scripts,' patterns or beliefs about what kind of persona we are and what to expect from life."*

With this in mind, if Uranus is not only opposite itself in this midlife phase but also aspecting other natal planets in the fourth house, you can expect a time of repeated transition in how you view and experience family, family matters, parents, and siblings. Within that context, you yourself undergo a maturing toward becoming an independent adult with new kinds of responsibilities and a fresh approach to those responsibilities.

*Howard Sasportas, *The Gods of Change: Pain, Crisis and Transformation*, Contemporary Astrology (London and New York: Arkana, 1989), p. 93.

5. Fifth House Midlife Transit/Natal Eleventh House: I Am My Hopes, Wishes, and Dreams

Since your midlife transition is from Uranus transiting the fifth house, and opposing your natal eleventh, it is a time of contacting your creative spirit and using it more personally and individually.

With natal Uranus in the eleventh house of "hopes, wishes, and dreams" you have always sought out dramatic results from your efforts. In a more contemporary sense, your relationship with groups and tribal affiliations, and your personal investment in collective movements and ideas is radically changing. The fifth house is personal, in that one's creativity comes from deep within, a wellspring of Eros and "seeds" in the soul. The fifth house is about *you* as a unique, creative being, and having your midlife transition begin with the fifth/eleventh house axis could mean that you withdraw your energy and focus from society and group dependency and become more *eccentric*—literally, "away from the center."

A strong urge to branch out and find new ways of expressing your inner self—your passions, romances, desires, and longings for pure creative force—initiates you into your midlife transition. This has to do with feelings of love and being loved. The fifth house is love given, while the eleventh is love received. If we get what we give, then, if you have given out more love or energy to the collective, and not enough to yourself, you are likely to find yourself burnt out or close to collapse.

Also, it is important to assess your capacity and willingness to take risks at this time. With an eleventh-house Uranus, you may have been a risk-taker and an adventurer but now find that your wanderer or explorer nature is tired of applause from the world around you and wants more meaningful, inner adventures. It is not unusual to find oneself in a passion about something new in a creative field. Art, music, play, love, emotional freedom, and other deeply creative urges to explore uncharted interior terrain will lead you across the midlife threshold to numerous alternatives.

With the caveat "All life is a risk," remember that the initial crack in the life egg is only a wakeup call, not a lifestyle, so it is essential that you take stock of the things that are truly of value and not throw everything

THE ASTROLOGY OF MIDLIFE AND AGING

out that *appears* to hold you back from an exploration of love, art, passion, and so on. This initial half-Uranus is a revolution, *not* yet a status quo.

The awakening of one's *genius*, ones *daemonion*, plays a huge role in the half-Uranus in the fifth house, as if the desperation of the soul demands individuation through creation and creativity. Not all one's friends or even one's spouse might find this as enchanting as the midlifer himself, so it is imperative that one keep one's head on. However, if one has lived out a life of soulless conventionality, then breakout is vital to a long and happy life.

The midlife trigger brings restlessness for all—but in this house axis, it is about your own natural talents crying out for attention. You may have become rigid and stultified in your relationships with your children, or fear losing your children as they grow older. If you chose or fate decreed that you not have children, this first stage of midlife may precipitate a period of biological grief and mourning.

Since rites of passage now are virtually nonexistent in contemporary society, natural transitions are often not received well. Thus, a woman who, for any number of reasons, passed into maturity with no children, must honor her body's natural relinquishing of its fruitfulness, and respect her own grief and mourning. This too shall pass, but better to pass with conscious collusion than suppression and depression. The supreme outcome of a woman's midlife is her menopause and, ultimately, her rational freedom in maturity.

Men with this midlife trigger often rekindle old passions, for example playing the guitar or hiking, and need to spend time alone, playing in the mind. The male archetype is aligned with action, and thus midlife can precipitate an opening of emotional experience with which they may not be well equipped to deal. That's okay, too—after all, their counterparts, women, are finding freedom in the world of objectivity and non–emotionally based action.

6. Sixth House Midlife Transit/Natal Twelfth House: Mind, Body, and Soul

Uranus in the twelfth house of the natal chart can pose a mystery to astrologers. I find that individuals with this placement have a deep bond with the collective unconscious, a connection that ties them into the revolutions of all times. A sense of global change is imprinted into their psyche. Their individuation process is bound to the collective and thus may not have been active in a personal sense, depending upon the rest of the horoscope. In fact, their "individualism" can remain totally unconscious and unrealized until the "shock" of the half-Uranus jolts them awake.

Twelfth-house Uranus people have a consequential ancestral link, one that means their existence is profoundly enmeshed with the history of human evolution. Their "league of ancestors" is often strongly present in their lives and assertive in the personality of the individual. However, as said before, losing individuality to the collective can result in *lack* of self-awareness.

The very concepts of the collective and the personal are fused and enmeshed, as the twelfth house is the area in which "everything happens all at once" and/or "we are all one" and/or "the universe in the cells." That kind of thinking is millennia old, and the base of all spiritual dogma, but to *live* it is not always comfortable. Planets in the twelfth house can actually remain "unborn," and latent, waiting for some revelation or passionate link to an external force to activate them.*

Often a twelfth-house Uranus person seeks the divine through unorthodoxy, and becomes dedicated to a path of inner wisdom and spirituality. He or she seeks alignment with institutions of a progressive or experimental nature. Church, synagogue, temple, meeting house, or mosque do not shelter the Uranian spiritualist. Only the constant *seeking* of soul will meet their needs. The problem with this is the lack of embodiment of the soul, a condition where the person's uniqueness, individuality, and personal qualities remain in utero, indeed unborn; that is, until the half-Uranus.

With Uranus triggering midlife from the sixth house to the natal twelfth, the soul is *forced* to enter the body and realize that the "game is up" . . . that is, the game of whatever it was one did till now. If you were attuned to the inner world of spirit, you might find the outer world of body

*See Erin Sullivan, *The Astrology of Family Dynamics* (York Beach, ME: Weiser, 2000), pp. 170–180.

just gripping now. Periods of solitude can bring spiritual renewal, because the inner world becomes a source of active imagination and can then be brought out in new ways of relating, working, thinking, and being.

Body and soul are reflected in the sixth and twelfth houses, respectively. And the body carts the soul around, and does the mundane (worldly) tasks needed so that one can eat, sleep, love, work, and so on. When the half-Uranus enters the sixth house, it often awakens the soul in the twelfth, toward a more embodied life. It can mean such things as abruptly changing jobs or dropping all previous commitments or moving to a new location.

The *soma*—body—is enmeshed with the *psyche*, and the two Greek words form the word *psychosomatic*—literally, a body/soul condition. If either the body or the soul are engaged in a battle, then symptoms arise. Much of our symptoms are bred in the bone, but equally they are bred in the soul. In midlife, we begin to notice the body's decline toward aging, and choices need to be made.

An interest in health or healing is likely to arise—a new desire to improve the body's structure and form. Also comes an awakening to the body in a new way, possibly to the understanding that the body is also a "spiritual thing"—not a bad thing to be ignored or punished but a good vehicle for one's deepest beliefs, ethics, and life goals.

This could be a very exciting and awakening time for the twelfth house Uranus person—a time of physical discovery, a journey into the world of form, work, and the simple joy of being a person in a body, with things to do and places to go—a place to put the iconoclastic beliefs and work them into daily life, or cultural life.

7. Seventh House Midlife Transit/Natal First House: The One in the Many

If you have Uranus in the first house at birth, then by midlife, it will have transited the entire lower hemisphere in your chart. This signifies a "loner" quality, an introvert, but often with extraverted personality traits. By this I mean that regardless of the number of people you attract and enjoy, live with and work with, you remain encapsulated in your individuality. By the time midlife comes, you may find your attitude toward independence and intimacy changing radically.

Having spent the majority of your previous years learning, changing, and moving on in accord with an inner dictate, meeting your inner opposite can introduce you to an entirely different motivation toward relationships. You may discover, for instance, that independence does *not* preclude intimacy. It may just be possible to be committed, have a partner, *and* feel as free as you need to for your own individuation process.

In fact, part of individuation for a first house Uranian is finding a comfort zone in relationship to others, while still retaining that spark of self and uniqueness you so strongly need. As you are highly innovative and original, you can offer much in the way of objectivity and insights *to others*, but the big test is being able to receive such wisdom *from others*.

Since you are highly charged, even electrical, in your energy, you may have found it difficult to contain yourself according to other people's standards, and learning to "live alone" has played a significant role in your development. It may have meant building boundaries and barriers around your heart. The cracking open of this shell does not mean that you suddenly become needy and wet, soppy and emotional; it means that the heart chakra opens to accept others.

If you have allowed marriage or committed partnership to stifle your true nature and have actually sacrificed your "self" for the "other," it will no longer work as well for you at this midlife juncture. You will need to find new ways to declare yourself as a person in your own right. Often, in generations past, this was simply the way it was, and no amount of analysis, individuation, or astrology could open the door to a new way of relating. This is no longer the case, and many people have broken the paradigm of "hang in there come hell or high water," so if a long-term arrangement has to end, it is okay.

The closer Uranus is to the ascendant, the more startling is the natal structure and, thus, the midlife change. Many Uranus rising people are really so restless and electrical that learning to live with *themselves* is a life journey—let alone the sophisticated concept of individuating! The biggest problem that arises from this picture is if one doesn't accept oneself—for instance, there may be a highly conventional array of other planets with a square to Saturn, for instance, which creates a psychic split between one's acceptance of being "different" and a truly strong pull to adherence to the social norm.

As with all midlife junctures, the less one has been oneself, the greater the power of the revolution! This is so especially for first-house Uranian types, who often find their soul mate well into midlife, even into the mid-fifties, at the second progressed Lunar return.*

8. Eighth House Midlife Transit/Natal Second House: Love, Money, and the Inevitable

Uranus in the second house at birth means that one has to find a whole new and unconventional way to perceive money, self-worth, and personal assets. Certainly the value of money and materialism poses a philosophical question in the mind of the second house Uranus person! Indeed, if money as currency is valued at all, it is primarily for the freedom it brings.

Because of this innate attitude, one's security, and financial security especially, comes in a wide spectrum. From financial windfalls to great losses, from elation to depression, all can come in the space of a week, or in waves over the lifetime.

Part of this nonattachment to substance and materialism may be sourced to earliest life. The second house represents one's self-worth and feelings of personal value. If deep insecurities are rooted in infancy or childhood, say the loss of a parent, abuse or neglect, or constant upheaval or relocation, then it makes sense that the Uranian second house person finds "security" laughable, if not totally imaginary. To some degree—in fact, to a *great* degree—what convention calls security *is* an illusion. Uranus in the second house comes straight from this school of perception.

However, it is through our trials that our successes are made. And the midlife transit begins a time of refocusing and reassessing what security really means to you. And what money means. And what its axial reflection means—love and risk. It may be that you have always been the one

*See the list of ages and their corresponding aspects from midlife to old age on page 106.

who supported financially, and now in midlife can relax a bit and let someone else be the provider.

Conversely, if you have been detached from material security, then your midlife will bring a better awareness of what value money, home, land, possessions have for you. The eighth house is the house in which we merge our resources, whether they are time, love, money, or all of those things. With Uranus transiting the eighth house, you will need to let a lot of old concepts die a natural death, and be reborn with new insight.

Deep emotional rebirth is part of midlife for you, as your investment of feelings will change. And since the eighth house represents one's partner's resources and security, there may be substantial changes in your partner's work, status, emotional nature, and possibly financial status. This would cause your commitment to and position in the relationship to shift, and focus in new ways. You may find you can materialize some very original and innovative creations and ideas under this transit, and create a new future to support yourself through your maturing years.

If you have been a reluctant self-examiner and have eschewed navel-gazing and self-awareness, then your midlife juncture will be a real third-eye-opener. If you have toughened up and told yourself that you "didn't need anyone," you are in for a big surprise. The eighth house is a psychological house, in among all the "sex, death, and taxes" interpretations that are so carelessly tossed about in lay astrology. Because of its mysteriousness and link to the sleeping side of consciousness, it houses psychological content such as fears, complexes, anxieties, and repressed material in the psyche.

Up rush these lost contents, out fly the anxieties, and psychological traits we have pushed down irrupt from the depths of the soul/psyche. This is all to the good if one is willing to see this catastrophe (about-face) as a healing and purging opportunity. If mortality plagues you at midlife, then see it as a *memento mori*. Yes, you will die, as will all mortals, but what you do in the meantime is more important, and at this crux of life, you are programming your death!

By this I mean that the style of life you live, the care you get and give, the emotions you allow to have freedom, and the assets you share with others—all these things contribute to your life's quality and ultimately its duration. As for the night terror that comes with midlife—embrace it, love it, and let it go.

The reality of death is part of midlife as well. Parents die, older friends as well, and sometimes younger friends. The reality is that you are facing true mortality, and you begin to discuss body parts with your doctor and friends. Contemporary and traditional medicines combined have given us collectively a much better quality of life in old age, so midlife is the time to attend to your mortal coil, and make it last longer and stronger.

9. Ninth House Midlife Transit/Natal Third House: Education, Education, Education

Having Uranus in your third house at birth suggests an independent and original way to perceiving and approaching life in general. Your thinking, though obviously affected by environment and DNA and so forth, is original and unconventional. You may have had a hard time focusing on long-term projects in your earliest schooling, and found creative ways of avoiding the curriculum presented to you. The earliest years of rote learning might have been really difficult, but it is likely that you were ahead of your time.

Hopefully, you found some sympathy in the education system, a way to exercise your abundant abilities without stifling your bright mind. Being restless and highly strung, your mind travels and wanders and explores continually. Many brilliant contributors to ideas have a third house Uranus.

People with Uranus in the third house have a difficult time conforming to mental routine, and have minds that are more suited to abstraction, exploration, and independent thinking. And as if that weren't enough individualism, they have wayward attitudes toward discipline! You may not have felt your potential come to real fruition until you matured, and by the half-Uranus, your mind can take off to all parts of the mental universe with more credibility. Conversely to what Uranus itself implies, you may find you are more capable of mature thinking and embodying your ideas than ever before.

You will need to have numerous avenues and built-in options available to you—you do not need to throw in the whole mental towel but simply realize that there are outmoded thoughts taking up space. For instance, you can embrace the break from the past in a way that is "right" for you, by taking stock of what is still of value and currency and what is holding you back. Any course of action and endeavor must have various provisos for change in place, so when the half-Uranus comes around, and your ninth house is charged with revision, an innovative way of using basic ideas emerges.

The midlife might well bring up potentials that existed in your youth but were not actualized. Now you have the opportunity to possess and own those potentials! The quest for knowledge and a calmer mind—in part because of age and mellowing with time—is strongly featured in your midlife change. All your ideas from life experience and observation now can be appreciated. Out comes the philosopher in you; it is time to examine social and cultural ideas and laws, beliefs, and ethics—possibly in a formal situation such as college or university.

Your relationship with siblings, if you have any, shifts to another level. At midlife, you'll see your relationship to them in a much different light, and if there were splits, problems, and troubles, either you can let go of that part of your feelings toward them, or cross the bridge to a new, more objective way of relating. This phase of midlife is an opportunity to remeet your siblings in a new way.

There are times when siblings are troublesome to the third house Uranian, and their rebellion may have somehow fallen on you as a responsibility. If that is the case, the time has come to let it go, and be responsible only for yourself and your broadening of mental horizons. Ultimately, you are not your brother's keeper, but if you have chosen or have had to adopt such a stance, you may alter that perspective radically.

10. Tenth House Midlife Transit/Natal Fourth House: At Home in the World

You were born precisely at a time when your family needed a catalyst, a reformer, and someone to bring profound liberation to the myth and history of the lineage. Being a Uranus fourth house individual is often not easy, especially during adolescence, again at the first Saturn return, and finally at midlife. Those significant rites of passage call for extra effort to break away from the status quo, regardless of Uranus—and trying to do so without leaving a mess behind. Many fourth-house Uranus individuals feel they were born to rebel and therefore must alter the perspectives of their family as it has been for generations. Acting out what the family would *never* do and thus "individuating" the family.

Since the first "half" of life is spent with Uranus transiting the fourth through the tenth house, the specific focus in the Descendant hemisphere is creative originality within the core self, and the family is the basis for personal originality. The matrix of the family is the early "testing ground" for your individuation process. In some instances, the very conventionality of the family is the spur to novelty and independence, but in many other cases it can be the instability and the unreliability, or the complete absence of a "safe," conventional family, that you respond to in midlife.

Your need to rearrange the structure of the family dynamic has probably resulted in a wholly unique domestic arrangement of the people in your immediate environment. Your capacity to discover family among your friends, and love your friends with loyalty and familial passion, gives you a strong base for creative living. More often than not, a fourth house Uranus indicates a family of origin that—tacitly or overtly—thrust you out of the nest early on and set you on the path to finding security in ways that are nonconformist.

In this case, your midlife will be about security, safety, home, and independence issues that stem from those basic needs. You may get your first home on your own, or you may find that your life now allows more movement and more freedom for exploring the world—relatively, that is—and the possibility of a new lifestyle. The potential for being at home in the world opens up your prospects, interests, and opportunities throughout your midlife transition.

11. Eleventh House Midlife Transit/Natal Fifth House: Getting Returns on Your Investment in Life

Uranus in the fifth house in the natal chart reflects the need to individuate through creative and emotional risk-taking. All aspects of love—especially the love you feel and give to others—involve risk. But then, so is having children, writing books, moving house, traveling, and all the adventures and unknowns in life.

By nature you are drawn to yet fearful of risk—indeed, it is the frisson of angst that underlies any undertaking of value that attracts you to it. Playful by nature, you might have spent your first half of life playing, and now see the value of serious investment in your life's goals and skills.

The half-Uranus from the eleventh house to the fifth emphasizes the growing need to see your hopes and wishes fulfilled—somehow. Since the fifth house core of individuation is about you finding your own self fascinating and the most investable resource to hand, then the eleventh house midlife will highlight the results of this investment to date.

Time, love, and money are our primary foundational resources, and they are inextricably enmeshed. Though you still need to feel free, you do need to compromise and invest yourself and your inner resources in other people, too. Anxiety may be reduced by accepting that aspect of yourself. If you truly work to come to terms with your needs to be unique and self-dependent, then midlife will open the door to profound returns in the way of friends, groups, social causes, collective action, and tribal affiliations.

By your own nature, the mutual dependency of intimate, committed love might feel stifling and cloying to you, or you may be ambivalent about commitment to a single individual in your life. This may have meant that you do not have children of your own but have the capacity to love other people's children, and to see all your friends as "children," in that you care for them in some responsible way.

We all are victims of social stereotype, no matter how inherently

Uranian we are—thus, if you have ascribed to socially received wisdom about love and relationship, then you may need to unwind yourself from that wheel. And as you are inherently a creative and self-inspired person, your midlife initiates you into the time when you truly can be who you are, with substance. If you are an artist (at heart or in practice) then be that. If you are a supermother, and it works, then do it with style as an elder. If you have longed to found a nonprofit organization in your spare time, do it full time.

Certainly midlife will bring you closer to the satisfaction of seeing your life in a clear light, and will open doors for both freedom and closeness. If there is a collapse of previous values in midlife, this is a good thing. Your inner system will not condone hypocrisy or insincerity now, and thus what irrupts as "bad" or false must be released.

Commitments now will not feel so restrictive, hypocritical, banal, conformist, or any of the other bugaboos you may previously have feared. After all, risk is also found in soulless conventionality—possibly the greater risk is loss of opportunity to expand and reach elderhood with peace and joyful satisfaction.

12. Twelfth House Midlife Transit/Natal Sixth House: My Body, My Self

With Uranus in your natal sixth house, you have an electrical system for a nervous system! This is an exceptional and complex place for Uranus, as it is so deeply entwined with the body/soul dyad. As a child you may have resented being coddled and babied, wanting to be independent before your time. Since the high level of physical energy that this placement (generally) brings can be hard on parents, who have to rush about saving you from yourself, you would have found exceptional ways to "work"—and, as a child and adolescent, to play.

For you, any job or career must provide many themes and challenges— otherwise, you would find yourself bored and unhappy. The "job" of the body is to carry yourself and your deep inner life around and to do practical, survival things. As you are inherently restless and in need of stimulation, motivation, and excitement about whatever it is you do, the likelihood of transforming and changing your job, work, and focus in your career can occur quite often, especially in midlife.

When Uranus opposes itself in midlife from the twelfth house to the sixth, you will have explored almost all the possible alternatives in your work and action—and when it makes its half-cycle, a retreat to a rich inner life could be your reward. This does not mean you go to a monastery or withdraw from work, but your interior life takes on a more prominent place in your nature.

It is highly possible for you to achieve independence and self-directed employment during any phase of your midlife transition, but the urge to break out is one of the crossover episodes; if you have already gone to self-reliance, then the opportunity to evaluate your satisfaction and happiness with that work will nonetheless take you in new directions. Conversely, if you are stuck in a rut when Uranus opposes itself, then your external world may appear to collapse around you, but it will have been coming along for a while, and you have probably sensed its arrival.

Uranus in the twelfth house transit phase often is a rude awakening. This is because the twelfth house contains the multiverse of the unconscious and, as such, hoards many secrets apart from our own conscious awareness. There is a profound collusion between your psyche and its deep unconscious Self with your actual experiences in life, and this must never be underestimated.

This mysterious relationship between the outer and inner worlds affects your own involvement in whatever happens to you. That is not to say that fate doesn't have a hand in life circumstance, or that you are in some way responsible for everything that occurs; but in many, many instances we can see how it is that we got where we are. This is the task at hand for your midlife lessons and growth.

Along with any Uranus transit comes a small spark of excitement, and this can ignite for you a revolution over the next few years, because the twelfth house transit addresses the degree of freedom you feel you have in life. You are preparing, both unconsciously and consciously, for the eventual crossing of Uranus over your ascendant. If you have put off dealing with or ignored the inner rumblings of change, then that crossing will certainly be useful for "hearing" the call to new ways of being yourself!

Change, in this instance, also involves your health and way of treating your body. Awakening to a more spiritual and psychological relationship between body (soma) and soul (psyche) can greatly enhance feelings of healthiness. Psychosomatic symptoms are key alerts to imbalance in your body/soul relationship. Being attentive and respectful of what your psyche/soul is calling out for can create a future with greater health, both mental *and* physical.

CHAPTER 6

GENERATIONAL IMPULSE:
PURPOSE AND VISION IN
CREATING THE FUTURE

PLUTO IN LEO SEXTILE NEPTUNE IN LIBRA

We are fast arriving at a time in society when the concept and relationship of families is charged with *angst* because no coherent picture exists of what, in fact, "a family" is. Families are becoming as individual and unique in structure and content as individuals. Family consciousness and consciousness of families is shifting forms rapidly, and the collective urge plays a tremendous parallel role, as it always has. Many of us born in the post–World War II period are still in thrall to the ideal of the Western family: Mommy, Daddy, little girl, and little boy—"us four and no more."

The American artist Norman Rockwell depicted this fantasy family brilliantly in his illustrations, complete with gamboling family dog and cat napping by the fireside. It was so adorable it hurt to look at it. The

---

*This chapter, including figure 4 on page 89, is drawn, with some editing, from my book *The Astrology of Family Dynamics* (York Beach, ME: Weiser, 2000), originally titled *Dynasty: The Astrology of Family Dynamics*, Contemporary Astrology (London and New York: Arkana, 1996). Permission to reprint granted to the author.

horror of this image is that not only does it emerge now as being patently untrue but also many of the largest group/generation to hit the planet (born 1939 and 1956) are still clinging to the Mommy-Daddy picture and are reluctant to let go of that interior image, though they are shattered and saddened by its lack of reality.

These people were all born with Pluto in Leo, the sign of the child, and will take their childhood to the grave. They (myself included in this generational imprint) may never leave off blaming Mommy and Daddy and the collective for everything, physical and psychological. The Pluto in Leo generation identifies with the child archetype, which ultimately needs a parental context within which to function.

Most of the Pluto in Leo generation have parents with Neptune in Leo—their (the parent's) dream of their children was dashed by the storming passage of Pluto over their collective Neptune and heralded the death of the fantasy child. The vast majority of the Pluto in Leo people did not want the burden of carrying the fantasy flame of their parents and, especially in the North American and European-origin cultures, they set about dashing the hopes, dreams, fantasies, and generosity-to-the-extreme of their parents.

Though in other cultures (Asian, Oriental, indigenous, and so on) this generation did not express this en masse as immediately in the 1960s, their collective unconscious contained it, and over the last thirty years they too have had the same catharsis, resulting in the slow rumble of mass rebellion (or inevitable loss of culture), and they have been just as destructive of their cultural histories as the noisy, colorful front-runners of the Western cultural revolution in the sixties. What we now know about China and its horrors in those years, for one example, illustrates the power of global consciousness.

In addition, the Pluto in Leo children have parents whose own Pluto was in Cancer, the sign of the family—to be specific, the indicator of the "nuclear" (isolated) family. This Pluto in Cancer generation was destined to have their children deny the traditional roles and make every attempt to decimate the image of the family that was lodged in the collective Western psyche. This disintegration has seeped into almost all cultures now, globally. Essentially, the Pluto in Leo generation was born to destroy

FIGURE 4. EVOLUTION

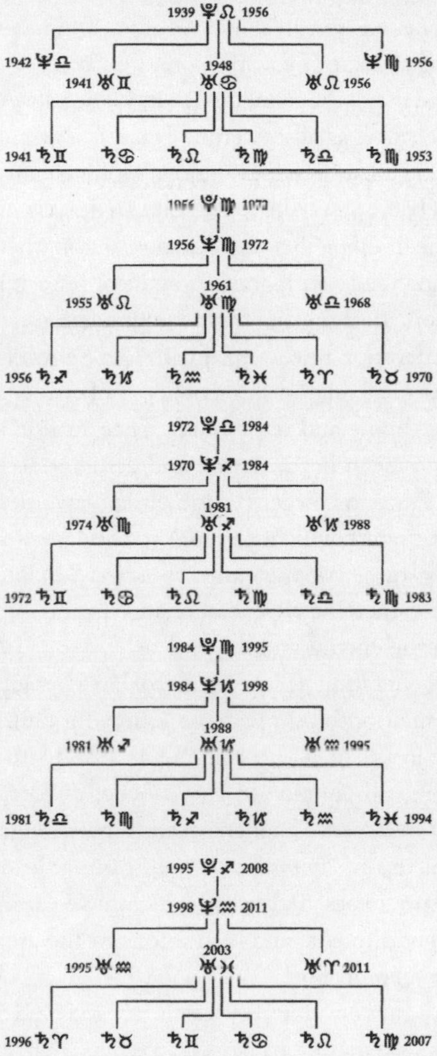

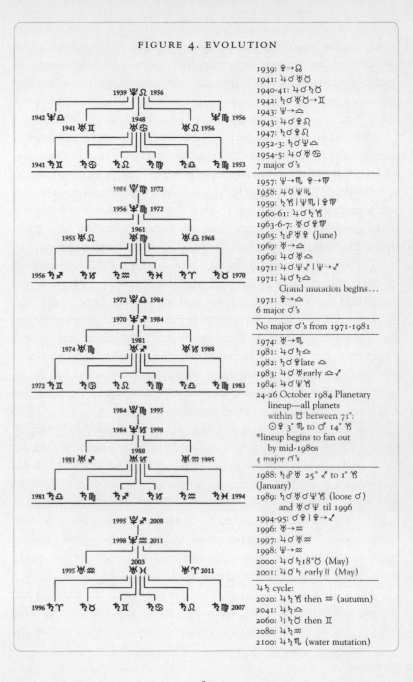

1939: ♇→♌
1941: ♃☌♅♉
1940-41: ♃☌♄♉
1942: ♄☌♅♉→♊
1943: ♆→♎
1943: ♃☌♇♌
1947: ♄☌♇♌
1952-3: ♄☌♆♎
1954-5: ♃☌♅♋
7 major ☌'s

1957: ♆→♏ ♇→♍
1958: ♃☌♆♏
1959: ♄♑ | ♆♏ | ♇♍
1960-61: ♃☌♄♑
1963-6-7: ♅☌♇♍
1965: ♄☍♅♇ (June)
1969: ♅→♎
1969: ♃☌♅♎
1971: ♃☌♆♐ | ♆→♐
1971: ♃☌♄♎
Grand mutation begins…
1971: ♇→♎
6 major ☌'s

No major ☌'s from 1971-1981

1974: ♅→♏
1981: ♃☌♄♎
1982: ♄☌♇late ♎
1983: ♃☌♅early ♎♐
1984: ♃☌♆♑
24-26 October 1984 Planetary lineup—all planets within ☋ between 71°: ☉♇ 3° ♏ to ♂ 14° ♑
*lineup begins to fan out by mid-1980s
4 major ☌'s

1988: ♄☍♅ 25° ♐ to 1° ♑ (January)
1989: ♄☌♅☌♆♑ (loose ☌) and ♅☌♆ til 1996
1994-95: ☌♇ | ♇→♐
1996: ♅→♒
1997: ♃☌♅♒
1998: ♆→♒
2000: ♃☌♄18°♉ (May)
2001: ♃☌♄ early ♊ (May)

♃♄ cycle:
2020: ♃♄♑ then ♒ (autumn)
2041: ♃♄♎
2060: ♃♄♉ then ♊
2080: ♃♄♒
2100: ♃♄♏ (water mutation)

the king, the *tyrannos*—leaders—of the times. However, the dictator that arose with the sighting of Pluto on January 21, 1930, was a penultimate archetype of the demon embodied, and his tyranny was of such large scale that all individuals born after the 1940s have the image of the tyrant-king imbedded deeply in their psyches and live in conscious or unconscious terror of their individuality being abducted by inappropriate authority.

Pluto in Leo symbolizes the rise of the individual to its highest level, its most grandiose imagination of itself as all-powerful. There is a deep fear embedded in the Pluto in Leo generation of losing one's individuality to the masses; an innate terror of being absorbed by the collective psyche. Yet, as this generation has Neptune in Libra, there is a paradox, in that there is also a general desire to fuse and merge with another and lose oneself in a dream-like fantasy of perfection, idealism, and harmonious relations.

That the Pluto in Leo generation have Neptune in Libra powerfully attests to their dream that the ideal relationship could exist between the sacred and the profane—the divine and the human. The idealism and values of this generation have been both exalted and denigrating. All the "radical" thinkers of the Pluto in Leo generation often conveniently forget that the other half of them have contributed to the loss of soul and defiling of Gaia, the very thing that the more "conscious" individuals have been in despair about since the advent of change in the sixties. However, we now have seen the enemy, and they are us!

The Neptune in Libra generation (Pluto in Leo) have projected their divinity onto human relationships and have suffered a crash in ideals and loss of innocence in the area of "profane" (that is, plain old ordinary) relationships, while still clinging to the concept of "divine" relationships—which do not necessarily happen on earth between mortals. Hence the phenomenal rise in "gurus," cult and spiritual leaders, the concept of soul mates, twin flames, and so on, which have paradoxically resulted in many disappointments and disillusions in the area of both personal and collective relationships.

The shadow lies in Leo: by our very mortality we are not gods and thus fall short of the mark, yet, in attempting to be gods, commit the sin of hubris. This is part of a deeply unconscious collective awareness that the shadow of the age, that is, Leo as polar opposite of Aquarius, is god-like and that the past Age of Leo, the Golden Age, underlies the coming "New Age." If the gods walked the earth back then, they are straining to return today. This collective impulse is manifested in individuals in ways both sacred and profane. Pluto in Leo/Neptune in Libra feels the resurgence of the gods and can mistake that for an individual personal godliness.

For example, the Neptune in Libra/Pluto in Leo vision is one of global unity, an ultimate fusion of cultures, along with the power of the individual in relationship with the collective. The axis for the individual-collective image *is* Leo-Aquarius, and with the quickening advent of the Aquarian Age (astronomically circa 2060), there is a collective anxiety afoot that heralds massive change.

As the first wave on the shores, the Pluto in Leo people inherently felt their work was cut out for them—to assert individuality (Leo) over the collective (Aquarius) and hopefully to institute a system in which the individual is responsible for the collective (Neptune in Libra). In some ways, this is still a rebellion against *auctoritas sine superioritas*—authority without superiority—because it is still one against the many. Massive ego inflation has occurred with this generational impulse—not only have there been multitudes of false gurus and deluded (lacking in playfulness) leaders, but also the generational stamp includes genuine resourcefulness and inventive genius.

On the darker side, the playfulness of Leo (*ludo*—"I play") is corrupted by the de-luded—unplayful—aspect of the visionary side: the deadly serious mien of New Ageism, a millenarian phenomenon that promises the advent of various types of messiah. In addition, the longing to remain in childhood, to play at life, has resulted in the paradox of the child-*senex*—remaining youthful in the aging process. These people are deadly serious about playing. An industry of leisure has arisen, one that has stripped the shores and beauty spots of nature to make adult playgrounds. Go any-where in the civilized world where there is a beach, a mountain lake, or a natural phenomenon, and you will find hordes of tourists lining up at arcades and clubs, booking into monolithic blocks of apartments stretching for miles, playing in the sun—and, like children, wholly unconscious of their impact on nature and the environment. Until the loss of natural resources have become so evident that the Pluto in Leo generation (half of them, anyway) now lead in environmental sciences.

All this affects our relations within the context of families. The greater family, the family of humanity, is deeply influenced by the "my toy" attitude of the supreme child, the collective psychology that is most currently in vogue and power. Changes evolve over time, and the movement of Pluto and Neptune in sextile for many generations yet to come (they begin to move out of orb of sextile around 2040 CE) will show marked attitudinal changes both within small collectives (the genetic family) and the global collective—the family of humanity. The collusion of Power-Pluto and Vision-Neptune will move toward new forms, mutate into new shapes, and contain new archetypal images for all. The Pluto/Neptune sextile has been and will be the subtext of the new era as it emerges over the next centuries.

We are still reeling under the impact of Pluto's sighting in 1930, but waves of its influence will continue to hit the shores of our consciousness in ever-increasing, further-implicating events and patterns for many decades. Though we might find the idea of evolutionary mutation a bit far-fetched, we are already experiencing it now and will see it quicken in this century. Fortunately, the planets move on, as do we, and each successive generation has its work cut out for it by the previous one, as each current generation sets the task for the coming one. The fact that Pluto spends a leisurely thirty-two years transiting the backdrop of the sign Taurus and a hasty twelve in Scorpio might suggest that its 245-year orbit can only sustain a short sojourn in its own sign— certainly, any longer in Scorpio, and little of life would remain!

In the generational sequence, Pluto symbolizes the collective purpose and Neptune the vision. What follows is a description of the evolution of the collective purpose and vision from the late 1950s through to the millennium. Families are set in the context of the *Zeitgeist*—but more momentous is their placement in the heavens. These comprehensive groupings show the timing of long-range shifts in collective values and perspectives that precisely demarcate global shifts in collective consciousness.

PLUTO IN VIRGO SEXTILE NEPTUNE IN SCORPIO

The Pluto in Virgo generation (born between 1956 and 1972) has Neptune in Scorpio. Their dreams were darkened while Pluto transited Scorpio between 1982 and 1995. The eccentric orbit of Pluto has some fated aspect for certain groupings of planets, signs, and people—the Pluto in Cancer people with Neptune in Leo (1915–1930) experienced their Pluto transit over Neptune during the 1940s and mid-1950s, and their dreams were powerful and grand; they built dynasties and created monuments to independence and the power of the individual—but, as I have shown, their dreams were not sufficient to support their children's needs for drama and revolution. This is not the tone of what Pluto in Virgo/Neptune in Scorpio people will experience. Pluto transiting Neptune is akin to having the anaesthetic shut off. There is no escape from *Weltschmertz*—world-pain. The scales do not drop slowly from the eyes, they are ripped away, and the stark truth of one's own personal self-delusion and the entire collective fantasy is revealed.

Generally, the people with Pluto in Virgo have not and do not find their nuclear families to be a nest of neuroses—even if they *are* such, the level of concern over parental influence is not as strongly focused as with the Pluto in Leo people. For the Pluto in Virgo people, individual families are unrecognizable by the old definition, and though many of them have emerged from exceptionally unconventional families (that is, the old norm is broken), some even from horribly dysfunctional families, they are largely disinclined to censure the parents themselves and are more inclined to lay blame on a more collective level and on a more existential, cosmic level. They are a more accepting group—they understand inherently that there is a fate to things, a time of life, and a job to do.

When I was studying classics in the mid-1980s, during my own midlife turning-point, my Greek mythology professor told me that he had suffered a great embarrassment when he was telling the Oedipus myth to his young students (generally all Pluto in Virgos—or 0° Libra—except for the odd "mature student" like myself), the one where the boy kills his father so he can sleep with his mother, the source of the now fa-

mous Freudian Oedipus complex. He interpreted the myth in the contemporary psychological fashion, admitting that it applied to him on an
archetypal level (he too has Pluto in Leo).

He then posed the question to the students whether or not they felt
this mythic triangulation in their own relationship between themselves
and their parents. He was met with a collective blank stare. The children
of the fifties/sixties did not know what he was going on about! They probably found him odd, and possibly deranged, to be "confessing" to Oedipal
feelings—*they did not resonate to the story in a personal, psychological way.*
He and I had a good laugh about this, but it set me to thinking and realizing that we must, as a generation, stop imposing our models on our children and burdening them with the guilt (sins) of our own pasts.

Though it is part of the survival instinct to indoctrinate our youth with
our own perspective and beliefs, it is impossible to infuse totally our own
generational values into succeeding generations, just as our contemporary
bias cannot serve the study of cave drawings. *As we do not know what archaic humans thought, we cannot know what future people will feel.* However,
with the planetary pictures in mind, we can arrive at some intelligent suppositions about what might be evolving in the archetypal mind.

Pluto in Virgo/Neptune in Scorpio brings new purpose and vision to
the world, one that is based on deep cleansing. Not only the old values
of family relationships but also the new values emerging in global relationships sit heavily on the shoulders of the Pluto in Virgo generation.
To speak frivolously, the function of Virgo is to clean up after the party
(the previous sign Leo) in order to create a new diplomatic equilibrium
(Libra, the next sign) within relationships, both personal and collective.
With Pluto in Virgo, your innate legacy is one that charges you with pu-
rifying and articulating more precisely the fabulous vision of the past
generation—but within the scope and limitations of reality.

The reality frame for Pluto in Virgo/Neptune in Scorpio is stark and
clear. The functional practicality of Virgo in dealing purposefully with
tools and materials at hand is tremendous, while the existentialism of the
Scorpionic Neptune is an asset in coping with the death of old ways—
part of the vision of Neptune in Scorpio actually includes endings. These
people's relationship to family dynamics is quite unique. Their perspec-

tive on the hapless limitations of their parents is fair and benign at best or cold, unsympathetic, and distant at worst. They recognize how human we all are, and that, in the end, death is the great equalizer.

It appears that the purpose of the Pluto in Virgo generation is to heal many wounds, and their awareness of their own parent's guilt and *angst* will work wonders for their future expectations of family groups. The Pluto in Virgo people will very likely be the healers of their family complexes and the nurses of the psyches of their Pluto in Leo parents' battered egos! In very plain language, the Pluto in Virgo generation does not and will not have the leisure, resources, time, or inclination to spend a great deal of their energy whining about their parents!

They are impatient to get on with it, and feel burdened by their parents trying to work out their own complexes through their children (i.e., them!). The leitmotif of Virgo is compassion (literally, "suffering with"), and their generational impetus is to throw off their parents' suffering and move beyond it toward a future fraught with uncertainty and potential chaos. The underlying unconscious theme in Virgo is the descent into collectivity and primal chaos (polarity: Pisces), which annihilates individual order, hence ego-loss in favor of soulfulness. Essentially they are here to resurrect what the Pluto in Leo generation has crucified.

The vision (Neptune) is Scorpionic—both fatalistic and realistic. The generational psyche faces the death of the old bravely, seeking solace both in spiritual and practical matters. Through work, diligence, humanitarianism, awareness of the *terminus* of the old way of life—a way not long passed—they are the nascent foundations of a new type of family dynamic: a dynamic that has been forced to include the concept of a global family.

It appears that the global family, though idealistically envisioned by the Pluto in Leo generation, really only began to emerge with the Pluto in Virgo generation. The efforts to decentralize the nuclear-family concerns during the years of their maturing, which opened up into the perspective of relationships of "families" to include larger, more culturally and internationally centered values, will still take several generations to become stabilized into a new status quo, and firmly established.

It is this generation that took the vision of the previous generation of Pluto in Leo/Neptune in Libra to the edge of the information superhighway, the global network, and perfected technology to move the world toward a seamless, organic whole—*unus mundus*. Though admirable in its technology, there is a paradox within the vision of Neptune in Scorpio.

Scorpio is a reclusive sign, singular and morose. It is water, so it is deeply feeling and needs emotional contact with others, but often it is repelled by prolonged intimacy and tries to kill the thing upon which it grows dependent. The global network that this generation has brought to maturity has two sides. On the one hand, theoretically, everyone is in connection with everyone else—but only so if they are alone in their room at their computer.

The awareness of psychic entropy, the gradual decline of energy, is strong in the Virgo/Scorpio combination. Nihilism cannot sustain itself in groups but can only find solace in the quiet isolation of aloneness. Generally, their expectations of happiness are not high—they do not recall the Golden Age, as did their immediate predecessors. But this is the reactionary aspect to their legacy from dramatic, flamboyant, demanding parents—parents who have not yet overcome their anger at *their* parents; parents who, at the age of fifty-plus, are still crying about their own dysfunctional families!

PLUTO IN LIBRA SEXTILE NEPTUNE IN SAGITTARIUS

There is a shift, yet again, with the next group, who were born between 1971 and 1983. Pluto in Libra and Neptune in Sagittarius people come in with an overwhelming desire for freedom and a new futuristic vision. It is significant to note that *there were relatively few births in that decade (the seventies) in relation to the number of potential parents* (the Pluto in Leo/Neptune in Libra people). It is fascinating to note that in parallel to this decline in birthrate, *there were no major conjunctions* between planets from Jupiter out to Pluto from 1971 to 1981 (see figure 4). Whereas in the previous generational periods there were *seven* major conjunctions between 1939 and 1955 and *six* major conjunctions between 1957 and

1971, there were *none* from 1971 to 1981, *four* from 1974 to 1984, and *six* from 1984 to 1997.

And then all the planets from Saturn outward fully changed signs by 1998. The 1970s were a dormant, incubating period, unremarkable on the outside but deeply fruitful on a gestating level. Everything went underground. The children of the 1970s are a potential "lost generation," one that seemingly fell through the cracks.

Even though they are few in number, real objectivity enters the picture with the Pluto in Libra/Neptune in Sagittarius group. They embody a great move toward liberation from the confines of old mores and dictates of all the previous generations. This is coupled with a strong commitment to relationship and ideals that can be met more realistically—a reaction to the "Love the one you're with" parents. These are the majority of children born to the Pluto in Leo/Neptune in Libra group—and they too will disillusion their parents, but in a very different fashion. Pluto is in the sign of their parent's Neptune, and just as the Pluto in Leo group dashed the fantasies of their parents, so it seems that history will repeat itself, yet again in a new way.

This group arrived on the planet as many of the Neptune in Libra generation were becoming uncomfortably aware that their fairy-tale attitude toward relationships was not working terribly well, and perhaps rethinking or refeeling the whole picture would be a good idea. As with all generational issues, those complexes that remain unresolved in the parents are passed on to the children to be further processed, and hopefully broken and reintegrated in new forms.

The fantasy of the ideal relationship, one that does not require work but can be jettisoned when it lacks idealistic perfection, is the shadow of Neptune in Libra. Neptune in Libra sought to recapture in adulthood the primary relationship found only in the womb, where two hearts beat as one. However, the subsequent people with Pluto in Libra were born with the inherent awareness that harmony, balance, and fair play are *not* automatically inserted into relating and that it requires civilization and work, mutual philosophy and beliefs, to keep a relationship or group or family together. The collective *ethos* of this generational motif is one that contains the possibility that because individuals are *not* perfect or identical, relationships between these imperfect, dissimilar beings are bound to be fraught with imperfections and contrasts. This sound philosophy can result in very fruitful new types of families and relationships.

The combination—Pluto in Libra and Neptune in Sagittarius—they produce is essentially an objective perspective arrived at by doing and thinking, rather than feeling and hoping. Naturally, individuals in this collective image are of various types and are distinctly individual and have deep, emotional, feeling natures, but their generational imprimatur, stamp, or archetype is one of emotional detachment, with strong collective social values, rather than of individual supremacy or personal gain. Their family patterns will probably be based more on tribal or even global humanitarian values—they are the real fulcrum between the past and the future, the connection to the global family.

Neptune in Sagittarius has a strong inclination toward idealizing the global family, possibly to the detriment of the deeper, feeling tone. They would be far more inclined to abandon family systems altogether as we know them, and mark the true separation from the pre–World War II values that were so badly mangled in the sixties. The high-mindedness of Sagittarius can become pathologically impartial and unbiased, treating all things as the gods of myth treated mortals. Like puppetmasters pulling the strings of their puppets, their attitude can be disdainful of emotion and human individual need. This prevailing wind would certainly shift the tide of family consciousness if it took that tack en masse. The vision (Neptune) of "one world, one family" (Sagittarius), will need to undergo the test of Pluto's full transit of Sagittarius from 1995 through 2008, and, hopefully, people will still be reading this book to see if things have, indeed, changed much at all! We will probably be experiencing the marriage of heaven and hell—the deepest, inmost self connecting to the highest, most cosmic mind.

PLUTO IN SCORPIO/NEPTUNE IN CAPRICORN

When Pluto entered Scorpio in 1983–84 for twelve years, Neptune also began its fourteen-year transit of Capricorn, and they trotted along in sextile together for around thirteen years. But toward the end of their reign in those signs, a major conjunction of planets took place on January 11, 1994—seven planets in Capricorn with an eclipsing moon conjunct Mars retrograde in opposition to the Capricorn stellium.

The entire transit of Pluto in Scorpio is a period now seen as one that signaled the death of the past age; the disintegration of a flagging system; the loss of cultural integrity; the pandemic AIDS virus; the muting of boundaries, borders, and cultural distinctions; and the final death knell of the old ways. But we are not clocks, it would seem. The heavens may impel, but humans delay. It takes about (or once took, shall we say) sixty years for a new idea to enter the mainstream fully—approximately two generational maturation cycles. The process of assimilation is necessarily slow and thorough. It must first move through the one and *then* the many.

There are times in history where the significance and power of the individual is greater than at other times. The astounding developments in science have been prolific. Individuals in the race against time, ideas in the collective brain are continuing to be funneled through human minds at a most incredible rate. Information that has accumulated over decades, centuries, millennia has been and is being collated and is producing some very sane, open-ended deductions—a revolution in evolution is on the doorstep.

How, then, in the light of such fantastic happenings and such truthful transits, can we possibly adhere to hypocrisy? Evidently, with great ease. However, if that is so, how long can this be supported? Probably not for long. If anything, what does this portend for families in the future decades to come? With hindsight as our lens, let us turn our scope on the future of families and, using pure astrological symbolism, moving beyond psychology, let us see what the planetary family has in store for its human representatives—a form of astropomorphism, we might say.

The AIDS virus is still a chilling messenger—that the immune system, once so reliable in humans and animals, can actually break down completely is a horrific biological metaphor for the loss of immunity to invasive forces that our very Earth has sustained. In effect, if the pollution rate isn't balanced by a radical correction, Gaia herself may turn

HIV-positive. This is the reality that the Pluto in Scorpio and Neptune in Capricorn people are born into, and will carry imprinted in their collective consciousness. It is no wonder that a scorn is felt for sentiment and nostalgia, both rather wasteful emotions, though both Scorpio and Capricorn are known for their sensitivity to deep and historical issues. With imminent threat of global disintegration, these people want to place their values in areas other than in small, secretive, insular, nuclear family conclaves.

Pluto in Scorpio and Neptune in Capricorn (conjunct Uranus for many of those years) gives birth to a generation of wise or jaded people, whose souls have come in with the knowledge of the ages. Nothing shocks them, nothing amazes—only the future is open to them, as the past is closed. The models of the past have been shattered beyond redemption, *nothing* works as it "used to in the old days," systems are limping along, hoping for reconstitution. And it will be this generation who will, indeed, repair and redo, resurrect and reclaim, regenerate and renovate. Able to work with the minimum of resources and capable of accepting the few viable routes left from which to carve a future path, these people are the hope of the long future. The images that are presented in this configuration symbolize a total restructuring of politics, money, resources, and relationships.

The combination of Scorpio and Capricorn is not a terribly cheerful image, and considering the mundane events of the time in which this transit occurred, we would be fools to consider that the product of those times might be a lighthearted, happy-go-lucky bunch of puers and puellas. To the absolute contrary, they contain a very serious, terribly realistic, senex consciousness.

Theirs will be the job of re-visioning power, social order, and a new status quo, with a dissolving trust in "history" as a great teacher! The disenchantment with the way things are will lead to a new way of creating a world system and order.

Their approach to relationship is filled with pragmatism and awareness of the power of love to transform all rigid states. Their allegiance to their groups will be undying, everlasting, and profoundly tribal. They instinctually know their tribe and tend to cluster around and within it, nourishing and protecting their own. Though other tribes are acknowledged, they will generally stick faithfully close to home; they will create working systems that will allow "handshakes" with other tribes, but they will not integrate. This is not a signature of "one world, one people." It would appear that the deep, systemic shocks that occurred to the collective psyche between 1983 and 1995 have locked a generation of people into defense and protection mode, which will result in a complete review of the concept of loyalty. It is not that they don't think globally—as I have already pointed out, this concept is now fully assimilated and integrated into the psychic whole—but that they know inherently that each of them as individuals are made up of and make up little collectives, which in turn make up the whole. They are aware of the cellular makeup of all things. And they see themselves as an essential cell in an organic whole. This is the fruit of the Gaia Theory in human form. This is individualism at its most intense and focused—awareness of individuality, but acknowledging its relationship within its tribe.

In 1984 there was a *true* planetary lineup—a harmonic convergence—as opposed to all the popular "harmonic convergences" advertised at odd times during the eighties and nineties in New Age magazines. Between October 24 and 26, 1984, *all the planets, the Sun, and the Moon were between 3° Scorpio and 14° Capricorn*. A 71° orb! All the planets—starting with Sun and Pluto at 3° Scorpio and ending with Mars at 14° Capricorn! The bunching formed a stellium contained within a quintile—an aspect that suggests the seeding of deep knowledge. This was the turning-point toward the future—this was the last "harmonic convergence," and the harmonic it struck was the fifth.*

This fifth-harmonic group of individuals have a Mandelbrot for a brain. (Remember, we are walking transits.) In a sense, they are all psychic manifestations of the Pythagorean philosophy. Tied into the Golden Section, they embody all knowledge ever passed before and to come after. It is a mystical yet terribly practical—the number of Man—

---

*For other references to the astrology on fifth harmonics, see Michael Harding and Charles Harvey, *Working with Astrology*, Wessex Astrology (Bournemouth, United Kingdom: Consider Publications, 2004), chap. 12, and Erin Sullivan, *Retrograde Planes: Traversing the Inner Landscape* (York Beach, ME: Weiser, 2000), p. 88.

configuration. They *think* differently from any other generation before or after them. This could be said of all of us, but this is a unique, turning-point generation—they mark the death of the past and the conception of the future. They live in a world in which anything might happen. Nothing can happen that will be shocking or amazing—unless, of course, it is in their lifetime that the unified theory is proved or the visitation from other intelligence takes place at last. This characteristic, the Uncertainty Principle inherent in the consciousness of the collective group, will result in a backlash, a conservationist and traditionalist-minded group of people.

The major configuration that marked the passing of this generational period was the Uranus/Neptune conjunction. This aspect, occurring only once every 171 years, created an atmosphere of total chaos in both the collective and in individual people's lives. Between the years of 1991 and 1995, Uranus weaved its way toward, through, and beyond the orb of Neptune. That Uranus is the planet of individualism and individuation and Neptune the planet symbolizing the ultimate loss of individual identity in the zone of the group-consciousness and the collective speaks of a massive identity crisis on a global scale. A loss of group identity was balanced by the extremist organizations forming and declaring supremacy.

Whole countries lost their identities. Individuals lost their concept of a personal future and a coherent purpose in life. Dreams were no longer sufficient stuff to live on. Capricorn is a harsh realist, and with Neptune dissolving realities right and left for fourteen years, then challenged by Uranus crying out for distinction among the confusion, all systems teetered, and many collapsed. People born under these configurations will have tremendous tolerance but little in the way of anaesthetics to prevent them from seeing through pretense. Hence their family structures will probably be based on a vision of stability, coherence, loyalty, inheritance, and continuity. This is a reaction to the independent nihilism of the previous group—they will want assurance of their continuation and will probably re-form the nuclear family archetype.

Neptune is like a giant sleeping pill, and Uranus an alarm-clock . . .

while one is wanting to descend into the arms of Morpheus, one hears the bell going off! Those who were born with Pluto in Scorpio sextile the Uranus/Neptune conjunction will find solace in chaos and uniqueness in sameness, will want security, and will create it in ways that seem unfathomable to their parents. The underlying uncertainty of Neptune will forever change the criteria for convention, standards, status quo, and authority. And the passage of Uranus through the Neptune zone in 1994–1995 shattered the dream of a spiritual leadership. However, it did begin to reinstate the power of the individual, which seemed lost. Families were shattered by a wave of sexual allegations in this era, a real crucible period. Children born carrying this stamp will have a vision of a highly moral culture with strong laws for conventional behavior.

PLUTO IN SAGITTARIUS SEXTILE NEPTUNE IN AQUARIUS

Pluto and Neptune moved into these signs in the 1995–1996 period and will stay there together until around 2009–2011, weaving in and out of perfect orb of the sextile with each other. The planet Uranus, like the previous configuration, was in Aquarius for part of this time as well, until 2003 or so. The conflict generated by ideas has been a historical fact—and most wars have been based on ideology, not territorialism, as is commonly thought. More people have killed other people for what they thought or believed than for what they owned or governed. Here we have a group of ideological warriors, ones who organize their groups around philosophy, religious views, cultural fluidity, international attitudes, and global-unity beliefs.

People born in this grouping will come into their maturity—Saturn return—roughly between 2025 and 2040. It is in these years that the Pluto-Neptune sextile will truly be over. After almost a century of being in the sextile formation, Pluto will begin to lag behind, and its movement will begin the slowing process as it heads toward Pisces through Taurus, on through the most apparent elongated point in its orbit. Pluto in Sagittarius/Neptune in Aquarius people will step over the threshold into the new world. With this in mind—being that we are made up more of our futures than our pasts—the seed of the new world lies in the psyche of this group of people.

This aspect does, finally, speak of "one world, one people." In this period, the seeds of such a potential take root, lending the people born during this time strong ideologies and a global-thinking attitude. How this occurs is not terribly clear, but there are some inherent horrors in Pluto in Sagittarius that must be addressed. Sagittarius has to do with formalized and legislated ideologies; it also has to do with the shadow of internationality—xenophobia. Zeus was the god of "guests" and "strangers," and he was ruthless with any who transgressed the laws of the guest-host relationship. One of those laws was this: in the liminal zone of transition, or travel, or unrootedness, one must never own an ego; to have the hubris to declare individuality or independence from the "gods" who guide (i.e., political heads) is a breach of mortal law. This configuration of Pluto in Sagittarius/Neptune in Aquarius could lead to a highly moral culture that abhors interracial and interreligious exchange or even travel among foreign nations! The potential for extremist reactions and dictatorial cultures is very, very strong.

Family dynamics are not deeply, psychologically enmeshing—this is an air/fire combination that leaves a lot of room for growth, change, movement, and space. Families will be very important, but relationships within the family will need to be based on values, beliefs, ideas, relevance, and participation in the larger collective—the culture, the religion, and further, the world itself.

These people will speak out against false values that their parental generation might subscribe to, and will override them, creating new laws and new boundaries within which to execute laws. They are a reaction to the previous conservative group and will break away from the fears of loneliness and establish families that are crosscultural and international. There is a strong adherence to philosophy, law, dogma, and various cultural ties that supersede family bonding. A phase of cultural loyalty is very much a part of this group, which does not hold the old "family values" in any esteem at all.

Theirs will not be a loud revolution but one that takes place covertly, and intellectually. Outrage will be marked by thinking, teaching, and creating, not bombing, invading, or oppressing by force. There is a kind of cold objectivity and high idealism (not romanticism) to this generational stamp, a lack of feeling tone or emotion. Fire and air are largely rationality and thinking based.

The technology developed during this time will be a double-edged sword that will cut society-at-large in two. As previously mentioned, there is a paradox inherent in the technological family dynamic. On the one hand, the computer technology will connect individuals to individuals on a global network; on the other hand, it serves to further alienate human beings from each other as regards emotional interaction. And the technology will connect those who have with those who have, and will further separate those in the know from those who do not have the resources or the abilities to take part in the cultural revolution that will be a direct result of online and Internet cultures. So the split between individuals and cultures will be even more vast.

Obviously, each person will react in his or her own way to the ethos of the time; however, as a stamp or an archetype, we are looking at a rapid movement out and away from the main themes of the Piscean Age, even as early as the millennium. People of this generational stamp will come of age during a time when the era of brotherhood and love (Pisces) has already become a thing of the past, and the age of technology and information is just beginning to reach its ascendancy.

FIGURE 5. TRANSITS OF MIDLIFE: 37 TO 60

*

The Half-Uranus—A Meeting at the Crossroads
The Generic Aspects from the Half-Uranus to the
Second Saturn Return and Their Meaning

THE PREPARATION PHASE PRIOR TO THE HALF-URANUS ♃♄

Age 36: Jupiter and Saturn—Preparing the Way to Midlife

ACROSS THE THRESHOLD—
URANUS AND NEPTUNE (AND PLUTO) ♅♆♀

Ages 38–44: The Big Leap Forward
Age 38: Second Return of the Lunar Nodes
Age 40: Saturn Trine Saturn—Familiar Boundaries
Age 42: Neptune Square Neptune—Beautiful Dreamer

PLUTO—THE NUCLEAR DILEMMA
AND THE EXISTENTIAL EXPERIENCE ♀

The "Problem" with Pluto
The Power of Pluto—for some of us
So, what does that mean?

MIDDLESCENCE ♄♅☋☊♃

Ages 44–46: Saturn and Uranus—Success in Limitation
Know Thyself and Nothing Too Much
Ages 47–48: Inversion of Lunar Nodes and Jupiter Return—quo vadis

---

AGE 50: THE WATERSHED ♄

Age 52: Saturn Square Saturn—Return of the Repressed & Liminality

---

AGES 54–57: INTEGRATION ☽♄☋☊

Age 54: Second Lunar Return; Saturn Sextile Saturn
Ages 55–56: Uranus, Neptune & Pluto Trine themselves; Third Return of
the Lunar Nodes

AGES 59–60: THE SATURN RETURN ♄

Sans teeth, sans eyes, sans everything?

CHAPTER 7

A Meeting at the Crossroads

Howard Sasportas says in his book on the transits of the outer planets:

> In a nutshell, [the midlife turning point] is a time for disassembling ourselves and then putting the pieces back together again, but in a different way. Parts of our nature we haven't integrated yet into our conscious awareness, and which we have been ignoring or not looking at, demand to be acknowledged and examined. Facing the conflicts and crises of this period increases the likelihood of a fulfilling second half of life.*

If we think of ourselves—in a rather Uranian fashion—as a "system" constituted not only of intrinsic attributes but also acquired traits and

---

*Howard Sasportas, *The Gods of Change: Pain, Crisis and Transits of Uranus, Neptune and Pluto*, Contemporary Astrology Series (New York: Arkana, 1989), p. 74.

characteristics, then we can take these words of Howard Sasportas to another level. Essentially, one is a mobile continuum of vast proportions that are contained within one's own psyche. The contents of the psyche are infinite, it seems, but for the sake of an organized and organic whole, are not available all at once. There is a necessary boundary between the self we are superconscious of and the Self of the unconscious psyche.

At midlife, the "system" that one embodies undergoes a radical chaos, which is a precreative time of collapsing the rigid structures of one's extant system, while still retaining all the attributes thereof. That is, we are still who we are, but not as well organized and contained as before the Uranus opposite Uranus transit. This half-Uranus cycle means it is time for our whole system to undergo simultaneously an expansive and a contractive episode.

For instance, if your own system has been organized around a specific kind of core or center—the nucleus of your identity—which has a social position to maintain, you might well find yourself losing your interest in that identity! It is more than possible to outgrow yourself; in fact, it happens all the time. But the half-Uranus is a critical juncture when we meet ourselves halfway through life, and we may not like all of what we meet. Similarly, we will like parts of ourselves very much, and give those aspects of ourselves more dominance or power.

The undoing at half-Uranus is not intended to be a complete collapse, though many people initially describe it that way. It is meant to be a legitimate and authentic rite of passage for all adults. All rites of this nature have a shocking impact—to get our attention. Somewhat as in adolescence, we experience a whole-system shock, and a period of adjustment. How the inner and outer shocks are met, however, is unique and individual to each one of us.

So a "midlife crisis" is about you meeting you in a new circumstance. Nothing more, nothing less; but what a great meeting it is! Depending on your personal life and circumstances, the cultural ethos, and the generational intent, there are many generic aspects that are synchronous with the entry into midlife. These aspects, from each planet from Saturn outward, define, demarcate, and offer meaning to the rites of passage that support our evolving life-changes throughout the twenty years of the midlife experience.

THE PREPARATION PHASE PRIOR TO THE HALF-URANUS

Age Thirty-six—Jupiter and Saturn: Preparing the Way to Midlife's Process

At thirty-six you have a Jupiter return, which brings with it an encouraging growth spurt. Jupiter returns to its natal position every twelve years, and this one, being the third return, brings you the first "adult" opportunity to review your core beliefs, expand your horizons, and learn more about yourself and your place in the world. Tribal affiliations and social structures now open new doors for you. A change in your life-path at this time probably is based upon a new maturity. Your Saturn return at twenty-nine and a half set the stage for departure from the womb of the family, and allowed you to separate more from family as a "dependent" (in many ways), and now the Jupiter return brings an exhilarating sense of freedom and opportunity.

The mid-thirties are a time when one feels empowered by the future, called toward it with an excitement of being authorized by self-confidence that the future is now truly in one's own hands. It is dependent no more wholly upon parental approval, or family obligations, but now wholly on one's own abilities. Jupiter helps us align with people of similar interests and parallel paths, and small collectives, groups, and organizations become more "personal," in that you can now bring a more meaningful sense of credibility to your stature in society.

Your political awareness also grows in the year of the Jupiter return, calling you to reflect on your ethnicity, religious background, political leanings, educational background, social "place," and so on, and from this reflection comes a renewal of your core beliefs and ethics. This upwardly or onwardly mobile period is not hampered by anxiety or generic transits that are fraught. Naturally, the transits of other planets to your natal horoscope will personalize this generic transit, and be more specific as to in which ways your growth, expansion, and forward movement occur—as will the natal place and "condition" of Jupiter.

This phase of the Jupiter return gives you a high point to approach your midlife with support, endorsement, and guidance. This guidance comes from within, your own teacher within yourself, but will often coincide with a remarkable meeting. A guru, counselor, friend, teacher, or mentor arrives with each Jupiter return but at this age comes in many forms. It can be a friend, a new neighbor, a movie, a famous personage—in whichever guise your exemplar comes, it is an indication of yet another threshold and a new perspective on a much bigger life.

Simultaneously in that Jupiter return year, Saturn will make a first quarter square to itself, an aspect that was in your life first at age seven or so. This structural transit, Saturn to itself, brings with it a sense of "arrival" at adulthood. The second Saturn return is the threshold of one's adult years, but the combination of Jupiter and Saturn bring both expansion and control into play.

If it were all about Jupiter, we might float off into the heavens, never to be seen again, full of inflated dreams and possibilities! However, Saturn is present in this threshold to adulthood as a guide, a parameter, and a governor on inflation and youthful adult hubris. Saturn requires a new set of limits and boundaries, based on a solid and serious reevaluation of one's true potential, rather than fantasy wishes.

Jupiter says "Go for it!" and Saturn says "But carefully." Jupiter is the youngest son of Saturn, and there is always a bit of a war between them in the psyche. Since the myth of Kronos/Saturn embodies the war between the young and the old, the puer and the senex, this Jupiter/Saturn period is about your inner child allowing your inner formative adult to assume a rightful position as the helper on the journey, not a throttle hold! Rather than let Saturn control all your impulses, you may well find yourself surprisingly moderate and conscientious about your directions.

Your more conservative side might want to squash your exuberant experimental side, so there is a struggle on this threshold, but it is one that is mediated by yourself. You become more interested in what you actually can do and less in imagining yourself to be something other than what you are.

The first stage of adulthood is crossed at this threshold, preparing your psyche, if not your conscious mind, for the midlife crossover events.

Note: If you were born between 1979 and 1995, you should read the section "The 'Problem' with Pluto" in this chapter, because you will have Pluto square Pluto at age thirty-six to thirty-seven.

ACROSS THE THRESHOLD:
URANUS AND NEPTUNE (AND PLUTO)
Ages Thirty-eight Through Forty-four: The Big Leap Forward

In American society, the idea of a midlife transition has always been something of an awkward joke; its mere mention provokes giggles and conjures up images of the gray, balding professor driven scandalously out of control by his love for the cheer leader or a fading housewife having an affair with her tennis instructor.

—JIM LEWIS, *Peter Pan in Midlife**

Quickly on the heels of the Saturn square to itself is the Uranus opposition to itself (keep in mind that those with Uranus in Aries, Taurus, Gemini, and Cancer have the half-Uranus at an earlier age than the rest of the signs). (See p. 63.)

This means that the initial crossover to midlife's journey is not only about breaking away from the past but also is a time of creative restructuring of one's relationship to oneself, so that a new, infant "future" is born. This is a phase in which individuation quickens, and a feeling of urgency and intense excitement infuses the soul and mind, creating a crack in the ego.

The interactions of three major life transits in this age—Saturn trine itself, Neptune square itself, and the lunar nodal inversion—span the ages of thirty-eight to forty-four, and all bring an increased intensity to

---

*Jim Lewis, *Peter Pan in Midlife*, Southwest Contemporary Astrology (Santa Fe/Silver City, NM: 2002), p. 49.

the inner life, and thus a major shift in consciousness. The crisis in consciousness can come with a crisis in action if life has been lived without at least an occasional self-analysis and truth quest.

To be truthful, *there is no preparation for midlife*. In fact, the Baby Boom generation felt, by and large, that they would not have midlife crises because they had "been there, done that." And, as Jim Lewis says, the stereotype emerged from the midlives of the Pluto in Leo's rejected parents, so "we" would not have anything that puerile and embarrassing! Well, my client load would not agree that the midlife is that simple, that ordinary, that silly, even if many—*many*—put off the so-called crisis till age fifty-plus!

So what does the half-Uranus actually do, then, if not send us off to the BMW dealership for a red sports car or to the health spa for a "ripped" trainer?

The ego, the "I-am," of who you think you are, will shift. After forty or so years of carefully building a personal identity, serious questions arise about what that identity serves. There is a rebellion against self-imposed limitations. If one has only just awakened to one's process of development (which is not uncommon), then the separation from the past is acute. A time of soul-searching, marked by frequent attacks of restlessness and desire for change, can disrupt the life of even the most contented or controlled individual. It is not uncommon for associates of a midlifer to announce that he or she is behaving differently, if not bizarrely!

A morbid preoccupation with aging and death is another symptom of midlifing. The biological peak and decline that is now clearly in process can be very depressing and frightening to the individual whose values are superficial, or related only to appearances and persona.

Often there are dreams that are classically associated with death and dying, because the ego is fragile and the inner Self is dominant. The unconscious is hyperactive and demanding. People complain of being tired, not getting enough sleep, but it is the body/soul reaction to the tremendous work being done in the unconscious. There are dreams of turning points, meetings at crossroads, tunnels, trains, numinous deities appearing, dead bodies (figurative of the dying ego), and the "procession of the ancestors" (literal archetypal memories of ancestral beings, complete with messages to impart).

Therefore a search for meaning is begun in earnest, and one feels an inner compulsion to examine the deepest and innermost recesses of one's soul. This is a time in which many "unexamined" lives head off to the self-awareness workshops, the analyst, the astrologer, and various soothsayers and professional helpers. Part of this death cycle is mourning, nostalgia, and recollection of early opportunities now gone forever. Mourning is necessary and healthy, because something has died, and it is healing to acknowledge this experience as you head into the full transition toward maturity. Any rite of passage involves the important question: "Who am I?" And at this juncture of life, this simple question contains multiple answers, all of which must be considered.

Age Thirty-eight—Second Return of the Lunar Nodes: Renegotiating Life's Purpose

While the core of your life purpose and your ultimate destiny do not change, the manner in which they are lived out most certainly will.

Symbolically, the nodes "recall" our soul's history (south node) and "remind" us of our life purpose now (north node).* The return of the natal nodes, for the second time, opens a door to renew our commitment to our core life-path, our destiny, if you like, and explicates a bit more of our core self into that life-path.

The lunar nodes are associated with the Saros cycle, that of the Sun and the Moon and the Moon's nodes. That cyclic return is the eclipse cycle—an eclipse occurs in the exact same position every nineteen or so years. Thus, we have a "nodal return" every nineteen years, and an inversion of the nodes about every nine and a half years.† The south node is a pointer to our vast repository of soul memory, while the north node points to where that archetypal knowledge is best directed in one's life

*See Howard Sasportas, *Direction and Destiny in the Birthchart*, Pt. 2, "The Moon's Nodes" (London: CPA Press, 1998).
†Fred Gettings, *The Arkana Dictionary of Astrology* (London and New York: Arkana, 1985), p. 439.

today. The north and south nodes of the Moon are exactly opposite each other, thus the "nodal axis." That axis is in retrograde motion, that is, they move backward against the Zodiac.

The Moon's nodes are the points in space where the orbit of the Moon around Earth intersects the orbit of Earth around the Sun. The nodes are frequently associated with *incarnation*—literally, entering the flesh. The Moon is the symbol of the mother as the container and, as such, its orbit's link to the earthly orbit around the Sun. These points in space symbolize our life on Earth as we move around the center of the solar system—the Sun, the focus, as it is connected to the Moon and our mother, our past, and perhaps even our soul memory of previous experience.

The return of the nodes every nineteen years engenders a spiritual, almost magical, element to the quality of time, and the fact that a nodal return occurs at the initiation to midlife simply adds to the urgency and feelings of "destiny" that irrupt. Often a major component in the midlife "crisis" is a spiritual dilemma, not a psychological collapse or breakdown! The spirit calls from within to express more of itself; the rushing early years of living—the ages from the Saturn return at twenty-nine to the midlife advent at thirty-nine—may have passed with either no spiritual focus or one that is inappropriate to the next phase of life. Hence the ensuing spiritual quest at midlife.

There is some validity to this idea of birth being an ending of one way of existence and the beginning of a new one. Certainly any new parents will attest to the innate wisdom and agelessness of their new infant, and the already powerful "personality" of the new baby. We don't arrive *a tabula rasa*, but with a history of sorts. The ancient Greek philosopher Socrates called the incarnated life a state of *anamnesia*, that is, one of constant recollection.

His belief was that we are born knowing everything from all time previous, and that incarnation was about remembering "lost" memories from previous soul experience. He called his method of getting to that place of recollection or remembering *maieutics*, which means "circling the hearth," literally, the central *focus*—and midwifing the truth.

This means that if we circle our center and seek the truth from the source, and work it conscientiously, then we will midwife our own new Self. The axis of the nodes of the Moon returning to the natal place opens the door to recollection of the soul. I find that people "awaken" to an enriched sense of their life purpose and the destined intent of their incarnation during nodal return times. There is also a checkpoint during the nodal inversions (when the nodal axis turns to meet the opposite of itself at birth).

Socratic philosophy or not, there is something magical about the Saros cycle (the lunar node cycle) that speaks to our soul purpose. And having the nodal return at this life juncture speaks to yet another reason to allow the deeper Self, or the intuition, to take a stronger place in conscious life. There will be opportunities to review your work, job, career, relationships, and lifestyle as you undergo this new period of "tailoring" your life to your true needs.

The previous nodal return at age nineteen marked the closure of adolescence, and the time in life when passion and focus are on "What do I want to do and be?" This second return is a maturing of that phase. What began at nineteen years now matures and is reexamined for validity in the new cycle of maturity. You have completed a cycle of development in your purpose in this life, and are now forging ahead with the new.

Within that span of midlife onset, between ages thirty-eight and forty-four, there are some specific helpers and tricksters on the path. Read on.

Age Forty: Saturn Trine Saturn: Familiar Boundaries, New Territories

At forty, Saturn makes a trine to itself, and this aspect is a point of encouragement. The planets in their generic cycles are very supportive of each other, and there are critical times when many aspects concur, but the general flow of the transiting life-cycle is supported and enhanced by the solar system's smooth, predictable regularity (with the naughty exception of Pluto). The Saturn trine says, "Now we begin slowly to evaluate our structures and behavior and patterns." With this evaluation will come a strengthening of will and force, so in the midst of the chaos that one might feel in this age period, there is a sense of structure and future.

The Saturn trine Saturn offers a leg to stand on, a respite from what might feel like a constant assault. Decisions to change careers, lifestyles, countries, or relationships are all hallmarks of the midlife transition. Deepening one's commitments is also part of that change, but only if the things to which one is bound are suitable for furthering one's life goals (whether or not you consciously know your life goals at this point is quite irrelevant). Your deeper Self, your core being, does know, just as an orange pip knows it's to be an orange tree, not a lemon tree!

The first time this waxing trine occurred was around age nine, which is a relatively peaceful time in childhood, but one when the civilizing process is very strong. Ways of behaving become essential to a child's acceptance and socialization. It is a time of growth spurts, physical coordination, and mental agility, and really taking on board a social responsibility.* The Saturn trine Saturn is the honing part of the process of becoming socially adept, which requires a certain amount of healthy repression and obedience to social laws.

In repressing the less socially acceptable or refined traits, which are inherent by nature, we create a repository of undeveloped attributes, aspects of ourselves that we do not like or want to acknowledge. These characteristics are relegated to the shadow—the place in the psyche that houses all the unacceptable aspects of the self that you cannot abide.† These characteristics can emerge and create havoc in a nicely ordered life.

Experiencing "childish" (read: a child's) reactions and emotional responses will shock you if you think you are "all grown up." So many times a client will say how embarrassed he or she is by his or her primitive and instinctual responses; one should be "over all that now." Simply not true. Taking that stance is dangerous to your evolution, because it is a stereotype. When you reach the aging section later in the book, you'll see how "grown up" some amazing eighty-year-olds are—or not!

---

*See Erin Sulllivan, *Saturn in Transit: Boundaries of Mind, Body and Soul* (York Beach, ME: Weiser, 2000), pp. 48–57.
†See Robert Bly, *A Little Book on the Human Shadow* (San Francisco: Harper Collins, 1988).

If you are shocked by your childlike responses because you are all grown up, and should be "over it," try not to judge yourself too harshly. We are never "over it," until it is over. Rebellion against socially imposed restrictions might seem adolescent, and the urge to cut everything loose may seem irresponsible, yet these natural responses need to be acknowledged. They are likely to have some healthy aspects to them, and indeed to operate as self-correcting devices.

So with that in mind, be careful of how sternly you treat yourself. By all means, remain as together as you can, but don't shut down your nature and your instincts—because the following phases require you to have those instincts to hand, if not on the surface!

Remember that Uranus is the backdrop to this *whole* initial stage of midlife work, and even within the bounds of a "good" Saturn aspect, there is still the rebellion to work with. The rebellion in midlife is not just about Uranus and the sudden impulse to do it again, only differently; it is also about being deeply angry that so much creativity was lost in childhood. Reclaiming and re-collecting your creativity and reinstating it into your life is a great project for the next ten or so years!

So while you are busy civilizing yourself, and coming to terms with getting older, thus not younger, keep in mind that while your rebellion against socially imposed restrictions may seem adolescent and the urge to cut everything loose may seem irresponsible, these natural responses need examining so as to apply healthy self-correction devices rather than fears, insecurities, or neurotic traits from old childhood messages.

Age Forty-two: Neptune Square Neptune: Beautiful Dreamer

You are now wondering where all the romantic fantasies and longings for divine oneness and self-perfection come in. And where are the imaginings that intrude into the midlifer's sanity, and the recurrence of lofty ideals that come and go with the speed of light? Astrologically, Neptune's realm is manifold, but it is one of the prime motivators for the imagination. Our imaginations are vast, limitless spaces in which we are capable of anything and everything.

The midlife imagination is rekindled with hope and possibility. At precisely forty-two, Neptune makes the first quarter-square to itself. This aspect symbolizes a turning-point in one's vision of the ideal. A loss of ideals, dreams, and spiritual direction can lead to a reformulation of personal ethics and philosophy, but not without much work and conscious awareness that this is the "work in progress." So many midlifers are riddled with anxiety and depression, feeling that their youth is gone (true), that they have crossed the threshold toward aging (true), and that their passions, dreams, potentials, and idealism have died (not true).

Many times midlifers have told me of the spiritual emergency they felt as they crossed over the threshold of forty-two. Indeed, it is a spiritual emergence—and the urgency of this critical juncture is profound. Neptune, as I shall show, is a symbol of much more than spirit, soul, archetype, and collective unconscious; it is the "place" where our longings for fusion with the divine are located. Each planet has its agency in the psyche, and, in a nutshell, Neptune's agency is to take us back to the place where two hearts beat as one—the womb. The perfect place of ultimate harmony.

In his book *In Midlife*, Murray Stein says:

> At midlife, there is a crossing over from one psychological identity to another. The self goes through a transformation. . . . But, I consider midlife to be a time when persons are going through a fundamental shift in their alignment with life and with the world, and this shift has psychological and religious meaning beyond the interpersonal and social dimensions. Midlife is a crisis of the spirit.*

Keep in mind that Neptune square Neptune is an eighteen-month transit as it undergoes a retrograde cycle, transiting back and forth your natal Neptune three times. So, in the midst of all the other features of early midlife, Neptune is in square to itself from ages forty-two to forty-three and a half (depending on the exact dates relative to your birthday; but still consider it a good two-year influence in the transitional stage).

*Murray Stein, *In Midlife: A Jungian Perspective* (Dallas, TX: Spring, 1983), p. 3.

One needs not only to be realistic but also to continue with the dreams and rich imaginings. It is a time of intense soul-making, and sometimes the sheer exhaustion of being alive for forty-some years, in a contemporary society, calls people back to fundamentals of faith and belief. Just as much it calls them to escape into flights of fancy, or worse— drink, drugs, and other dependencies.

At this stage of midlife, you are still in liminality, the place between, the threshold position—not who you once were, and certainly not yet who you are about to become. In fact, the Neptune perspective is a strong aspect of liminal life. In this threshold place, there is no past or future but only a lingering sense of eternal transition. Again, this is a good thing, a rightful place. The *limen* of the ancient worlds were sacred spaces, places wherein the gods guarded the traveling journeyer. In this way the midlife journey is guided, too, perhaps no longer by gods appearing and giving cryptic signs but now more probably by your inner god, your *daemon*—in plain language, your gut.

Neptune has had far more wonderful things attributed to it than it ought.* It is the most deceptive of planets, lending its essence to everything from drug addiction to transcendental experiences; from colors to rivers; from dreams to icy reality; from the profundity of archetypal unconscious imagery to the mastery of arts and sciences. What is consistent about Neptune is its ambiguity, its nebulosity, its capacity to diffuse and confuse, to obscure and replace images one on the other.

In theater, the scrim—a sheer curtain upon which are painted images—is a vaguely obscuring screen behind which hints and suggestions can be seen of underlying features of the play and its characters. A hint, if you will, of something going on, but not clear or intensely obvious.

In psychological imagery, Neptune is the agent of slow, dissolving change, where one is vaguely aware of a subtle but effective erosion of sharp edges, absolutes, and concrete beliefs and systems. During this entry stage to midlife, this soft, gentle corrosion of your hard-won ego is part of the sense of disappearing, or loss of glamor. Some individuals ex-

*See Liz Greene, *Neptune: The Quest for Redemption* (York Beach, ME: Weiser, 1996).

perience their midlife as a slow process of slipping away—not the sharp shock of Uranus but the gentle fog of Neptune.

Ultimately, both Uranus and Neptune work toward permanent change. Because Neptune and Uranus are outer planets, their transits in this aspect will never repeat themselves in a lifetime. This means that an outer planet transit is a life-changing process, not an event. Two hard aspects from two big planets—Uranus opposite Uranus and Neptune square Neptune—work together to undo what has been done. Uranus is the shocking separation from complacency and stereotype, and Neptune is the fine dissolve, the softening of the hard edges of ego and conscious control.

And this brings us to the existential experience in midlife for certain generations.

PLUTO: THE NUCLEAR DILEMMA AND THE EXISTENTIAL EXPERIENCE

Awakening to one's mortality for the second time in life—the first time being adolescence—means dealing with the age-old problem of the existential experience as an adult. Pluto is the planet that holds our "aloneness," that reminds us that "naked came I into the world, and naked I shall go." In contemporary astrology, we see Pluto as the edge of the known solar system and thus the end of conscious knowledge—as Saturn once was the last planet known, now it is Pluto. And, to that we must speak. Pluto is a planet of the twentieth century, but it carries its *memento mori* still.

THE "PROBLEM" WITH PLUTO: A SPACE ODDITY

Pluto has such an eccentric orbit and inclination to the ecliptic that its own aspect cycles to itself occur in vastly different sequences of time, depending on the natal sign. It is not the tidy Jupiter, staying in a sign for a year and a month, or Saturn making neat seven-and-a-half-year cycles within its twenty-nine-year orbit.

Pluto was sighted on January 21, 1930, and immediately was being discussed by astronomers and astrologers alike. Pluto's unveiling, as it were, occurred at the depths of the global depression, and also inducted a short but effective epoch wherein the "underworld" was celebrated as heroic.

Its sighting initiated the nuclear age and the arms race, which by 1945 had reached evil proportions. The first atomic bomb was detonated on July 16, 1945, near Alamogordo, New Mexico. Weapons of mass destruction were launched, and since that time have been housed as a threat to the world by many countries. The fact that Pluto rules such things as waste, by-products, mines (deep earth resources), and plutonium is not a light use of metaphor. That plutonium is a by-product of a nuclear reaction (fission) lies at the metaphorical core of the planet Pluto's power. In and of itself, there is nothing wrong with a nuclear reaction; the solar system is powered by a constant series of them—on the Sun, mind you. The problem with nuclear power in its 1950s form (and today) is that it *still* belongs on the Sun and *not* on Earth.

And so the Pluto in Leo generation were born to the nuclear age, and many of them span the era of World War II, and thence the mid-1950s, when nuclear energy was explored and experimented with recklessly. Innate in the psyches of the Pluto in Leo generation is death by Pluto. How each individual manifests this death consciousness is dependent on myriad factors, not least of which is the placement of Pluto in the natal chart.

Leo is a fire sign, and the by-product of nuclear fission, plutonium, *is* death by fire—the polar sign is Aquarius, death by fire *and* aetheric ice! This monumental content in the collective unconscious became absolute on August 6, 1945, in Hiroshima and on August 9, in Nagasaki, Japan. From that moment on, there has not been a moment of peace and security that hasn't been based on nuclear death threats.

✳

Just because Pluto was not sighted before 1930 does not mean it was not "there." If we cover our eyes, does the environment disappear? Such as the way of a very small child, still in the "I am the world and it is me" stage, playing hide-and-seek, covering her eyes while standing in the middle of the room, calling out "Come and find me." She thinks because she can't see anyone, they can't see her!

The advent of a new planet (or anything of this magnitude; for example, the discovery of DNA and now the genome) is always preceded by sudden advances in psychology and technology and followed by huge leaps in the social/global arena. It is likely that there is some mysterious collusion between the inventor and the invented—where human behavior and phenomena conspire in a universal scheme. We understand synchronicity to some degree—well, perhaps not understand it, but are well aware of it.

Synchronicity is summoned to explain why it is that four people submit the same "original" idea within hours of each other, or in the case of the advent of a new planet, actions on Earth are intertwined with the symbology of the new planet.* Jung called it "an acausal connecting principle," and he wrote much about such links between subject and object in synchrony.

Just as Uranus and Neptune were there before they were sighted, so was Pluto, but *what was it doing*? Same old thing, *but* without any human consciousness of its orbit, influence, and so on. As with Uranus, it was there, just one orbit beyond Saturn, but it took an invention, a telescope, to allow us to see it. The rest is industrial, technical, and consciousness history.

The moment a new entity is observed or discovered, it enters the collective psyche. Pluto, regardless of the Disney dog tag, is one of the Roman names for the god of the underworld. Pluto's origin lies in Hades, the Greek Lord of the Shades, and his name means "the unseen one." The myths that surround and involve Hades are many, but the origin myth of him as an entity has to do with love and loss.

One such myth involves Persephone, whom Hades abducted and made his lover and consort—the queen of the underworld—when she was a maiden, just a teenager in school.

Her mother, Demeter, who was queen of the seasons, agriculture,

---

*This is not the place to launch into a dissertation on synchronicity, but there have been many psychological evaluations, as well as chronological and "scientific" works on it. Most people refer to Jung as the popularizer of the word. He continued to develop his exploration of synchronicity until his death, with no absolute understanding or conclusion to the mystery of it. Some books on it are listed in the bibliography. As Jung would have it, once is an accident, twice is a coincidence, three times is synchronicity. See Carl Gustav Jung, *Synchronicity: An Acausal Connecting Principle*, in *Collected Works*, vol 8. Bollingen Series (Princeton, NJ: Princeton University Press, 1975).

and domestic nourishment (Ceres in Latin), responded to the violation of her daughter by shutting the earth down into *permanent winter*. This is the *very* description of what would happen if there were a nuclear holocaust much greater than the one in 1946—a constant blizzard and well below freezing temperatures on a global scale. For eons. So Demeter's revenge is the result of a Pluto meltdown.

No wonder the Pluto in Leo generation, the first to know mass death of a Plutonian nature, and the first in an epoch to have the Pluto square Pluto at midlife, took it to the maximum and created an icon of the midlife transition. Many of the Baby Boomers, when still very young, had strong fantasies of never reaching the age of thirty! Existentialism was bred in the bone. So not only surviving thirty but also the shock of turning forty and *aging* was monumental!

THE POWER OF PLUTO—FOR SOME OF US

Figure 6 is a listing of the primary ages in which each Pluto "generation" receives the Pluto square to natal Pluto (with the *approximate* number of years of Pluto in each sign, and the span of each Pluto "generation").* The figure shows that the Pluto in Leo, Virgo, Libra, and Scorpio generations receive their Pluto square Pluto in the initiation stages of midlife. Figure 7 (p. 124), depicts the fact that Pluto will oppose itself only in the generation from Leo to Aquarius at the age of eighty-four—at the same time and age as the generic Uranus return!

The other signs all receive the Pluto square at an advanced age, and in many cases, these individuals will never experience their Pluto square Pluto.

Earlier in the book, I discussed the Pluto in Leo generation making an ideology of their midlife crisis and transition to their aging phase. How powerfully the idea of midlife gripped the largest generation of its time, introducing a complex psychology along with it! Many books written on the climacteric, menopause, and the midlife transition feature an intense inner struggle, one in which it seems as if the arrival of old age

*From Neil F. Michelsen, *Tables of Planetary Phenomena*, 2nd ed. (San Diego: ACS, 1995), p. 64.

FIGURE 6. PLUTO IN SIGNS WITH AGE OF SQUARES

♈ Pluto in Aries	29 years	1822–1851	Pluto square ages 90–93
♉ Pluto in Taurus	33 years	1851–1883	Pluto square ages 86–88
♊ Pluto in Gemini	30 years	1882–1912	Pluto square ages 74–75
♋ Pluto in Cancer	26 years	1912–1937	Pluto square ages 59–60
♌ Pluto in Leo	19 years	1037–1956	Midlife square ages 42–44
♍ Pluto in Virgo	15 years	1956–1971	Midlife square ages 39–40
♎ Pluto in Libra	13 years	1971–1983	Midlife square ages 40–41
♏ Pluto in Scorpio	12 years	1983–1995	Midlife square ages 36–37
♐ Pluto in Sagittarius	13 years	1995–2008	Pluto square age 48
♑ Pluto in Capricorn	15 years	2008–2023	Pluto square ages 58–59
♒ Pluto in Aquarius	20 years	2023–2043	Pluto square ages 72–73
♓ Pluto in Pisces	25 years	2043–2068	Pluto square ages 86–87

FIGURE 7. PLUTO OPPOSITIONS IN:
GEMINI, CANCER, LEO, VIRGO, LIBRA, AND SCORPIO

♊ Pluto in Gemini	Pluto opposition at age 102
♋ Pluto in Cancer	Pluto opposition at age 88
♌ Pluto in Leo	Pluto opposition at age 85
♍ Pluto in Virgo	Pluto opposition at age 90
♎ Pluto in Libra	Pluto opposition at age 105
♏ Pluto in Scorpio	Pluto opposition at age 124

and death were imminent, rather than the robust middle years we really have and are experiencing between forty and sixty.

Two factors are strongly suggestive of the power of Pluto in Leo:

1. This particular Pluto in Leo generation (1939—1956) is the first one to have the "newest" planet, Pluto, in its collective unconscious.

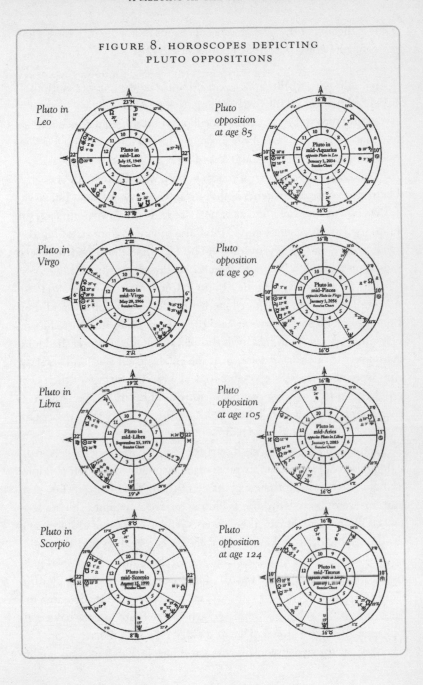

FIGURE 8. HOROSCOPES DEPICTING
PLUTO OPPOSITIONS

Pluto in
Leo

Pluto
opposition
at age 85

Pluto in
Virgo

Pluto
opposition
at age 90

Pluto in
Libra

Pluto
opposition
at age 105

Pluto in
Scorpio

Pluto
opposition
at age 124

2. It is the first of the next three generations following it to have Pluto configure powerfully in its midlife onset years.

So, although within a 245-year cycle there are four generations of people who enter midlife with a bang, this post–World War II generation with Pluto in Leo sets the precedent for all subsequent generations to come. Out of 245 years, only fifty-eight have Pluto squaring itself between the ages of thirty-six and forty-four!

Think about it this way: if you were born with Pluto at 15° Leo, it is likely that your grandparents had Pluto in Gemini and would have experienced Pluto square Pluto at or near the end of their lives. In fact, the Pluto in Gemini generation had the Pluto square to their natal Pluto at ages seventy-four to seventy-five. (The fact that Pluto had not been sighted in that era yet is another factor, as already mentioned.)

And your parents, with their Pluto in Cancer (and Neptune in Leo), may well have been born not long before Pluto was sighted, and their Pluto square Pluto occurred around their second Saturn return, at ages fifty-nine to sixty. They had lived through the depression and the Holocaust and the nuclear devastation at the end of "their war" and, by sixty, they were not very willing or able to deal with the outrage of their own children. In fact, the big complaint for the Pluto in Leo generation is that their parents (generally) did not have the intensity and concern for them that they "should have had."

In the United States and all over the world, parents of hippies, radicals, and social reformers were more often intimidated by their children, and angry with them, than supportive of them. The Pluto in Leo generation were born with their Plutos on their parents' Neptune—essentially born to "nuke" their parents' 1950s fantasy of children and dream of how their children were to be. It is revealing that the child-rearing manual *Baby and Child Care*, by Dr. Benjamin Spock, was published in 1946. That book was the bible by which almost all Pluto in Cancer parents raised their Pluto in Leo children—and inaugurated the beginning of "cookbook psychology," which the Pluto in Leos have multiplied as they have grown older, and older, and even older.

Now, all the generations previous to Pluto in Leo have had midlife crises and midlife transition periods, according to biographies of highly creative and inventive people, but they didn't have them while Pluto squared their natal Pluto. Crisis, yes, but death fears, and the psychological "death" of the ego, no. And of the generations preceding Pluto in Leo, none had the image of the mushroom cloud burned into their psyche. The bubonic plague, smallpox, and syphilis—though to the previous generations they were devastating—were death by Saturn, not Pluto.

Their grandparents, with Pluto in Gemini and Cancer, received their Pluto square Pluto at age sixty-six—not only well after midlife but in the years following the second Saturn return.

This puts in a different light each generation's experience of Pluto, because each generation experiences the critical Pluto square to itself at very different age phases—all except those born with Pluto in Leo, Virgo, Libra, and Scorpio, who have it in midlife's initiation years between thirty-seven and forty-two.

So What Does That Mean?

People who are born between 1937 and 1995 have Pluto square Pluto in midlife's initiation period. The Pluto in Leo, Virgo, Libra, and Scorpio generations have to incorporate this profound collective aspect both into their generic as well as their personal midlife.

Metaphysically, the Pluto in Leos underwent in midlife a psychological death, a time in which their parents and previous generations actually died.

It came to the Pluto in Leo bunch as a great shock not only to have a midlife crisis but also having to experience the generic aspect that occurred at the previous generations' deaths. Essentially, this kind of aspect invokes a racial memory in which the ancestral experience is recalled to our current experience, if only unconsciously.

Not that the majority of us actually knew this astrology at the time, but the peculiar intensity and grieving that occurred for almost everyone I knew and worked with was different, somehow, from what was expressed by the old saws about the midlife crisis. There was a level of collective grief and mourning associated with the ages between forty-two and forty-four that was distinctly different in psychological effect from what other generations have described as midlife.

This may be why midlife has become such a powerful influence in the Baby Boom generation, and since most of them have lived beyond thirty, they have carried on their search for eternal youth, disregard of death, and unwillingness to face the harsh realities that their grandparents did. Each generation has an existential "problem" unlike every other one.

My astrological "seasoning" to date has been working with people who have Pluto in very late Gemini, Pluto in Cancer, Pluto in Leo, and Pluto in Virgo in their midlife experiences. Subsequent to Pluto in Leo, each successive generation will feel the power of Pluto in its midlife initiation, but differently, because the global social network moves rapidly, so the *context* of midlife changes. Once something is absorbed and fully incorporated into the collective psyche, it becomes less charged; we become inured to the "old" shocks and a bit jaded. That does not mean less meaningful or portentous. As the Pluto in Leo generation absorbed and integrated the nuclear age, each subsequent age will need to redefine it for themselves. Each age following the advent of Pluto adds increasing meaning to its collective experience.

Thus, it isn't as if the Pluto in Leos have "taken care of it"—indeed, to the contrary. It is the Pluto in Leo generation that brings the nuclear age to a dangerous peak. Subsequent generations will live in its perilous shadow, but we hope there will materialize a positive role for nuclear energy, and, more important, that ways will be discovered to regenerate the massive destruction of resources that are a direct result of the Pluto in Leos largesse, overexpansiveness, and heedless greed. Pluto in Leos have been big spenders—vast amounts of ecology have been swallowed in their pleasure and play in the fields of the Earth. Perhaps to be restored by the Pluto in Virgo and Libra generations, so that the Pluto in Scorpio generation will have resources? We shall see.

CHAPTER 8

MIDDLESCENCE

AGES FORTY-FOUR TO FORTY-FIVE:
SATURN AND URANUS—SUCCESS IN LIMITATION

The Saturn opposition to itself at ages forty-four to forty-five initiates a seven-year cycle in which the only other outer planetary aspect that is made is Uranus quincunx to itself (150°). These two aspects are another midlife juncture, but by this time the midlifer has accommodated much experience and is more seasoned in life, so moves into this phase with a bit less resistance. However, the aspects have no less of an impact on one's ever-changing worldview.

It is no wonder that the midlife transition is commonly called the "second adolescence." The phase of development from ages fourteen to twenty-one is notable for its lack of major aspects from the outer planets, Uranus, Neptune, and Pluto, to themselves, as is this adult phase. (The adolescent cycle contains only Uranus square Uranus, and only at the very end, at age twenty-one.)

The opportunities to restructure one's sense of authenticity and authority are based on the adolescent period, when the first Saturn opposition to itself occurred. The astrological "second adolescence" begins only with these aspects, because they replicate the aspects that launch adolescence. The rebellion of the adolescent phase has formed a foundation in the psyche of the middlescent adult, and this foundation is excavated during the Saturn opposition to its natal place.

First, a good part of this phase recalls the adolescent rebellion against authority and oppression (though one hopes that one is more conscious at forty-five of what this rebellion is really about), and further evolves unfinished business from the past. The return of the repressed is the most startling and interesting aspect of midlife because, by the very nature of the unconscious, we do not know what it is that must resurface until it does. Middlescence disinters the first encounter of Saturn opposite the natal Saturn with such a profound biological, psychological, and social change in status that it literally recalls the tumult of adolescence.

Once again, the father/son dyad of Ouranos/Kronos, or Uranus/Saturn, engages in a struggle for ascendancy. The struggle may be reduced to a single factor: the need for true individuality to rise over and above imposed or received wisdom that has been swallowed wholesale in the hurly-burly of living.

The interpretation of any natural cycle disintegrates at certain times. This phase of the Saturn cycle is entirely dependent upon what one has been doing for the first half of life and, more specifically, what the Uranus opposition brought up as critical for change. There is, therefore, no pat answer or description that will satisfy any one individual at this stage. It is simply a period of time in which personal development needs to include a keen awareness that the future is entirely dependent upon what one creates. As it has been and will continue to be.

The persona *is* important. So is personality. Nothing is wrong with anything until it stops working positively. You don't have a problem unless you have a problem, and the minute you come up against an issue that is conflicting with your inner self, you might accept that the problem is real. Psychological complexes are significant in the creation of anything of value, whether it is art, a project, an idea, or a lifestyle. Complexes also are at the core of behaviors and patterns within oneself that one finds troublesome and that have both a repetitive and a destructive quality.

The same old problem disguised as a new one is something that we can recognize by midlife. This business of self-discovery now can be very exciting, can produce some of your best work, and can provide your future with endless activity and ideas, new philosophies, and ways of being.

I say this keeping in mind the qualification of self-conscious awareness. In the privacy of one's own mind, one can grapple with the kinds of difficulties that truly are repetitive and unproductive, causing one to feel unhappy, dissatisfied, difficult, and rebellious. The initial stage of the Saturn opposition can give you the courage to shrug off social expectations and pressures, returning instead to what it is you really want to do and when you wish to do it.

So this phase is about making adjustments to your already well-developed self that will allow you to continue to be effective in your own unique way. Or, if you have found that the bottom fell out at midlife onset, then this is the reconstructive period, when your accumulated wisdom and the fabric of your life can be rewoven into a more comfortable material in which to cloak yourself.

Thence to Uranus, where we encounter our unique thread among the millions of other threads we live among. And in the Uranian fashion, we balk at Saturn's limits. This too is good. One must bump up against the boundary to determine its effectiveness. If life has been hard, and work has become worn, or the wild and fun aspect of adolescent experience has been nullified by trauma, then the desire to recapture "lost years" is important. At this stage it is quite possible to do this, by the way, and still retain one's dignity.

For instance, if one's childhood was robbed by abuse or neglect or adolescence lost to circumstances such as the death of a parent, poverty, or early parenthood, then there are genuine opportunities to heal those wounds, and experiment and explore. There is an opportunity in this phase to recapture a period in life that was truncated or never lived at all.

The more repressed the individual, the more likely he or she is to break out in ways that seem "uncharacteristic." The more "uncharacteristically" a breakout midlifer seems to behave, the more repression he or she has lived. Friends see them shrug off the persona, and fly into the winds of change. Others are suspicious and often jealous of the sudden adventurousness of their contemporary but perhaps fail to understand that it is not madness, or selfishness, or even irresponsibility but necessity that pushes a forty-something person to relive a lost youth.

If our boundaries and limits are either externally or personally imposed but are psychologically unworkable, then Uranus will operate to find ways over, around, through, or under them. If no way is found, then it is time to assess "who you are." And if you find that you are greater than the limit you have accepted or placed upon yourself, Uranus will find the way over, under, around, or through the wall.

Transiting Uranus opposing natal Uranus is the forming, or eighth house type, quincunx. It foreshadows the trine to itself at fifty-five to fifty-six. The quincunx that follows an opposition has both a sexual and financial tone to it. The adjustments that are made under this quincunx have a lot to do with sexuality and resources, both personal and available resources in the environment.

Since the opposition, and now at the quincunx, there has been a seven-year itch—that is, an itch that has lasted seven years. The yearning is to succeed, to break through, and to mature with as much dignity as possible, using one's innate gifts and unique abilities in a superfunctional way. It is at around forty-six that we truly see ourselves as either having succeeded in life, or not. That is a big threshold to cross, bigger than any so far.

The kinds of adjustments that can be made are social and personal. The serious (but not depressed) seeker for self-fulfillment is prepared to make lists, prioritize, let go of the things that will not be possible, and focus in on the things that are possible. Many people seek professional guidance for their career direction, their financial security, their psychological state, and their future options. This age is often one in which the combination of the Saturn opposition (structuring) and the Uranus quincunx (adjusting) brings a sense of real control over one's life, and a sense of pride in having arrived at this point.

"KNOW THYSELF" AND "NOTHING TOO MUCH"

This title is a roughly translated version of what was inscribed on the Delphic oracle. Once Apollo took over the sacred precinct, and imbued the perfection of masculine, Apollonian values into the previously feminine-ruled Greek psyche, these two dicta were the prime cautions for mortals. Gods, of course, needed no such cautioning.

"Know thyself" does not mean having years of psychoanalysis, and "Nothing too much" *might* refer to chocolate cake or sex, but it actually refers to not overstepping your mortal bounds. The seed meanings of the Delphic phrases are exactly what you feel they are—you must learn to accept who you are and not overextend yourself into oblivion, or obliteration.

Today these important mortal codes mean that we simply must accept who we are and not pretend to be someone we are not. And, too, we must not commit the high crime of hubris and overstep our bounds. Saturn is one agency for our boundaries and our limits.

Ultimately, this passage through mid-midlife is about one's moira, or fate. The triple goddesses, the Greek Fates, were called the Moirai, a name that derives from the Greek word *mora*, which is an astrology term, too. The Greek *mora* was the "lot" or the allotment of time, the portion or degree that one carries as one's own fate. Astrologically, the *mora* is the actual degree of a planet. From that core meaning we have the entire philosophy of accepting one's *mora*, or one's "lot in life" or fate. The Fates, triple in form—Clotho, Lachesis, and Atropos—are the spinner, weaver, and cutter, respectively. One spins the life thread, the other weaves it into the fabric of the life, and the other cuts the thread to complete the life. Middlescence is midway in the weaving, and thus perhaps far from the cutting, but it is always the same thread from birth to death.

By this time in middlescence, many people have come to a place where they have achieved a greater sense of their own authority and authenticity in the world around them, and thus make choices based on this important individual place. In an ideal world—which this one seems not to be—you can look at your inner Saturn (your own "governor") and see if you are operating out of rote learning or still listening to your parents, or what you think other people want you to do.*

Next, we can look outside ourselves, and see whether or not we agree with the various parental archetypes that underlie our society, such as politicians, law enforcement, major corporations, religious dogma, to name just a few, as well as the prevailing views (received wisdom) furnished by social hierarchies such as science, law, ecology, government, and so on.

Ages forty-four to forty-five is a period when one comes to a peak of personal power, when time and circumstance meet. The subtle restlessness that is felt at forty-five can be the final resistance to maturity. It can signal a focused attempt to "get ahead" and make the most of these next many valuable years. By this time, one is acutely aware of one's limits and can use the phase to come to terms with them, making the most of one's true abilities and letting go of the fantasies of youth. Saturn plays a major role in success because of its capacity to edit and limit—*it is within the circle of our parameters that we find our strengths*.

The potential for true success is high at this time because one realizes that there is little time now for fantasy or extreme experimentation and one becomes more conservative with investments of time, love, and money. In all, most people in mid-midlife find that they can let go of their child dreams and take on the adult realities in creative and productive ways.

AGES FORTY-SEVEN AND FORTY-EIGHT: INVERSION OF LUNAR NODES AND A JUPITER RETURN—*QUO VADIS*

As I mentioned earlier, the nodes have a return cycle of nineteen years, which means that every nine and a half years from birth, the nodes reverse by sign and degree. At forty-seven, their north-south axis inverts—

---

*See Jim Lewis, *Peter Pan in Midlife* (Santa Fe/Silver City, NM: Southwest Contemporary Astrology, 2002). Part 5, Chapter 2 of this book, "How Not to Turn into Your Parents," is both enlightening and cautionary.

that is, the transiting north node conjoins the natal south node, and vice versa. What you inherently carry as a destiny or fate in your life has a background of knowledge, and the inversion of past/present soul opportunities creates a harmony.

The metaphysical interchange of nodes brings an opportunity to become more consciously connected to the source of one's being, and to reevaluate one's accomplishments in relation to one's gifts. If indeed the north node is "where you are going" and the south "from whence you came," then the interchange is about a collusion between your fate and your circumstances. Within the bounds of real possibility, anything is possible.

But travel forward is not always constant; the planetary model as experienced from the earth-view has both retrograde and direct motion. So do we as people. We are ultimately going forth, but periodically backstep. The retrogression periods of the life-path are needed to recapitulate and redirect our life steps. Though the essential self and the life goals may remain constant, the way to fulfillment will change in accord with your age, the times, and the world in which you find yourself in midlife.

Renegotiating your contract with your destiny seems to be part of this age period, during the inversion of the lunar nodes. Often an opportunity will arise that offers you a chance to step forward and promote yourself; if you are prepared to take the responsibility and do it with full knowledge, then it is a successful venture! Crossing the threshold to adventure is exciting at this time, because it has a strong historical basis from your previous years of life experience.

Along with this nodal reversal—within a year of it—comes a fourth Jupiter return. Options, paths, and horizons open, and the chance to make another leap into your future occurs.

The Jupiter return heralds more potential and growth over the next year or so—Jupiter is accented because it is the only other major cyclic activity in this age range. Jupiter, depending on its natal relationships, can activate an interest in travel, education, and career goals. One has reached a prime age for stable and consistent growth, and sure, steady progress can be the result of new ambitions, perspectives, and lifestyle changes. One's sense of adventure and courage rises, giving the impetus to take risks in life and to take on new ventures and projects. If life has moved relatively smoothly to this point, then one can realize the greatest power in one's chosen field, setting the stage for a long and satisfying phase right through the second Saturn return around fifty-nine.

This can be a deeply philosophical period in life, when introspection and contemplation are healing and strengthening. The one major drawback to inner searching is what it does to a relationship if the relationship is not based in shared visions and ongoing communication.

Not all relationships are threatened at the half-Uranus, but they can be difficult at this time. If the confidence of one partner is not matched in the other—that is, if the balance of power has really polarized—then the Jupiter return partner can feel really trapped, and may need to "fly." Often a healthy examination and rejuvenation of a longstanding relationship comes about here, when the adjustments of the previous Uranus quincunx slowly begin to evolve toward the Uranus trine.

CHAPTER 9

AGE FIFTY:
THE WATERSHED AND
THE CHIRON RETURN

A T the extreme ends of the spectrum, there are two ways people can approach the age of fifty—either with genuine excitement and anticipation of a true rite of passage or with actual dread. Between those two poles lies the truth—most of us approach the age of fifty feeling a combination of both, and periodic vacillation between the two.

This age mark is met by biology winning out in the end. There is no way back, and regardless of how genetically beautiful one is, one is getting older, if not already appreciatively showing it. This is the point of no return, where the biological imperative, if nothing else has, begins to nudge the maturing midlifer.

Again, there are two extremes. First, either turn into a crone or senex; second, become, as my upper-class, London born grandmother would say (with a sniff), "mutton dressed as lamb!" But my grandmother *did* look old at fifty, with a robin bosom and her flowered housedress covered by the "pinny" she donned each morning to stuff the hopper of our sawdust-burning stove in the wilds of Canada. With her grey hair tightly permed and sluiced with a lovely violet rinse, my grandmother had sagging elbows, with which I played, and skin with "squares in it," as I so ruthlessly, childishly noticed out loud.

A man can get a bit silly, too, dying his hair when he looks better with it speckled, wearing leather bomber jackets zipped over his paunch, and buying the inevitable sports car. Would he be a "goat dressed as a stud," laughing loudly in the dark as his youth recedes along with the formulaed hair?—his restlessness becoming an irritant to his wife, who may well have found herself a new job, or a new involvement with studies or social work, or possibly a new heart throb, further driving him to consider sexual alternatives, if not actual divorce?

Then there is the man who falls into midlife depression and sinks into his aging with a sad, limp feeling of acceptance. Rather like my grandmother, but in a male way. He becomes quiet and uncommunicative, letting his wife do all the social arranging, and he sits silently, smoking, brooding, or building things in the workshop.

Again, these are the extremes one can experience, but even in the classic mid-midlife crisis—for that is what we have at fifty—it is an experience that is deeply personal, profoundly tailored to the individual.

The astrology of the age of fifty is marked by Saturn trine to itself and then, by fifty-two and a half, Saturn square to itself again, as it heads into the second return. This aspect is one of tremendous support for positive aging. Since the Saturn opposite natal Saturn at age forty-four, hundreds of years seem to have passed. In fact, Saturn is the old god of time—and, by fifty, time *is* an issue.

Women, regardless of their inclination, have left behind their childbearing years. These days, with in vitro fertilization and so on, many women choose to have children quite late in their cycle. I have many clients who are in their mid-forties with children under ten! And not only do they have to deal with midlife but also postpartum and childraising issues! It is a new dynamic, coming into midlife in the third millennium with the options for living and lifestyle so varied and vast.

However, on the biological level, the fertility cycle is closing; there are new hormonal signals and adjustments going on. Menopause is real, and it is liberating. The phase of menopause itself is riotous with changes, and is the only other biological, neurological, and psychological upheaval that women have besides the onset of adolescence and the menarche. An old joke I used to say before I reached fifty was "menarche, marriage, motherhood, and menopause—the four Ms of womanhood." During and after menopause, women have time to contemplate their own directions and futures. If it was not already an open option, it is now, and the completion of immediate family or relationship responsibilities has arrived, or will soon.

A woman's instinctual nature is toward interconnectedness and relationship. In A Women's Book of Life, Joan Borysenko says: "Midlife testosterone levels are high in a woman, but in contrast to men, so are our levels of estrogen, even though they are lower than they were premenopausally."*

In most feminine lifestyles, a woman has been focused on the core function of nurturing and family management, and then at this age period she undergoes a long but diminishing sense of the empty nest. Her natural instinct to care for others is hard to elude, and ideally should not be lost in aging. But the focus and the breadth of her caring nature must contract. Often if a woman's life primarily has been about nurturing and family management, she feels lost, and if she rises to the call of the "unlived life" now, she will grapple with feelings of guilt about this newfound freedom. Moving from other-oriented to self-centering is hard but positive work.

In midlife, one does meet one's opposite, and in the case of the old traditional and highly instinctual paradigm, a woman's outreach for assurance from outside the family unit can result in deeply ambivalent feelings. Again, to quote Dr. Borysenko, "the prodigious physiological changes of menopause . . . have let the genie of the yang, or the masculine, energy, out of the bottle." She continues:

> Many women are afraid of power and success, afraid of taking
> leadership roles, and I believe that one of the underlying reasons
> for this lies in the fact that we are aware of how power has been

---

*Joan Borysenko, A Woman's Book of Life: The Biology, Psychology, and Spirituality of the Feminine Life Cycle (New York: Riverhead Books, 1996).

abused through millennia, most often by men, who have been in positions of political and social ascendancy (p. 196).

So power in the feminine function is vastly different from power in the masculine function, and this differentiation only really fully emerges in the menopausal period of women and the climacteric in men. The women suffragettes of the 1920s were the originators of women's rights—primarily to vote and to own land, and to keep one's children if one chose divorce. The 1960s women's movement was more about the "inner woman," addressing the sexual freedom to choose motherhood or not, to choose career over home management, to achieve equal pay and promotion opportunities. All have been steps forward in the natural evolution of the power balance in the world. However, there was a strange feeling about the strident, infuriated feminist movement in its most extreme—I often felt it was an attempt to create just another patriarchy that was run by women.

However, as a women acclimatizes to her "new" biological balance, and the freedom from the lunar-based cycles and feelings, she can begin to feel less guilty about personal success. Many women advance their education or retrain, entering the world of success-oriented industry. Others, however, will continue to rule their families like aging generals, unable to let go gracefully and develop the "other side" of themselves. Or they adopt a long-suffering martyr's attitude—I like to tease my grown daughters by saying "Be nice, I don't have long." Their response? "But how *long* do we *have* to be nice?"

Frequently men find their feelings surfacing during midlife in ways that are foreign to them. Traditionally, the man must provide for his family and is by nature inclined to "part-time feelings." Not only is the male disposition one that is solar and idea oriented but also the man is trained to be so. His training is such that feelings are to be shelved, compartmentalized, but between forty and fifty his "opposite" emerges, and his contrasexual feminine side irrupts. He becomes moody, emotional, needy, and quite the opposite of his female counterpart, who becomes increasingly independent, impatient with his needs, and, well, like *he* always was!

The impetus of male psychobiology and archetype is toward compartmentalizing and containing various and sundry life factors, either in boxes or hierarchical structures or both. This is not bad nor evil but simply nature's way. Whether or not it is rewarding, satisfying, or even compassionate is the most important criterion for *any* change in one's character or behavior.

All of which means that men and their feelings are more typically segregated from the gestalt of their personality but become more urgent to come to full consciousness, while a woman has a difficult time separating out her feelings from everything else. So the woman's midlife and onward is about becoming increasingly aware of her choices in feeling and doing. And men find themselves at sea in their newly arising need to integrate and synthesize their feelings, emotions, and responses within their actions, so that post-midlife they can choose to integrate increasingly more of themselves into themselves in their journey toward wholeness of mind, body, and soul.

RELATIONSHIPS: TO BE OR NOT TO BE?

At fifty, and in the years to follow, individuals find themselves changing so much that relationships of all types are radicalized. There is so much at stake in this phase of life, that many friends, group associations, and partnerships are examined for their value.

Relationships are a mirror of one's own self, and when we are in transition, our relationships are too. Because of the homeostatic principle— the "stay the same" regulatory function in the psyche—we don't change friends, groups, or love objects as easily after a "certain age." But the changes that occur at the watershed of fifty will demand that some old relationships will pass away and very few new ones will develop. It is crucial that if you have a deep, old friendship and it hits a rock in this phase, you truly examine both it and yourself for what is happening.

We find ourselves being more cautious and less easily befriended after fifty, and quite naturally so. As we age, our time is increasingly precious. And thus, we are less risky about our friendships, and certainly about our intimate friendships.

It is a natural progression in the first half of life to have loads of experimental relations, but that natural youthful carelessness declines with time. By midlife, one is less interested in the risk and more interested in the investment. By fifty, we have run our thread, really, and need to be very deep about those we have around us, and be true to our inner self, not paying as much attention to what others want—or, more important, what we have been trained and habituated to do.

This can be a painful process, the pruning of our emotional life, because it may well mean that associates, kin, friends, and so on of many years' standing fall away—either by choice or by circumstances. If we are lucky, we don't lose the ones we most cherish; if we are typical, then we do give up relations that are not part of our deeper Self's plan for us. In contrast, we often find renewed contact and profound feelings for members of our own families. The numbers of people who reconnect with cousins, elders, or family who may still be in "the old country" is amazing.

There are times when the outer world and its happenings are an eventful mirror of one's inner life. If one does not heed this natural law, then deep, scarring, emotional tears can take place in the fabric of one's soul. For example, if you have had a strong bond with a group of individuals who form a collective or tribal function for you, and you have outgrown them, then "things" begin to happen. Ultimately, a projection of any unresolved issues or contents of the shadow realm of the unconscious will emerge, whether one is "innocent" or not!

Many Pluto in Leo people who followed a devotional path and had a living master or teacher, lost that guru and found themselves undergoing spiritual crisis. Often the questions about "faith" and spirtuality are profound and have huge impact on them, resulting in having to "leave home" all over again.

Similarly, in personal relationships—formed from love or other bonds—there are opportunities to reevaluate and either change or drop them. It appears that we cannot take everything with us—we cannot take into the future all that has been our history, if it is not all still functional or useful for our own individuation. Some previously valuable

---

tools from one's past *must* be left behind on the threshold of change. The task is to know what those outmoded traits are and when to leave them!

The numbers of people whose partners ask for a divorce, or walk out on them, or spring a surprise lover on them at this juncture is stunning. More often than not, the husband, wife, or partner who does the "leaving" is doing it for both! This is reciprocity in the unconscious. Generally, the departing partner is fulfilling an unconscious request from the abandoned one.

If people have a strong bond and a good relationship at this stage in life, and they continue to grow together, then there is no need to be divorcing. Divorce is an option that has been increasingly abused with the Pluto in Leo/Neptune in Libra generation; it is *not* a prime choice for the Pluto in Virgo generation, and is likely to become less so as we move on. There are now more opportunities for both men and women to really live out their true natures, if they so choose. And the generational imperatives of Pluto in Virgo, Libra, and Scorpio are not to be the center of the universe but an integral part of it.

Once the shock and excitement of turning fifty has come and gone, a sense of settling in will occur, and by the time one reaches the mid-fifties, there is a marked shift in psychological perspective.

THE CHIRON RETURN

In Melanie Reinhart's masterpiece on Chiron, she says:

> At the Chiron return, if we have not already done so, we begin orienting toward death, the end of our physical life on earth. The half-way point of life has now passed. . . . The Chiron return poses the question: "What am I going to do with the last part of my life?" . . . If a personal sense of connection with the numinous and spiritual has not yet been found, denial and fear of death may invite the insidious and draining experience of meaninglessness. However, for many people, the Chiron return brings a very real sense of participation in the overall process of

life as a whole, resulting in conscious commitment to their individuation and spiritual life.*

Chiron is the bridge between the social planetary realm and the collective planetary realm. The linking of the classical planets, from the Sun through Saturn, and the modern planets Uranus, Neptune, and Pluto, will have been complete by this age. And now, with the inclusion of the Centaurs in the Kuiper belt, incorporating the realms of both desire and abstinence, the quality of the Chiron return is rendered even more profound.†

Here one realizes one's relationship to one's own tribal unit, whether that be aboriginal or secular or religious. One realizes one's limits within culture and its cosmos, as well as one's own role in that collective. The "wound" associated with the myth of Chiron is both personal and collective. Not only was Chiron mortally wounded personally, he sacrificed his immortality for the greater good. If our culture has been unsatisfactory to us as individuals, then we suffer not only because of it but also on behalf of it. But the most important thing about the Chiron return is—as with all planetary returns—that it reiterates birth. That is, it begins the journey around the zodiac again, forming the same aspects as it did in one's first fifty years.

Here is the chance to review and re-vision things that hurt us so as youngsters—infants, even—and heal those hurts or wounds by giving birth to ourselves as adults. This opportunity for rebirthing one's true nature is the real message in any recurring trauma, pattern, or impulse as an adult over fifty. This should not be done as a self-destructive or masochistic reliving of bad stuff but as taking time to see objectively and clearly what you are and how you got to that, and to fully embody yourself—all your warts and gloriousness included.

Recapitulation of one's life seems to come at this stage whether or not it is desired. Along with all the other influences, Chiron adds an urgency to this life change by offering a choice. The choice is between as-

*Melanie Reinhart, *Chiron and the Healing Journey: An Astrological and Psychological Perspective*, updated ed., Contemporary Astrology Series (London: Arkana, Penguin, 1989), p. 268.
†Melanie Reinhart, *To the Edge and Beyond: Saturn, Chiron, Pholus and the Centaurs*, vol. 4 (London: CPA Press, 1996). Reprinted as *Saturn, Chiron and the Centaurs: To the Edge and Beyond* (2002).

suming your own destiny and character and living it out fully or finding ways and means of avoiding that responsibility. Melanie Reinhart calls the second alternative "perpetrator energy." The dilemma that accompanies this recapitulation period arises in the form of alternatives— either you can see your own life as your own, or you can project it onto others. There is a point when your mother/father/sister/teachers are no longer culpable in your own discomfort or pain.

Chiron acts as a watchdog of the solar system; it parabolates in and out of the personal zone, and links us to our responsibility to the collective. In this epoch, since Chiron was only sighted in 1977, it is particularly important for each one of us to recognize that by improving one's own self, one improves the collective by that much.

Many people find themselves called to "higher ground" when they are passing through the Chiron return—that is, they are filled with direction and purpose that transcends the personal.

Alternatively, there are people who may have spent the first fifty years of life dedicating themselves to the collective—to groups, beliefs, politics, and so on—and have arrived at this stage with no personal life. They feel unloved, alone, unmasculine/feminine, and unfulfilled in the most intimate aspects of life. I have a client who, though she raised three children on her own, spent the first sixty years of her life establishing human ecology foundations and so on, and now, at sixty-one, seeks to find a personal intimate life—in her own words, "to be a woman, a grandmother, and a person in the world." In fact, she seeks to be a human being, not a human doing.

Many of us find that we avoided our "wound" in a personal way, transferring it to cause-related action. Whatever it was you did before your Chiron return, and, more significantly, why you did it, will alter radically, and your deepest, interior motives for life and action will change.

AGE FIFTY-TWO: SATURN SQUARE SATURN— LIMINALITY/CONSOLIDATION

The next phase, potentially introducing the prime-time period of life, begins with the Saturn square to itself. This aspect is reminiscent of the first square at twenty-one. The initial stage is infused with uncertainty, because one is at an age that is "in between"; one is not yet categorically old, but it is evident that youth has passed its bloom. Many people do experience a depression at the onset of this phase of their lives, being forced to contemplate the deeper issues that may have been ignored in the previous stages of midlife.

Similar to the depression that befalls the newly adult twenty-one-year-old—when one is expected to stand on one's own, express independence, and be all grown up—this brief juncture has a critical seriousness to it. At fifty-two and a half, one is certainly an adult, but tottering in liminality. The square is a forming square, that is, a square that is returning to the conjunction at Saturn return in seven and a half years, so it presages real aging. One can actually perceive oneself as an old person.

This particular Saturn square initiates yet another phase of liminal or threshold experiences. Generally, society does not endorse astrologically marked rites of passage, and if you tell people you are feeling a bit odd, a bit off center, because you have Saturn square Saturn, you likely will be *thought* odd on top of it all! The awkwardness of the liminal adult is usually contained, but the inner feeling of displacement is disturbing. Here you are, not old, not young, not really anything, but definitely in between the past and the future. The context in which you find yourself, obviously, is crucial to what you can do to get through this and into the fast-paced next phase.

It can be an introduction to the wasteland, insofar as there is a two-year period after the initial aspect in which there is *no other cyclic activity*. It is oddly consistent with liminality that one of the biggest questions that arises for an individual at the age of fifty-two is "Now what? I am supposed to be all grown up, but I don't feel it." From the ages of fifty-two through almost fifty-five, the lack of other major cycles contributes to the experience of thresholding, drifting, seeking and questioning authority and one's own authenticity.

During the social revolution that occurred in the mid-1960s, when Uranus and Pluto conjoined opposed by Saturn, an amazing number of fifty-two-year-old people "dropped out" of mainstream society to explore their inner world and liminal fifty-two-year-old people, all hanging about in the same park, doing the same thing, and revolting against the same issues, but for entirely different social and personal reasons. At fifty-two, dropping out is *very* different from rebelling at seventeen or separating from the family at twenty-nine.

If one's life has been governed by the status quo and one has subordinated one's individuality to externally imposed values, this stage of development can result in revolution or depression or a bit of both—and both are healthy stimuli for change.

If you discover that over half of your life has passed with no sense of deep, heartfelt satisfaction, the anger that arises can be profound. This phase of Saturn square to Saturn can precipitate one of the most dynamic life changes—because there is not only a good history but also a stronger potential for true and rapid change. The astrological cycles are relatively quiet for the next three years, so now is a time for a vital soul-searching, and a rearranging of life's priorities.

It is never too late to set off on a quest. And the quest for identity can mean many things. Indeed, by now, in this phase it is essential to be realistic about life and your role in your own life. Feelings of disappointment need to be realistically viewed. For instance, to see life as an experience rather than as an accomplishment is valuable in itself. If this is a time of accounting, then it is good to see yourself as who you are, not what you think you should be, or in relation to others' mysterious destinies.

This type of square—a waning or tenth house square—symbolizes consolidation of practical matters and gathering of resources in preparation to make changes in perception of one's self as it is in reality, not the imagination. Our primary resources are time, love, and money, so intimacy, age, and personal resources are paramount in one's consciousness now. Have you looked at your bank account lately—have you saved up for this time? Or have you spent your time, love, and money in ways that show no return at this stage?

Nothing is *ever* too late, and this is an optimum time to reconstruct your environment—including the people within it—so as to suit you better in this next phase of your midlife journey!

AGES FIFTY-FOUR TO FIFTY-SEVEN: INTEGRATION—FREE AT LAST!

In his book *Facing the Fifties*, Peter O'Connor says:

> By one's mid-fifties, a fundamental shift occurs, with time already lived outweighing time left to be lived before death. This shift is, in my view, the great initiator into a more fully realized life, since it brings with it the possibility, if we allow it, of altering our orientation from an outwardly directed one to an increasingly inward one. . . . In short, if a successful shift is made to the centre of psychic gravity, then *one begins to experience* **oneself** *more directly, rather than exclusively in terms of relationships with others.**

This is a *most* wonderful thing—to be able to see oneself as an organic whole, an integral entity, and not an extension or projection of others. This is an experience I hear about repeatedly—the great joy a person feels at being free of dependency. This does not mean isolated and uncaring about others, or not responsible for others, but rather being "clear" about who one is regardless of what others might think, or what one might *think* they think.†

To be less concerned about others and more about life itself is the greatest gift of this threshold crossing. Relationships, intimacy, love, friendship all continue but without the sense of ego attachment, and thus is experienced by most men and women as a time of great liberation and deeply enriched relationships.

It is primarily one's ego and persona that require less shoring up from outside, and a more introspective life is enjoyed. It may be as simple as feeling okay about declining a party invitation, or deciding not to go to the company picnic—this fundamental life change is not always a great revelation but is always a less stressful feeling. Relating in the mid-fifties and beyond—if one is "doing the work"—is about true generosity and

*Peter A. O'Connor, *Facing the Fifties* (St. Leonards, New South Wales, Australia: Allen & Unwin, 2000), p. 16. Emphasis added.
†See R. D. Laing, *Knots* (New York: Pantheon, 1970).

true love. Most obligatory-type relationships should begin to diminish, enhancing the quality of the ones that are truly satisfying and reflect common ethics, values, and goals. Recall Heather's experience at fifty-four when she found herself operating out of old patterns and blinded her inner eye to the intuition she had.

Between the ages of fifty-two and fifty-seven come a flurry of developmental generic aspects, and with that a sense of urgency to "get it together." One feels an imperative toward self-fulfillment and self-honesty that must come to pass by the second Saturn return.

Age fifty-two, there was the transiting Saturn square to natal Saturn; then, at fifty-four, is the second return of the secondary progressed Moon and Saturn sextile Saturn; this is followed by Uranus trine Uranus and Neptune trine Neptune at fifty-five to fifty-six. (And for the Pluto square type of midlifers, Pluto trines Pluto in this phase too!) And at fifty-seven, the Lunar nodes return for the third time.

The plethora of big aspects in this five- to six-year period can be summarized in one sentence: There is an emotional coming of age (secondary progressed Lunar return), along with a rise in energy and excitement about simply being who one is (Uranus trine Uranus); a more realistic grip on one's true creative being (Neptune trine Neptune), a reorientation within one's life destiny (third nodal return); and, for all who have Pluto in Leo, Virgo, Libra, and Scorpio, a time of tapping into one's core power (Pluto trine Pluto).

FIFTY-FOUR—LUNAR NO MORE

The second Lunar return by secondary progression recapitulates the first one at age twenty-seven and a half. This means that when you were born, your natal Moon was in a particular sign and place. At the instant of your birth, and your emergence from the womb (Moon), the heavens did not halt but carried on . . . or the Earth continued to rotate, that is.

In the continuum of the birth moment, astrologically, your natal Moon was "fixed" at the place it was at the time of birth, but the transiting Moon—the actual Moon in motion—carried on in its orbit around Earth. It is this motion that describes the progression of the Moon and its return to its natal place every twenty-seven and a half years. Secondary progressions use each day, starting with the day of your birth and subsequent days, as a microcosm of a single year. So the actual Moon in the sky makes a full cycle through the zodiac every twenty-seven and a half days, and from that follows the idea of the day-for-a-year measurement.

The second Lunar return is a truly significant rite of passage, and it is centered in the focal point of one's emotional, biological, and instinctive life. Around the age of fifty-four, one has come to a place in one's body where the hormonal dictates change—both for men and women. Biology recapitulates ontology, and it brings with it a renewal of all things that the Moon symbolizes—both generally and specifically for each one of us.

The Moon is the container of the biological and reproductive, thus creative, core. It represents not only one's womb experience but also the mother as the container of you in your gestation. In the womb we are conceived, and outside of the womb we develop in accord with that ontological creative process. There are even hints that the embryonic experience actually is relived in various ways throughout one's life in the form of gut reactions, instincts, inexplicable feelings, moods, and personality traits. For instance, if your mother was seriously ill, or depressed, or suffered a shock when she was pregnant with you, your gestation is affected, and the transference from mother to child is held in the body as a visceral memory.

So the Moon as a static natal position holds vast amounts of encoded information about who you are in a deep, emotional, private, and instinctual way. From that your needs, wants, desires, and habitual patterns are formed. Some things don't change. There are even very dramatic aspects of this lunar memory or DNA code that emerge periodically in life, such as unexplainable habits that are embedded in your system and are so exactly like your mother/father/aunt or other blood relative that everyone comments on it. There is no real understanding of this, though we strive for it—both in hard science and in astrology. And the Moon as it progresses to its second return to its natal place recapitulates one's emotional origins, development, and maturation.

For now, let's just say that the Lunar return at this mature age is a time when you can accept yourself truly—for who you are, and as a bonded member of your family of origin and the result of the long lineage back through the immediate ancestral realm. The needs and demands of your body and soul at this stage are more about you, however, than anyone else.

For once in your life, you are in the process of becoming free from old emotional habits and deeply entrenched needs that are not truly yours but are acquired or have been demanded by others, and in this way the Lunar return can re-turn you to your moment of birth, and allow you to "bring yourself up" again—as an adult.

Coming of age in the emotional sense is the precursor to the second Saturn return, at 29½, read about in the next part of the book, but if you think back to the last years of your twenties, at 27½, you may well recall something important. It was then that your "inner clock" began to say that it was time to move on from being a child of your parents and toward being an independent person in your own right.

The second time we get this emotional maturation imperative, we are older and, if not wiser, much more experienced. With this second Lunar return, the mandate from the psyche is to move on from being in relationship to others based on dependency, old patterns, and family dynamics. This is not as easily done as it is said. To really mature with emotional grace, it means letting go of one's children as dependents, letting go of one's spouse or partner as a habitual necessity, and renegotiating these relationships so that they are based on choice, not need. That does not mean that you stop needing your spouse, or your kids and grandkids, but you *choose* to be with them or not when you want to or not. Without guilt and obligation.

The Moon rules the body fluids and secretions, and the reproductive system in women, so there are the obvious changes that occur around the mid-fifties, such as menopause for women and the climacteric for men. The physical aspect of the Lunar return includes the annoying and sometimes pathological drying skin and mucous membranes, the beginning of cartilage and "joint" problems, and all the normal body changes in late midlife. One's hair grays, the skin wrinkles, and the joints stiffen—but there are attitudinal and physical ways to maintain optimum health while the natural progress of time continues. These are the more important lessons in the Lunar return—you must make conscious choices about the quality of life and how those choices can be made into new habits!

New habits are harder to keep than old ones, just as a good habit is easier to break than a bad one. The Lunar return will emphasize the habits you know are not healthy and allow you to think more positively along the lines of reconstructing your life so that the next five or six years are optimally productive, and get you to where you want to be by sixty.

SATURN SEXTILE SATURN: GRACEFUL BOUNDARIES

In the same time frame, the transit of Saturn is sextile itself, as it moves toward the Saturn return at age sixty. The Lunar return and the Saturn sextile is the best time for renegotiating your incarnation contract. Both the Moon and Saturn are planets that are agents for our worldly habits and our ways of being in the world. The outcome of our future depends on the way we approach this phase in maturing, because many of our more deeply unconscious habits that have been "okay" till now stop being "okay."

The only way one will know this is when one sees those habits at work in one's relationships, work habits, and diet—drinking, smoking, lying around, not doing what we really deeply know we should be doing—nags at one. This is the best time in maturity to do what we "should" do! It is during this time that you can really get to a place of being on time, in the groove, doing what you ought to do—thus preventing too many "I should have's" in your sixties! So if you feel the urge to get it together, to take control over yourself and your bad habits, then this is the optimum time to do it, since the impetus to actually change dramatically any of the things you really need to change decreases after the age of sixty.

Similarly, establishing new patterns and habits in this period—of about a year or two, really—is much, *much* easier than it was before. So plan ahead, think of your work patterns and where you would like to be in ten years, and begin to reorganize around those future needs. Some people who have worked a straight job for thirty years begin to chafe badly. If at all possible, begin to line up alternatives and things to do that will give you encouragement and excitement about retiring.

Those who have pursued independent careers or creative lives—with all the attendant anxieties, unless one has been fabulously successful— may need to seriously buckle down to the reality of aging and the practicalities of that process. For the inevitable now draws more closely to you and your conscious way of being. Thus, if you haven't already, begin to map out a financial and activity plan—think of yourself and your family and what you and they might need; and if you can foresee any changes, begin to act on those now.

Uranus Trine to Uranus and Neptune Trine to Neptune: If at First You Don't Succeed, Trine and Trine Again!

Though both these planets are in a trine to themselves at fifty-five and fifty-six, the trines are very different in quality and intent. Neptune spends fourteen years transiting each sign, while Uranus has a seven-year period in each sign; thus, the actual "type" of trine is vastly different in quality and intent.*

Uranus

Uranus, in this post-midlife trine, is highly stimulating mentally. The mind is electrified with new charges, and there is a real surge in exploratory ideas, innovation, pioneering, and surveying new horizons with a sense of excitement and potential. Typically, the angst of middlescence has shifted, and one has become more interested in the ongoing aging process with a sense of future and renewed desires for the future.

---

*Neptune being fourteen years in a sign and Uranus seven means that Uranus covers twice as much "ground" as Neptune in as many years. Thus, there is an interesting collusion between the two at this stage of life, with Neptune being in a "separating" trine (from conjunction to opposition) while Uranus is in the "applying" (from opposition to conjunction) trine. The quality of the separating and applying aspects (sinister and dexter, respectively) are very different, as we see in the descriptions here.

There may be a longing for travel and experiencing new cultures and horizons. This trine aspect is what is referred to as a "one-to-nine trine," that is, a first house to ninth house trine, which immediately brings to mind all aspects of Sagittarius and the ninth house qualities. If you have lived a traveled or restless adventure to date, your new excitement is about stability.

In an ideal world, this is an interesting age for exploring the world—or at least spending more time traveling and scouting for places in the world, or your own culture, that open new doors to the next part of life. Many people are retiring and spending more time away from the primary home at this age, and finding ways to spend periods of time in other places. Often a mobile home or recreational vehicle will help with this, so that it doesn't mean only the wealthy can feel the open road and the excitement of a new way of living.

This trine stimulates the desire to be "free," to move on and think in new ways. By this age one has well-formed philosophies and worldviews that have a lot of history and experience underlying them. This phase can open a closed mind and encourage a wider view of the world and its happenings. A new surge of mental youth arrives, and through the next few years may even mean studying and learning new subjects, or devoting oneself to an interest or passion on a greater or even full-time basis.

When I was in midlife, and studying the classics at a university, there was a seventy-year-old woman in my Latin 200 class—and she was taking a degree in German literature of the classical period. She had begun her university work in her mid-fifties after her children had got settled, but then had come a long period of home care for her ailing husband. After he died, her longtime interests and the desire for such a mental journey were being completed and fulfilled at seventy. So why not at fifty-six or fifty-seven?

Neptune

Neptune's qualities are a polarity to those of Uranus. While Uranus is about clarity, objectivity, specifics, and alertness of mind, Neptune is more mystical and embodies the intangible values of soul and spirit. The

Neptune trine to itself brings a quality of playful imagination to this time, and the fact that it is coupled with the adventurous sense of exploration of Uranus adds the benefit of childlike playfulness to any new thing. Exploring art, music, theater; gardening, alternative health, and body regimes; finding spiritual and philosophical beliefs more intensely satisfying and interesting; reading, walking, seeing life in a new and more positive way—all these are part of the duality of having such positive aspects from the two most transformative planets.

Finding a sense of comfort in the most simple things in life is part of this trine of Neptune to itself. It is a "separating" trine and is called a "one-to-five" aspect, which means that it embodies the characteristics of the first house and Aries to the fifth house and Leo. I believe this is the aspect that begins the softening phase in the turning-point from maturing to aging—wherein acceptance is a grace and not a failing.

Gently the trine allows the soul to accept the benefits of a lived life, and encourages the spirit to be more playful and experience a greater sense of confidence in the face of life's "slings and arrows of outrageous fortune." More than ever now, the psyche begins to prod at the ego to encourage it to let go, move on, and accept the true benefits of much of life lived with still a very great deal of life left to create within.

Breaking out of the mold, thinking differently, taking risks with ideas, projects, and work brings a burst of life-force to the late fifties. This natural, generic "boost" is the very energy needed to cross the threshold to the genuine elder years, where vitality is still high but the level of ambition and aggression has softened.

PART II

BEYOND THE BOUNDS OF SATURN

✳

CHAPTER 10

INTRODUCTION TO AGING

A PRAYER FOR OLD AGE
God guard me from those thoughts me think
In the mind alone:
He that sings a lasting song
Thinks in a marrow-bone;

From all that makes a wise old man
That can be praised of all;
O what am I that I should not seem
For the song's sake a fool?

I pray—for fashion's word is out
And prayer comes round again—
That I may seem, though I die old,
A foolish, passionate man.*

—WILLIAM BUTLER YEATS

*William Butler Yeats, *Collected Poems* (London: Macmillan, 1933), p. 326.

Very few people truly think about being sixty-plus until they are. Nature has a self-preservation clause, what I call healthy denial, inherent in its codes that prevents us from knowing anything until it actually happens. Oh, we have an imagination, and a tendency to use it, but we know that life happens as it happens, but certainly imagining sixty-five is not being sixty-five.

Ultimately, this has been a difficult part for me to write, partly because I am "only" fifty-six as I write it, and partly because I am profoundly unhappy with the way our culture has evolved toward the treatment of the aging and old. This is not to say that it was better in the "old days"—probably not—but culture has not improved much in the acknowledgment and respect and true care for the aging and elders as a class.

I do not mean treatment as a geriatric patient, but treatment as a human being, still alive, still growing, and still essential to the collective consciousness. In writing the astrology of Part II, I faced something ahead of time, something that lip service is paid toward but nothing so far has been done about. I am hoping that my small contribution will be heard and changes will be made, and aging will become a recognized place in society.

This will mean radical re-visioning of what an "old person" is, and how one matures and evolves toward the inevitable. By this I mean sanctions that will acknowledge the old person's real place and standing in our world. So many of my contemporaries and, thus, the future middlescent generations, are facing the aging of their own parents. So many of them go to help them out and discover that no homeowner's taxes have been paid for a couple of years, income tax filing is undone, bills are left on the table or in the drawers, they are being seduced by telephone solicitors posing as "financial planners," and so on. The elder people of all societies have to have new rules for their self-governing, and for those who live in their realms.

There is a point it seems, in aging, where the interest in advancement, and even maintenance of ones' practical life, stops. There should be a time when people of a certain age can opt for less mundane responsibilities and move into their elder status with fewer tasks, such as filing taxes, paying bills, and so on. This is not to say that electric bills should be absorbed by all people under seventy for those over seventy, but there need to be changes in how old people actually live their daily lives.

We are gradually introduced to the responsibilities of adulthood starting in the adolescent years. There is a natural urge in the human being to take part in the "grown up" world, and in the course of time, to a greater or lesser degree, we pick up and use the tools of advancement, achievement, payment of dues, and so on.

However, there is no gradual introduction to aging! One is led to believe that one's interest in maintaining society and running one's life as a high-powered midlifer should continue to death. But it does not.

Jung says:

Aging people should know that their lives are not mounting and expanding, but that an inexorable inner process enforces the contraction of life. For a young person it is almost a sin, or at least a danger, to be too preoccupied with himself; but for the aging person it is a duty and a necessity to devote serious attention to himself. After having lavished its light upon the world, the sun withdraws its rays in order to illuminate itself. Instead of doing likewise, many old people prefer to be hypochondriacs, niggards, pedants, applauders of the past or else eternal adolescents—all lamentable substitutes from the illumination of the self, but *inevitable consequence of the illusion that the second half of life must be governed by the principles of the first.**

The more I wrote, the more concerned I became about insulting my elders, being an upstart, and talking imperiously about that which I do not know. The first third of this book was easy because I have been there

---

*C. G. Jung, *The Structure and Dynamics of the Psyche*, in *Collected Works*, vol 8, Bollingen Series XX, (Princeton, NJ: Princeton University Press, 1960), para. 784. Emphasis added.

and done that. In this part I am humbled by my own unknowing and total naivete, though I am supported by empirical evidence and the work
of others.

However, the more I wrote, the more engaged I became with the
process—the natural process—of aging. In doing so, I realized that it is
not aging that is a problem but our contemporary attitude toward it.
Something that we need to reclaim has been submerged, and it is within
the power of the individual to reclaim it. The problem is our culture and
its desire to "disappear" the aged, and marginalize them, rather than acknowledge their role in the transmission of myth and legend—of personal and family and social history—for posterity.

The astrology in this part—in the fruitfulness of latter years—takes
into account the natural cycles of aging as defined by time and cycles.
The rising of life—dawn; the refinement of life—noon; and the integration and fulfillment of life—vespers. If we could design a culture and a
world in the same elegant, evolutionary, and ever-changing fashion as
that in which the solar system moves, then we would be in the Utopia
of Thomas More's imagination. That we cannot live in Utopia is acceptable, but that we cannot improve the world is not.

As Joseph Campbell said:

> The modern hero, the modern individual who dares to heed the
> call and seek the mansion of that presence with whom it is our
> whole destiny to be atoned, cannot, indeed must not, wait for his
> community to cast off its slough of pride, fear, rationalized
> avarice, and sanctified misunderstanding. It is not society that is
> to guide and save the creative hero, but precisely the reverse.*

In addition, the more I wrote and immersed myself wholly into the
viewpoint of aging—the astrological theory and my own gut response to
what I was seeing and writing—the more I became aware of the unique
timing of the Pluto in Cancer people (born 1912–1937), Pluto in Leo

---

*Joseph Campbell, *The Hero with a Thousand Faces*, Bollingen Series XVII (Princeton, NJ:
Princeton University Press, 1949), p. 390.

people (born 1937–1956), and the three subsequent generations and what is happening with them.

In Part I, I clearly explained how midlife is different now, as shown by Pluto's involvement in the generic cycles of development, and the astrological generational intent of Pluto's movements and cycles. And now we are moving into the aging factor of these generations of the future—those born between 1937 and 1995.

Another thing I encountered, when my own idealism came up against the reality of aging, was that every single person I spoke to about his or her own aging, or his or her experience with aging patients or family or in work with elders in community situations, said something that was a real eye-opener for me.

Not once have I encountered in my surveys and research a single person over the age of sixty-five who said they enjoyed getting older physically at all; but spiritually and psychologically they felt increasingly more "at home." In many of the Platonic dialogues, the ancient Greek philosopher Socrates says that the whole of one's life should be a preparation for death, and that life was about recollection and reflection. And that death (thanatos) was the liberation of an imprisoned soul. The body becomes an increasingly Socratic tomb in this philosophy, and most elders know this well. In my discussion of ages seventy-five through ninety, I relate the tale of Er, told in Plato's *Republic,* in which there is a lovely metaphor for this spiritually uplifting time.

The Greek words *sema* and *soma* are very similar and form a sophisticated pun in Greek—*soma* is "body" and *sema* is "tomb." So the philosophical content of the idea of the body as tomb of the soul is very rich in the original, but it is certainly not lost in the translation. This viewpoint seems somber and, in the days of New Ageism, possibly even "negative." But it isn't really. The soma/sema analogy is okay if one realizes that it is about the soul, not the body, and that real life and growth continue—that within the soul, the psyche, we evolve in a natural and pleasant way toward our freedom.

This is all very fine and well if you have the financial resources and the familial support that aging demands. The problem is that the majority of old people do not have a comfort level that gives them peace of mind to enter their aging with philosophy and spirituality as the prime focus or *modus operandi*.

＊

A spectacularly timed life and death was that of Joseph Campbell, who was born on March 26, 1904, and died on October 30, 1987.* He was just five months short of his Uranus return—the final pass was November 1988—when he died. To cap his monumental achievements, he did a series of interviews with Bill Moyers *just* before his death, and in 1988 those interviews became *The Power of Myth*, a six-hour PBS special. I will say more about his Uranus return later.

In an interview in *Modern Maturity*, Ram Dass, who had a stroke at sixty-five, was asked by his interviewer, Amy Gross, how he first came to terms with his disability: "To see things that way [spiritually] you have to shift to what you call soul perspective?" He replied: "It's also the witness. It's like: I have a stroke. I witness me having a stroke. The witness doesn't have any fear of death. You stand outside the action. Shifting perspective takes the suffering away." She asked: "How do you make the shift?" He replied: "By being in the moment—by not dwelling in the past and not anticipating the future."

---

*March 26, 1904, 7:25 PM, New York, NY (birth certificate). Died October 30, 1987.
*Modern Maturity, August 2000.

CHAPTER 11

SANS EYES, SANS TEETH, SANS EVERYTHING?

In *As You Like It*, Shakespeare wrote:

> All the world's a stage
> And all the men and women merely players:
> They have their exits and their entrances;
> And one man in his time plays many parts,
> His acts being seven ages. At first the infant,
> Mewling and puking in the nurse's arms.
> And then the whining schoolboy, with his satchel,
> And, shining morning face, creeping like snail
> Unwillingly to school. And, then the lover,
> Sighing like furnace, with a woeful ballad
> Made to his mistress' eyebrow. Then a soldier
> Full of strange oaths, and bearded like the bard,
> Jealous in honour, sudden and quick in quarrel,
> Seeking the bubble reputation

Even in the cannon's mouth. And then the justice,
In fair round belly with good capon lin'd,
With eyes severe and bear of formal cut,
Full of wise saws and modern instances'
And so he plays his part. The sixth age shifts
Into the lean and slipper'd pantaloon,
With spectacle on nose and pouch on side,
His youthful hose well save'd a world too wide,
For his shrunk shank; and his big manly voice,
Turning again toward childish treble, pipes
And, whistles in his sound. Last scene of all,
That ends this strange eventful history,
Is second childishness, and mere oblivion,
Sans teeth, sans eyes, sans taste, sans everything.

—Act II, *scene* vii

These famous lines on "ages of man" are poetically descriptive of the classical planetary sequence—the infant lives and nurses in the arms of the Moon; the schoolboy with enquiring mind is Mercury; the "lover" embodies Aphrodite's call in the planet Venus; the heated and armed soldier is a minion of Mars; the justice, his "belly with good capon lin'd" is, of course, avuncular Jupiter's era, and the last, final, and dismal age being in the realm of Saturn, tottering toward the grave soon after age sixty, if not before.

We now have three more planets beyond Saturn (and we also incorporate Chiron, the Kuiper belt, and the Centaurs, and maybe more to come?), so there is more to the life story for us than there was for contemporaries of the bard!

The "modern" planets, those beyond the bounds of Saturn, are the agents for options in consciousness and opportunities for innovative advancement or novel ways of viewing the world. Even many contemporary students find it a chore to get a grip on just what these outer planets, Uranus, Neptune, and Pluto, "do."

Like all planets, the outermost do not "do" *anything*, but their inclusion in our consciousness and their presence seen through telescopes have extended both our vision and our inner options in life. Each of the

FIGURE 9. GENERIC ASPECTS FROM 60 TO 75

AGES 59–60	♄ ♃ ☽ ☉

Second Saturn return
Fifth Jupiter return at 60
Secondary progressed Moon and Sun repeat their natal phase at birth
(for the second time) in the year

AGES 63–64	♅

Uranus square Uranus returning back to its natal place
(waning from the midlife half-Uranus)

AGE 67	♄ ♆ ♀

Saturn square Saturn waxing from the Second return (third time)
Neptune quincunx Neptune(150°), toward the opposition in fourteen
years, at the Uranus return
For the Pluto in late Cancer (15° and later) and all of the Leo generation
only, the quincunx of Pluto to Pluto (150°)

AGES 68–72	

There are no generic aspects of planets beyond Saturn between 68 and 72

AGE 72	♃ ♅

Sixth Jupiter return (6 cycles x 12 years each = 72)
Uranus sextile Uranus (60°)

outer planets in their discovery heralded new realms of experience that prior to their known presence were unheard of.

Since the outer planets are agencies of consciousness, they "do" things that are intangible. For instance, a flash of genius, a great idea, is intangible. So we go back to Saturn to manifest the brilliant idea. To make it happen and be useful, we still need to operate within the agencies of the classical planets—the Sun through Saturn. Beyond that, we are in outer space, though still within our solar system, and thus, since the mid-1700s, the options for future life are infinite.

Uranus is associated with the options and freedoms of individual choice. Its sighting coincided with the Industrial Revolution, the American Revolution, and the French Revolution. It also was the gateway to the universe, in that once the telescope was invented, our vision extended not only beyond the bounds of Saturn but out into the vast and unknown universe. Uranus is the ethers and the heavens—the open path to exploration and endless vision.

Neptune opened the gates to bringing in options in spiritual, psychological, and physical experiences. Gas, ruled by Neptune, became the new way of lighting the night; the "spiritualists" claimed to have visions of and communication with those "gone beyond"; new drugs, like nitrous oxide, cocaine, and other anaesthetics, were discovered to aid in surgeries; mesmerism and hypnotism were employed to heal psychic problems; and so on.

Pluto is the "new" Saturn, in that it represents the edge of the solar system, the final place. The advent of Pluto shifted the "grim reaper," death, from Saturn's realm to Pluto's realm. We now consider Pluto to be the planet of the great equalizer and the place where souls reside and where the mystery of life and death is held.

So as we age, beyond the realm of Shakespeare's Saturn and the old social terminus, the outer planets are part of our extended lives. The choices we have in our lives now, and the psychological growth that increases in depth and magnitude, are even richer after the second Saturn return.

FIFTY-NINE TO SIXTY: CROSSING THE NEXT THRESHOLD

First the young, like vines, climb up the dull support of their elders who feel their fingers upon them, soft and tender; then, the old climb down the young and supporting bodies of the young into their proper deaths.

—LAWRENCE DURRELL, *The Alexandria Quartet**

This age threshold introduces a period when the opportunities to pass on the gnosis of age and time are paramount. Even if one has no chil-

*Lawrence Durrell, *The Alexandria Quartet* (London: Faber and Faber, 1962), p. 214.

dren of one's own, one is subject to the natural and evolutionary experience of birth, life, death, and the cycles those mysteries contain. It is essential to crossing the threshold to realize that it is time to prepare to pass the torch of the future on to the next generations, and to reap the benefits of a life lived.

Artists, musicians, creators, and family people of all kinds all have a gift to pass to the children who survive them. As we all stand on the shoulders of our forebears, so are we the forebears of those who are to come.

The second Saturn return recapitulates the first one at twenty-nine to thirty. In my book *Saturn in Transit*, I mention various qualities that emerge for young adults at that stage in life.* The primary "intent" of the first Saturn return is to separate from the parents. This does not mean, nor do I encourage people, to "kill off the parents" in any way at all, but to renegotiate one's relationship within the entire matrix of the family of origin. Nor does it mean to cast off the family or parents, but to once again enter that core and retrieve more of one's own character and nature.

Reentering the family matrix is something that must be done on a periodic basis, in response to either the demands of circumstance or inner impulse. We all do it, and we all *should* do it. The family is our biogenesis, and our psychological training. The return to the matrix is a work done within one's own self; many people, when turning sixty, will have put their parents to rest, but increasing numbers of us have elder parents to concern us as we ourselves reach "elder" status.

As we grow older, we are more our parents than we ever dreamed of when young. Saying "I'll never do that! I won't turn into my dad/mom/grandma," and so on, is vital to individuation for the young. But anyone who is over the age of fifty is already deeply impressed with the DNA imperative—we are not only our parents but also the entire genealogical line back from those two beings . . . *their* parents, *their* parents, and so on back down the line as far as it reaches. Thus, here you are slipping into your sixties, and realizing just who it is your parents were—or at least to

*Erin Sullivan, *Saturn in Transit: Boundaries of Mind, Body and Soul* (York Beach, ME: Weiser, 2000).

a great degree—and you can make conscious choices about the next phase of your life. Most of our parents—the prewar parents—could not.

And if you are reaching your majority as a senior adult, you may ask yourself some serious questions about the quality of your life now, even considering how it is you would like to feel as you age and approach the closure. Do you want to assume the role of senex (old man) or retain your puer-ism (youth)—or is it possible to arrive to this age of sixty with your youthful flexibility intact, and with the wisdom of age firmly in place?

Senex or Puer? Or a Youthful Maturity?

This is the biggest issue at sixty. There are astrological aspects, and for this transition, they are rich in symbol and myth. The primary one, as I already mentioned, is the second Saturn return. During one's Saturn return, the planet itself repeats the same aspects—as with all returns—as it did from birth onward to thirty, at which time it recapitulated the ontology of your own status and place in the world.

In Part I, I mentioned that the Pluto in Leo generation is bound and determined to take its youth to the grave, and in doing so have established a new paradigm for the aging process. Ideally, one wants to find paths to move with the times as well as with the demands of one's own body—and hear what one's body tells from its voice of experience and authority. From the mid–twentieth century onward, increasing consciousness about constitutional health and well-being has resulted in more vigorous health as we continue aging.

Saturn is a planet that demands embodiment—the very fact that we are incarnated, learn, grow, structure our lives, and maintain a level of relatedness and common sense is Saturnian, and if we have our best interests in mind, we respond to Saturn with some acceptance. Saturn rules our bones and skin, the very stuff that keeps us upright as well as contained. The "bones and skin of our psyche" are reflected in this physical image of the body. Without inner supports, such as principles, standards, accountability, and responsibilities, we have no humanity. Without external psychic supports, such as family, culture, society, and a worldview, we also have no humanity.

Saturn is related to the inner and outer support systems with which we are born, but we also assimilate wholesale "supports" (and barriers and boundaries) throughout our lives. At sixty-ish is the next major juncture in life when one has the opportunity to divest one's Self and ego from false and inappropriate coping mechanisms and controls that are not one's own, but have simply been absorbed through social pressures.

If you are true to yourself *as well as* to others, your Saturn is "good" to you. If you lie, and you know it, then your inner balance is tilted, and the feelings of hypocrisy are strong. If you push yourself to places where your ethics are not being lived or met, then you are using your Saturn in a negative way.

At this age, the Saturn return is about letting go of superficiality, and moving to a more "real" or more basic life. This does not mean to give up your creature comforts, or join a monastic order—you can keep all that you have, while letting go of its previous meaning. It is another threshold crossing, whereupon the hero and heroine must leave behind tools that no longer serve, and bring across the threshold tools that are for the appropriate age.

Most people arriving to this age say that they feel a sense of freedom from having to strive for validation and approval. The primary structural change at this crossover is one of relaxing the mind, body, and soul from an attitude of striving. Rather than this being an indication of giving up, it is an indication of a more authentic way of being. One can still work, achieve, excel, and overtake oneself, but the motives for doing so undergo vast change from this juncture onward. The function of Saturn, always, is about finding one's own inner authority and, thus, external authenticity. The second Saturn return, ideally, brings this objective closer to the heart, and thus reduces the stress on accomplishment as proof of existence or self-worth.

My most successful elder friends and clients, once over sixty, say they don't give a damn what others think! And just as often, they follow up by saying they never thought that this kind of inner security and authenticity was to be theirs, ever! Obviously there are the body complaints—stiff joints in the morning, dietary changes, no more late parties; certainly drugs and alcohol take a greater toll. And the need for social input and existential validation on a constant basis declines.

Ideally, then, the *senex*—the "old man" in us who is very resistant to change—needs to be honored. As does the *puer*, who plays an immense role in the balance of respectability and maturity, with open minded-ness, excitement, and ongoing interest in life.* Gods are jealous, and want propitiation—so we must honor both Saturn and Jupiter, and their little brother, Hermes/Mercury.

Resistance to aging is found in individual charts where there is a pre-ponderance of air and fire signs, especially the signs of Gemini and Sagit-tarius. The adherence to youth even in the face of balding, thickening, and wrinkles is not bad in itself, but if it means not progressing toward a place of contentment, then it is not good. Puers and puellas have a *very* hard time individuating into their aging process. There is a great re-sistance to it, as they fear loss of physical beauty and the choices that physical beauty brings. And, regardless of whether or not one is brilliant and has "been there, done that," there is always something not been to or done!

In contrast, a strong Saturn in aspect to the personal points, such as Sun, Moon, Venus and so on, predispose one toward the senex. That is, these people are often old before their time, and in the case of Capricorn people, actually get younger in spirit as they age! Their homeostatic principle overrides their wild or primal instincts in the first half of life, but as they age, becoming more self-credible and, usually, socially ac-ceptable in their own eyes, they "lighten up."

The puer is honored by people who are primarily mutable, especially Gemini and Sagittarius, as well as those having strong aspects from per-sonal planets to Jupiter. Psychological and physical aging is not easily adjusted to by the freedom fighters in the zodiac. The drive to stay young, free, and boundless becomes increasingly at issue. But does it have to? Can one not mature without cementing and crystallizing one's beliefs? Apparently so!

---

*See Jim Lewis, *Peter Pan in Midlife* (Santa Fe/Silver City, NM: Southwest Contemporary Astrology, 2002).

The natal aspects that Saturn receives and makes in the natal chart have everything to do with the character and tasks that the psyche assigns to you at this Saturn return threshold crossing. If you have Saturn squaring your inner planets and/or the Sun and Moon, then the return of Saturn will question how well you have learned to accept that you are not perfect, never will be, and thus, so what! You will find you revisit your family of origin and its influence on your attitudes toward maturing and aging. Because you had a Saturn return at twenty-nine, there will be some interesting reflections on that time, and how you broke out of the family mold and began to individuate toward where you are now.

The second Saturn return brings yet another family issue to bear, and usually it is from the family you have created for yourself. Your role in relationship to your children and, possibly, grandchildren becomes more important in your new place in society. In some dignified way, you may need to rebel against them and their stereotype of you. Better than rebelling is coming to terms with the fact that you have crossed the line into a new generational imperative, and thus need to adjust your attitude and behavior accordingly. Becoming an elder in the family and community takes work, too.

Perfection exists only in the Platonic realm of the ideal forms, and bridging from the Ideal to the Real is another quest of the sixty-something person. One does not have to give up one's beliefs, ethics, and ideals; indeed, one needs to retain the core essence of those. But one needs to become more practical. This way of being results in a healthy balance between one's inner senex and puer.

Relationships that form after the second Saturn return hopefully are based upon uniquely individual needs. There is no social pressure, really, to conform to standards outside ourselves. Those who have the good fortune to meet love in the latter years have the freedom to take that love and cherish it without the disapproval of parents.

SECOND RETURN OF YOUR NATAL LUNAR PHASE

The transit of Saturn and the secondary progression of the Moon are closely aligned, in that they stay in the same aspect relationship for about the first seven years of life. After that the progression of the Moon, moving a little faster, begins either to separate from Saturn in transit, or to draw toward it. This is partly why our instinctual habits are so profound, and so difficult to alter by conscious choice. Both the Moon and Saturn are strongly involved in the establishment of rote and instinctive habits.*

Your second Saturn return coincides with the repeat of the birth Lunation cycle. For example, I was born with natal Saturn at 22° Leo. My natal Lunation cycle is "balsamic," that is, in the very last phase before the new Moon. So in the year of my second Saturn return, I set up a chart for my precise Lunation cycle return—when the natal moon is exactly 39° behind my natal Sun, as it is in my chart. And in my *sixtieth year*, the Lunation cycle return occurs eleven months before my actual sixtieth birthday, and the planet Saturn is in its returning phase: 22°–24° Leo.

For love of precision, then, I would consider my actual Saturn return in two ways: first, the very day it first returns to the degree and minute of its natal place, and if there is a retrograde cycle associated with it, the second pass of Saturn to its natal place. That is the technical Saturn return.

Second, and possibly more significant during this period, is the exact return of the Lunation cycle with which one is born—in the same year of returning Saturn. That time, the very month and day of the natal Lunation cycle return, I consider to be the most important month of the Saturn return year.

Because the Moon and Saturn have so much to do with our deep, ingrained habits and survival mechanisms, the chart that is set for a secondary progressed Lunation return in the transiting Saturn return year shows what the real issues are regarding your next phase of life. Our gut (Moon)

---

*In *The Lunation Cycle* (my first astrology book), Dane Rudyhar presented the Lunation cycle as a paradigm for all planetary phases, but in particular related the Sun/Moon phase at birth as the prime motivating force for life. There are eight lunation phases, from the new Moon through the full-Moon phase and back to new. It takes the Moon twenty-seven and a half days to move through the zodiac. If it starts in Aries, say, then it returns back to Aries in twenty-seven and a half days. However, the synodic cycle, which is from one conjunction to another, and because the Sun moves a degree a day in that sidereal cycle, from new Moon to new Moon takes twenty-nine and a half days. Your secondary progressed Lunation cycle is also repeated—the phase in which you were born is repeated between the progressed Sun and the progressed Moon—in the course of that year.

responses to our purpose in life (Sun) is returned to its own place, while the stabilizing Saturn gives an important structure to that basic life-force.

So this complicated dynamic symbolizes a renegotiation with your soul—a reissue of your natal promise. And thus, many changes can be implemented, especially around the maturation and acceptance of who you are and how you are with that.

Many individuals at sixty-ish truly do "mellow"; mind you, though, biology begins to win out here, and mellowing is also part of that process.

JUPITER AND SATURN — AGAIN!
FIFTH JUPITER RETURN

This return, occurring at the second Saturn return, is most interesting, because it too exemplifies the struggle at the threshold of the young/old crossover. The ancient Greek Kronos (our Saturn) was the father of Zeus (our Jupiter), and their relationship was as bloody as Kronos's was with his father, Ouranos—whom we met at midlife. In fact, the afore-mentioned return of the Lunation phase and the Saturn degree also puts Jupiter in the same sign!

Thus, in your sixtieth year, you have the second Saturn return, the secondary progressed Lunation return, *and* your Jupiter return. It is also possible to have a Mars return in the course of that year, too, depending on its natal place, and the retrograde cycle of Mars. In my own case, as I mentioned, Mars did return to its natal place, but a few months ahead of my exact Saturn return; therefore, it was a few degrees later and out of sign in the Lunation cycle return chart—but that was because I was born just prior to a Mars stationing period.* Indeed, my own second Saturn return will herald the actual secondary progressed station retrograde of Mars!

So there are a lot of return dynamics at this profoundly significant age.

---

*Erin Sullivan, *Retrograde Planets: Traversing the Inner Landscape* (York Beach, ME: Weiser, 2000), p. 119, for the cycle of superior planets retrograde, wherein we find that Mars is "rebellious" and is the least retrograde of all planets. See p. 163 for the transits and natal Mars retrograde cycles, with examples.

JUPITER AND SATURN:
OVERTHROWING THE TYRANT

In the ancient Greek origin myths, the birth of Zeus was a tremendous threat to Kronos because the Fates had warned him he would be usurped by his youngest son. With that uppermost in his mind, he began to swallow each of his offspring as they were presented to him by his wife, Rhea. After Kronos devoured five of her beloved children, she got very fed up with it and tricked Kronos by feeding him a great stone, hiding the sixth-born in a cave on the island of Dicte, where he was raised by wild women and nurtured to adolescence.

That sixth son was Zeus. Indeed, the Fates do know all, and do not lie. When Zeus came of age—the age of the natural "father battle" for sons—he induced the birth of his other five siblings from the "womb" of Kronos, and set to war against him, his own father. *The War of the Titans* is a terrific old movie, and true to the myths, if you care for lots of beheading, incest, lightning bolts, and dark gods and monsters.

Now, having mentioned that Saturn/Kronos is the astrological senex, I can introduce Jupiter/Zeus as the "next generation," the exuberant and warrior youth with a new vision for the future. Jupiter is not a puer, as is Mercury/Hermes; rather, he exemplifies the emergence of the new era (in this case, of Greek mythology) from the belly of the outmoded elder generation.

Passing the torch from one generation to the next, though it is not always as bloody as was Kronos/Saturn's assumption of his father's power, nor as epic as Zeus/Jupiter seizing the power from his father, is still fraught by a necessary struggle between the old and the young as they pass each other in the line to ascendancy.

Once the epic war between Saturn and Jupiter was concluded in mythology—and badly for Saturn, who was sent to Tartaros in Hades to welcome "returned" or dead heroes—Zeus/Jupiter enthroned his liberated siblings and a couple of other immortals, giving them the Olympian status they still enjoy to this day.

The father-son battle, between Saturn and Jupiter, is an internal battle that we all experience when we have to depose our own inner tyrant and let the new and more contemporary self emerge. This myth is so powerful that it can be rendered to apply to almost all psychological conflicts. This is because myth is archetypal, and thus not restricted by stereotype, and in the case of you or me or a friend, "hitting sixty" is a reenactment of the War of the Titans.

When our own inner Jupiter wants to overthrow the inner Saturn, there is a huge internal struggle. And the fact that the second Saturn return and the fifth Jupiter return occur in the same year means that you are on the cusp of vanquishing your old attitudes in favor of new, and liberating ones. This battle occurred around the thirtieth year of life.

The primary difference between *that* juncture and *this* one is that it was Saturn that had to be overthrown at thirty, while Jupiter took ascendancy. Now, at age sixty, it is Saturn who must assume a dignified place, with Jupiter as a benefactor of the aging process—as Shakespeare says, "belly with good capon lin'd."

LIFE AS A SEXTILE

One of the most powerful, precise, and significant aspects of predictive and timing techniques is the *Solar Arc Direction* of each planet.* This measurement is very specific and means that each planet is directed about one degree per year, or technically, each planet is directed as if it were moving at the same speed as the Sun *per diem*.

The Solar Arc, in totality, has a profound impact in a couple of specific years of our lives, because it means that at key years—which are measured in astrological harmonic "numbers"—there is an exact Ptolemaic aspect link between the Solar Arc–directed horoscope to the natal horoscope. For instance, at age thirty, all the Solar Arc planets are semisextile (30°) the natal planets. How irritating, on top of all that other work at twenty-nine and thirty!

At age forty-five, the Solar Arc planets are in a semisquare to the natal, which brings lots of hard work and many adjustments, and this is

*See Noel Tyl, *Prediction in Astrology: A Master Volume of Technique and Practice* (St. Paul, MN: Llewellyn, 1995).

combined with the middlescent phase, when transiting Saturn is opposite itself. If you live to be ninety, then all your Solar Arc planets will be
in a trine to your natal planets; the next contact of this variety is at age
120, but this book doesn't go that far.

So, at sixty, all the Solar Arc–directed planets are in a sextile to all
the natal chart planets. Every single natal imperative is in harmonic res-
onance with a creative and communicative boost from the "third house
type" sextile from the Solar Arced planets.

SEXY SIXTIES

It is well known that people actually die from lack of love and emotional
or physical contact. They pine away. If you are not touched, loved, or
needed, then why bother? I have several clients in their late sixties—
both coupled and single—who have become "grandparents" to little
kids who are lonely in isolated situations or fostered out. Their own
grandchildren are in their late teens and twenties, and they have found
wonderful satisfaction and amusement in having visits from or taking a
young child out on a regular basis.

Meeting a new lover or mate post-sixty is certainly more possible
now than ever before. The capacity to live life more fully and longer has
extended the potential *and* probability of people over sixty having love
affairs and late marriage or communal living. Intimacy is not just sex—
indeed, often far from it. But certainly sex in the sixties is very real, still
wanted, and, from what I hear, still loads of fun.

Aphrodite's remedies in late-life sex have been broadly advertised
and are commonplace. Aphrodisiacs and sexual stimulants are as old as
humanity. Women who find their vaginal membranes dry from natural
maturing can apply remedial hormonal and natural creams, and so on,
while men who are passionate and have desire but simply are not "what
they used to be" have options too. Love and sex are not to be laughed off
or embarrassed about. Though by one's mid- to late sixties, sex is not a
major motivator, it still has depth and intimacy, which is important.
The thing to remember, at all times, is that by this age, it is a matter not
of one's "part" but one's "heart."

A close friend of mine, a vital woman in her late fifties, rang me up one day to tell me she had finally had sex for the first time in over a year and a half. She had been seeing a man who was seventy, and they shared everything, except he was unable to sustain an erection. Their relationship—because it was also a sexually desirable relationship—was deprived because of his physiological impotence. He was in that stage of "the spirit is willing but the flesh is not," so he spoke to his physician and, all else being well, was prescribed and took the new aphrodisiac Viagra. Thus the early morning phone call from my girlfriend.

The real issue arising in relationships during the aging process is not usually about sex, it is about meeting someone one can feel love for and receive love from. As we age, we become increasingly individuated. Although this is advisable, it does mean that we become increasingly individual. And so the old "stuck in one's ways" condition emerges as a block to opening heart and soul to one another. Though we are in the process of becoming throughout all our lives, it is by now that we are really, truly who we are.

Being on one's own often is a relief for women, especially after sixty. If one has had a full life of love, sex, children (or not), or one's art, creativity, or career has been deeply satisfying, one is more capable of living on one's own, and creating a social and personal life. Men, however, often do not have this skill well developed, and by the nature of the male archetype, find loneliness more sharp.

It is essential both for men and women, of course, to be active, but especially for men to do "men" things. Whether it is a formal club, a sport—tennis, golf, the spa—or an intellectual group or interest, it is very important for a man to nurture himself, and develop his "feminine" aspect, his anima, in a new way. For a man to "develop his anima" does not mean to feminize himself, but to feel his own creativity and independence.

Women find self-sufficient men far more interesting and desirable in later life, and are more consciously discriminating than when they are in their youth seeking a mate or a father for their children. Romance in the latter years is no less intense or demanding, but both men and women are far more discerning, simply because they seek partners based on companionship and not social hierarchies or biological demand.

SIXTY-FOUR—AND STILL WANTING MORE

Between the ages of sixty-three and sixty-seven, there is one major generic aspect only, and it is from Uranus to itself. The planet of individuation is quickening the process of finding increasing means of being fully oneself! Uranus makes a square (90°) to itself in the sixty-fourth year of life, as it begins the movement toward its return at eighty-four.

Uranus in a square to itself brings a crisis in consciousness, in which we are faced with the absolute necessity of individuation. We might have paid lip service to "becoming increasingly oneself," but any unfinished business that needs attending to at this age becomes urgent.

For instance, if one has emotionally and psychologically resisted graceful aging and maturing, then this age is a shock. The previous Uranus square to itself occurred in the twenty-first year of life. At this age, the rebellion against the social imperatives, and the assertion of self and individualism, is full of fire and light and Promethean promise. The first Uranus square to itself heralds a future vision of an idealistic world in which one has an important role to play. At twenty-one the square acts as a prod to meet one's own uniqueness in conflict with the status quo, or social acceptability.

At sixty-three, there is another prod from the Promethean Uranus, in that the opportunity to seize life and thrust it forward into a new phase is great. Having come through the Saturn/Jupiter/Lunation return, yet another imperative is issued from the deep Self to "be yourself." No, one is not twenty-one again, but one has earned the *gravitas,* through life experience, to find that same youthful flame of passion again to create a unique, very personal life.

In some reflective way, the Uranus square—forty-two years later!— may even reignite the flame of passion to create a Utopia! At this age, one cares more for quality of life than quantity of experience. The experiences of youth are no longer interesting or necessary at this time of life. This does not mean that if you love to scale sheer rock walls, you need to stop, but it does mean you will scale them for different reasons, as well as with differently applied physical skills.

Creating your own niche, finding a place in your life's work, your vocation, and so on, are all deeply significant acts at this time. Many people find they can stand up to the conservative forces that they have allowed to prevent them from speaking out, and demand to be heard. I have had many women who reach this age say to me, "It is as if I was invisible." Hmm. Whereas men, having overcome the midlife crisis, the realization of baldness, sexual maturity, and all the ego issues that go along with male aging, find they are actually more distinctive if they are active in their careers or in the community. They become "safe."

In *The Gods of Change*, Howard Sasportas writes:

The second Uranus square occurs in our early sixties, not far from the Second Saturn Return. The obvious concern is aging. Some people give up growing at this time, nail their coffin lid down and slide into an "is that all there is?" state of mind. However, statistics show that people who were worried about getting older in their mid-forties and fifties, stop worrying so much about it in their sixties.*

I have found that people who age consciously say they have entered a new phase in life that they can only call impersonal. By this they do not mean they have no personal feelings, or they don't care about people anymore. What they are saying is their needs are less personally greedy, and their actions more geared to transpersonal issues. One's emotional life demands less energy, and the impulse to argue fine points of feelings does decrease, so a sense of greater self-comfort arises.

Again, Sasportas:

We may begin to feel detached from (or not so bothered about) issues or concerns which previously meant a great deal to us, but this doesn't mean we are slipping into a state of indifference

---

*Howard Sasportas, *The Gods of Change*, Contemporary Astrology (London and New York: Arkana, 1989), p. 69.

where nothing matters. On the contrary, those things we still find important become even more important (p. 70).

For instance, by focusing on community needs, taking the time to explore hobbies and interests that have lain dormant, and looking toward your future as an opportunity to become more conscious and aware are now possible. Often this phase is associated with actual retirement from long years of employment. Now is the time when separation from the past heralds an exciting possibility of not only living out individual dreams but also having the time to explore new dreams. This phase of life, if it does involve retirement from a job or career profession, should be planned for. A sudden end of ritual, habitual, and rigorous activity is not always followed by elation and wild, gleeful freedom.

In fact, elder depression is a big problem for this very reason. Someone whose body has been "doing something" for forty years is hardly about to become relaxed about an abrupt cessation of drive, focus, desire, and movement. Often the man who retired was an imposition on his wife, who, after thirty or so years of married independence, finds her homebody husband truly in the way. This is not just an issue with previous generations; it is occurring in my own contemporary Baby Boom circle too!

Creativity often reaches a turning-point, and artists, writers, and musicians—not necessarily professional ones—leave the stage of striving, and find deeper meaning in the quest for creativity, not the actual results. There is less anxiety about identity now, and thus more room for experimentation. Novel ideas, innovative plans, and the added benefits of modern, healthy lives can actually precipitate a new vocation.

Although you have already experienced loss through death of friends and family members, this is an age bracket where that sadness becomes more frequent. Many young people lost many friends in their midlife due to the AIDS virus, through the 1980s and 1990s, and continue to do so, which is part of the Pluto square in their midlife advent. But when you find yourself losing the most intimate people in your life because of age and natural causes—those who needed no explanation for your existence and behavior—the loneliness is profound; those individuals are irreplaceable. There is no grief like experiencing the loss of familiarity.

Our friends and closest associates are "proof" that we exist, as well as being proof that we are known, cared about, and irreplaceable. We are meaningful, important, and essential to others. By this age, that grouping of unspoken support begins to diminish. The ties that bind become fewer, and thus the inner strength to carry on in a meaningful way is even more crucial. As we are closing in on our own mortality, and facing it through losses of contemporaries or intimate friends, it is absolutely necessary to have a "purpose" in life.

Sasportas says: "In accord with the Uranian nature of this period, the outlets which could prove most rewarding are ones that we can pursue independently of other people, yet which serve the community in some way" (p. 71). Clearly, this is not a venture that can be developed overnight, on demand, at the turning-point of one's mid-sixties because one wants to "do" something. It is something that must be prepared for and planned for and must actually serve both the individual and the collective.

Making some efforts to learn something new, to begin a program of action or civic duty, *before* the roster of automatic activities begins to diminish is part of individuation. We never leave off with the work of becoming.

One's mortality becomes tangible now—if not through one's own frailties, by example of others and their frailties. Not to be morbid, but to be more conscious: there is a time in this four-year open phase where one begins to program one's own death. By that I mean that one's lifestyle habits, thinking patterns, relationship links, and activity engagement all contribute to well-being (or not) and thus to a renewal (or not) of life commitment.

That is why geriatric depression is such a critical issue—it is important to notice if depression is part of aging. This is not something that the elder person may even realize, but others might. Family may see this. Many adult children are overworked and have stressors, so there is often an impatience in dealing with the aging parent. If at all possible, this is the time to restructure your own inner life, and be conscious of your level of need and demand.

If you are moving into your later years, finding alienation and lack of purpose an issue, and are falling into eccentric and unhealthy emotional patterns, it is essential to see someone about it, a professional who might offer some perspective on how you feel, and its significance in your individuation.

On the other hand, if you are aware of your parents, a friend, or a neighbor who appears to be falling into geriatric depression, inquire of them about it. Speaking with a professional in geriatric psychology, going to groups who are there to heal and discuss—all are good, but only if one is aware of depression.

Not being a doctor, or a big advocate of pharmaceuticals, I do however support the brilliant new treatments for clinical depression. Just as one might get a hip replacement at sixty or find a need for blood-pressure medication, or take insulin, it must be taken into consideration that the level of serotonin uptake in the geriatric brain is greater than before, and depression can be a part of aging for certain individuals. If depression is a part of this aging phase, then see to it immediately.

There are more things now available to us as spiritual and psychological aids other than medications, for example, meditation, spiritual reading, enlightened books on aging and death and dying, and so on.

Distrust of "the new" begins to come in very strongly at this age—and one has to make a real effort to keep an open mind toward innovation and modernity. I recall again my grandmother, an expatriate, pre–World War I English lady, who in the mid-1950s could not for the life of her understand how "they got the people into the television," though she had her favorite programs with which she identified passionately: *As the World Turns*, *One Life to Live*, *Oral Roberts*, *Lawrence Welk*, and so on. I recall her constant companion in reading was *The Power of Positive Thinking* by Norman Vincent Peale.

I now know, from my own age perspective, that the book was a source of real spiritual support to her, as she was in her mid-sixties at that time. Her involvement with the Church of England and the Women's Auxiliary and singing in the choir were also vital activities in which she participated fully until her own death, a good decade after my grandfather had died. There was not then the plethora of information, support, and enlightened material for aging people in their forties, fifties, and even sixties that we have now. And sources of senior support need to be considered even at this early stage of eldering.

The most amusing and poignant story about my grandma was her absolute belief that if an empty light socket was not stuffed with tissue (or a light bulb), electricity would "leak" into the air and do terrible things to our brains and reproductive systems. This is not a stupid thought, it is a logical thought—if you don't know what electricity actually is and can do. This is a common occurrence; I call it the "new-fangled theory phenomenon."

As many aging people do, she stopped working at understanding her contemporary times. For some, this is a relief—a time to stop stressing about what is going on and stop "keeping up with the times." However, this way of being is increasingly unsatisfactory to elder people, and though they may not feel the need to truly understand fractals and chaos theory, they *do* want to stop being superstitious about progress and innovation.

CHAPTER 12

THE THIRD ACT

Elder in some cultures is a term of respect, an honorific, an implicit bow to the wisdom embodied in years of living. But among those peoples, it's not the word alone that confers this special status. It's the cultural context within which the word is spoken, the meaning it carries in the society, which, in turn, is related to the role and function the elders fulfill in group life. Among other things, the old in these societies are the carriers of culture and the bearers of their social history. Without them, group life would be immeasurably impoverished and the past would fade out of human memory. Can we say anything comparable about the elders of our nation?

—LILLIAN B. RUBIN, *Tangled Lives: Daughters, Mothers, and the Crucible of Aging*

THE greatest blessing that friends and clients have shared with me is the level of impartiality that occurs somewhere in this age transition. Not that there are no feelings of love, need, desire, and the acts of sharing that humanize us—but the *attachment* to personal goals is lessened. The greatest human achievement of age is compassionate detachment. This is why the "grandparent" role is so vital in society. When one crosses over the threshold to the impersonal, it means there is little meanness left inside, and this is a goal to achieve, if it does not arrive through the dictates of nature.

In *Solitude*, Anthony Storr, the British psychoanalyst and philosopher, says:

> It may also be a merciful provision of Nature, designed to lessen the pain of the inevitable parting from loved ones which death brings in its train. Man is the only creature who can see his own death coming; and, when he does, it concentrates his mind wonderfully. He prepares for death by freeing himself from mundane goals and attachments and turns instead to the cultivation of his own interior garden.*

My own mother died at age sixty-five. In her last six weeks of life, I lived in her small beach cottage, sleeping on the living room floor, monitoring her last days on earth, making her comfortable, supervising and delivering her meds to her, and so on—and dealing with home hospice schedules and the physician who had treated her for over twenty years. She was always a controlling person, acting more as an attacker/ defender in life than anything else. Though her personality was strong, her inner fortitude was fragile to the point of nonexistence.

I was struck by her sense of purpose in those last six weeks. I had never seen her so "in the moment," in the "now," comfortable with the inevitable. She didn't want to die, per se, but I had *never* seen her in all the years I knew her (forty of them at that time) operate with more purpose, calm, direction, and intent. I had the distinct feeling that she had finally met her match—that in death she found life and purpose. She was an exemplary model of the "last days." For all her earthly sins, her death redeemed her. It is never too late.

SIXTY-SEVEN THROUGH SEVENTY: ELDER WINE

Between the ages of sixty-seven and seventy there are two primary generic aspects for all generational groups. The first is the third waxing

*Anthony Storr, *Solitude* (London: HarperCollins, 1994).

transit of Saturn square to Saturn, and the second is the quincunx of transiting Neptune to natal Neptune.

These two aspects denote critical turning points in life's unfolding. The Saturn square happened at age seven, and again thirty-six, and now happens again at sixty-six or sixty-seven. The crossing of the threshold into elder status is complete, and the relinquishing of dreams or unrealistic fantasies is part of the process. Many people are vital and very active and alive at this age point, but they are also coming to terms with the true reality of aging.

This Saturn square is a time of serious reconsideration of one's social "place." At age seven, the first Saturn square was in the context of being in school for the first time, having to be more disciplined, and learning the social rules that either got one into the right place or got one into trouble. At thirty-six there is a jump forward in social place, too. At thirty-six, one crosses over the threshold toward serious maturity.

This threshold, when crossed, brings one into serious aging and the consciousness that comes with many years of witnessing, experiencing, and letting go. Thus, new social status, new organizational patterns, new psychological realities—and physical changes—are established that mark ongoing maturing. Jung was the first to suggest that adults continue to mature and grow, that the process of individuation is ongoing. Indeed, the word *individuation* is based on a verb—it never stops and is in constant forward motion.

Thus, the aging with this Saturn square is about both one's inner *and* outer structures—physically and psychologically. The bones become more fragile, one's skeleton undergoes transfiguration, the very skin on the surface of the body (all Saturn ruled) is changed. By now hair is fully grey or often, for men, gone! And, at this age, it matches the face and the rest of the body, and looks right.

The structures and limits within which one must operate begin to be rearranged. It becomes increasingly important to accept and create new boundaries for living. Expending too much energy is immediately apparent to most people after the age of forty! Certainly, it is not shameful for people at this later age to accept that.

There is more time for real reflection and philosophical consideration, deeper reading, more selective input, and recognizing the importance of allowing one's body and mind to accept the demands of the soul. Many indigenous cultures have distinct rites of passage into every age, and within those brackets of ritual, an individual is honored for his or her contributions, and is given a respect and position that relieves one of the stress of "finding oneself."

Brooke Astor's poem declares that she has found a sense of self that transcends "I" and "me." Her ego is still present and operative enough to write poetry and do "good works," but her deep, inner Self has grown larger, to oversee the "I am"—the *ego sum*—of her life at the mid-seventies. Her poem is a foreshadowing of the more relaxed inner life a mid-sixties person can anticipate!

Individuation continues on for the full life—it never stops—but the decreasing intensity of self-discovery is natural. Around this time in life, the journey toward wholeness is less striving, less angst ridden, and has a more natural flow. People begin to accept themselves, but if they are still working a conscious life, they do make major changes in their relationships with their friends and family. A responsible and conscious aging process requires a level of true compassion—not only for oneself but also toward those who care for and love one.

One's outward appearance may not reflect one's sense of inner resilience and enthusiasm—and this can be difficult for a vigorous mid-to-late-sixties person to cope with. It requires tremendous dignity and forbearance for a truly energetic and alive soul to exist in the body of an aging person. But that is what this third Saturn square is about—accepting the boundaries and limits of age and assuming the dignified posture of a senior human being. In that conscious acceptance, one's beauty and handsomeness radiates—others see it, and admire it. One does not have to degenerate into a mass of osteoporotic crumbling and a psychological crystallization! Not any more one doesn't!

Limits and boundaries include one's DNA and, thus, the aging patterns in the family of origins and its ancestors. By this time, it is apparent that if your mother had arthritis, and you do, little can be done but improve your physical functioning to the degree that is possible. There are many traditional as well as modern conventional ways for "loosening" up the joints, softening the hard arteries, and so on. At this age many individuals experience their first really serious health problem. So the Saturn square is about mortality and how that mortality can be managed more healthfully. And the resources are virtually limitless. However, life is not, so once again one's quality of life and one's personal attitude toward one's body come to the fore.

For many of those reading this book, who are in the select generational span of the "special Pluto" years—having been born between 1937 and 1995—a unique collective aspect occurs between sixty-seven and seventy. There was a first-quarter square at midlife onset, which most people I have interviewed have described as exceptionally painful. It has been characterized by the non–astrologically literate as a death, a feeling of dying and purging. There seemed to be no real "personal" sense to it—that it might have coincided with a divorce or a loss seemed almost beside the point. Every person says about the Pluto square Pluto that it was about a struggle for survival—a soul struggle—that had all the earmarks of a mythic dragon battle or an Atlantean struggle with Thanatos.

PLUTO QUINCUNX PLUTO:
THAT OLD PLUTO "PROBLEM" AGAIN— FOR THOSE BORN 1928—1956

People who did have personal grief or traumas during the time of their eighteen months of Pluto square Pluto at midlife said there was "something else" going on other than the divorce, death, house fire, unemployment, and so on! What *was* this something else? Even the most eloquent and literary of clients seemed stymied by this struggle for survival and basic purging of their souls—but all equated it with something going on in the collective, and with the planet itself.

Pluto forms a quincunx (150°) to itself in this age bracket, *but only for people who have Pluto in late Cancer and all of Leo.* But, because of Pluto's apparent negative acceleration during its transit from the sign of

Sagittarius through Cancer, this is a phenomenon *only for these two signs.* (See figure 8.)

The quincunx of Pluto to itself, at this writing, in 2003, with Pluto in mid-Sagittarius, has been experienced only by people who have Pluto in the sign of Cancer (born 1912–1937). The combination of the novelty of Pluto—being sighted only in 1930—and the fact that it has only made this aspect to one sign, that is, to Pluto in Cancer from Sagittarius, means there is little empirical evidence of "what it means."

No astrologer *ever* has seen this aspect occur in his or her contemporary time, until now. In Part I, I talked about the "problem" with Pluto and explained the phenomenon that the Pluto in Leo generation embodied, and in this phase the Pluto transit is also present for this generation *only*—as it will be at the age of their Uranus return at eighty-four.*

I think it is safe to say that the adjustment that the quincunx requires from the Pluto in Leo generation is perceptual, and that the ways of the world are moving so quickly for these two Pluto generations (Cancer and Leo) that the adjustments necessary may be too great to fully comprehend. The capacity to contain the whole of intellectual progress is impossible.

There once was a time when it was possible for a major intellect to know everything—perhaps the Renaissance was the last time in which a "Book of Knowledge" could contain the full knowledge of all time. This is not possible now, and hasn't been for a few centuries. But the progress in information in the twentieth century is phenomenal, and has become so detailed and specific that it is truly impossible to comprehend the totality of even one phylum subspecies of a single subject.

This means that a lot of suppositions and hypothetical "truths" must be accepted at face value; we are wholly dependent upon "experts" to

---

*The Pluto in Leo generation *is the only group* to have the Pluto opposition to Pluto at the same time as the Uranus return at eighty-four. This is because of the elliptical orbit of Pluto, as well as its 17°+ inclination to the ecliptic. In chapter 7 this is elaborated on as a "feature" of the Pluto in Leo generation. Because Uranus is seven years in a sign, and for the span of Pluto from Virgo to Capricorn its median traversal of a sign is fourteen years, we have this phenomenon. Neptune, by contrast, is always fourteen years in a sign, doubling Uranus; thus at the Uranus return at eighty-four, there is also the opposition of Neptune to itself.

tell us what they know—or think they know—in all specialist realms, including medicine, science, economics, and politics. It is necessary to operate on the assumption that things are as the experts tell us they are. For many individuals—especially the strong-willed, self-oriented Pluto in Leo—this kind of trusting assumption of things would be unpalatable and frightening to them as they age. And thus, sometimes an aging person lives in a state of mystery and fury over the sense that he or she is being "kept in the dark." All very Plutonian.

Since this is one of the most collective of the generic transits, although it is a personal experience, and thus is coincident with other personal transits and astrological timing, we can make some assessment of what it "does." There have always been conspiracy theorists and millenarianism thinkers, so this is not the only result of the Pluto quincunx to Pluto, but there are so many possible conspiracies afoot in the turn of the millennium that the number of "heretics" will increase in proportion. With the Pluto in Leo generation being the largest single grouping, we will find them at the core of both conservative and heretical—orthodox and heterodox—thinking!

Pluto, as we know, is the existential planet—it treats life and death with equanimity. It is the place in which we are truly alone. Hades of the ancient Greek world was not only a "god" but also a "place." Like Ouranos, the sky, his place is in many ways more significant than his job. The acts of birth and death are undertaken alone; it is a soul's journey, not a social experience. The place of Hades, or the realm of the planet Pluto, is a place in which souls reside between incarnations. It is not the hell of the monotheistic theocracy but is the place where one goes alone, and leaves alone, and throughout one's entire life one tries to stave off that existential aloneness.

Pluto as an agent of the soul, then, has to do with the recognition that we only feel close and linked to people on the basis of human experience—and soulful familiarity. It does not represent friendly, happy, socially acceptable things but rather deep truths that bring one closer to feeling whole within one's self, appreciating solitude and allowing for moments of deep isolation. It represents the part of one's psyche that safeguards the archetypes of the collective experiences that are housed in the "big mystery" place in one's psychological mind.

Since people over sixty-five have come to accept—willingly or unwillingly—the fact that death is inevitable, and that it may meet them at any time, it is likely that some of the adjustments for those reaching the latter sixties will involve extending their life as well as increasing the quality of an extended life. Postponing the inevitable seems desirable—even when the most uncomfortable body is housing the soul.

So the choices being presented to people in the aging stages are now vast and pose far more existential questions than ever before in human history. These questions are worth pondering, and it is in the latter part of our life that we have the time and the opportunity to do this. Indeed, it is within that the greatest intelligence is found, as we grow into our eldermost years, and from those years we have much to offer society and its younger generations.

SEVENTY-TWO: A ROOM WITH A VIEW

It is statistically proven that people who stay actively engaged in their lives and have control over their environments stay healthier and live longer than those who don't. I don't subscribe to "New Age guilt" in any way—this is a phenomenon created by the Pluto in Leo generation, which is a kind of elitist attitude toward living and dying. Many times clients, both women and men, have been grief stricken because someone has suggested that they caused their own breast cancer, or their own heart attack, because of their attitude or spiritual path. This is simply not wholly true. To compound someone's illness and problems by projecting the shadow of New Ageism upon their heads is simply cruel and ignorant. It is also a projection of Leonine childish narcissism and a denial of maturation, carried from the protests of the 1960s to the sickbed of the aging population.

Yes, attitude has a significant and measurable effect on constitutional health, well-being, and longevity, but it cannot alter the somatic, organic structure of one's body. If a lifetime of negative thinking, missed opportunities, and alienist behaviors caused death, then the average life span we have now would have dropped, rather than increased. We all know that crotchety, nasty old people can live on and endlessly on! And lovely, hopeful, and helpful people can die at fifty.

Statistically, optimists live longer than pessimists, and people who suffer from constitutional and clinical depression, if untreated, die younger than those who do not. Thus, diet, activity, and mental exercise are critical to long and pleasurable lives. Avoiding all foods, lifestyle habits, and emotional environments that cause illness and stress is vital to a healthy life—but there is no guarantee for how long that life will be, or in what way one is fated or biologically directed to die.

In his book *Man's Search for Meaning*, Victor Frankl, who survived four concentration camps in the Holocaust of Hitler's Germany, says: "A man who becomes conscious of the responsibility he bears toward a human being who affectionately waits for him or to an unfinished work, will never be able to throw away his life. He knows the "why" for his existence, and will be able to bear almost any "how."* This simple statement can be seen as a life tenet—in that a survivor does it not for him or herself but for a higher purpose—be that spouse, children, community, the divine, or art. Frankl's divine principle boils down to saying that suffering minus meaning equals despair. So loss itself is not the killer, but loss of *meaning* is.

In *A Woman's Book of Life*, Dr. Joan Borysenko says: "When we lack mental stimulation at any age, mental processes and the ability to create begin to deteriorate. And when we stop creating, life-force energy diminishes and depression sets in. The prevalent myth of aging states we gradually lose function and finally die."†

There are several age junctures at which we "program our deaths" in tandem with our allotment. The turning-point at sixty is important because that is the second Saturn return and the time when genetics begins to really win out over attitude and perspective. The family core, as the legacy from your antecedents down to you, begins to weave its unique place for you in its tapestry. Thus, I have always seen this period—sixty—

*Victor Frankl, *Man's Search for Meaning* (New York: Washington Press, 1963), p. 127.
†Joan Borysenko, *A Woman's Book of Life* (New York: Riverhead Books, 1996), p. 230.

as a point of no return. The saying "point of no return" derives from an aviation expression meaning that an airplane has now passed the time at which it has enough fuel to go back to its starting point.

Death is something that becomes an issue in one's early seventies, especially if you are still alive. Ultimately, one needs to prepare and "get one's affairs in order." This includes a living will, and legally endorsed instructions to your family and friends for how you wish to be treated should you become seriously ill or mentally incompetent and are unable to control your life. This is both to assure you of your continuing control over your own life after you may have lost control over part of it, as well as to support your family and friends so they can not only go on without you but also feel that they did right by you.

It means thinking about the reality that the average American woman's life span is now seventy-five, and a man's is sixty-nine. On the average, women live 7.8 years longer than men, and thus, being widowed is more common than being a widower. It is entirely possible that if you are a woman of seventy-two you have already outlived your spouse(s).

Widowed women tend to outlive their spouses, on the average, by almost seventeen years! In contrast, men have been shown to wane in the six months to two years after the wife or partner has died. If a man has a strong life-focus and social activity, then after that his life span increases. But generally a man has less potential to recover his life-force when his long-term partner dies.

My own uncle Tom, who was partnered with Uncle Ron for over thirty-five years, died within a month of Ron's heart attack. Ron and Tom had been bonded so deeply for so long that even with positive thinking, forward plans, and loving family, my uncle Tom simply dropped dead of a heart attack himself one morning a month after Ron died. Both men were in their mid-sixties. I was personally devastated, but at the same time I realized that Tommy would not really have had his heart in his life without Ron, and I was so moved and impressed with his love for his partner that I was also happy for him. If we were to genderize their archetype, Ron was the feminine and Tom was the masculine of the pair. I feel strongly that if Tommy had died first, barring the Fates, that by his nature Ron would have survived him more readily and for longer.

Men are not only loners by nature (the hunter archetype) but also by culture—the "wife" is the one who is the networker, the arranger of dinners, movies, yard parties, and so on (the Gatherer). She (or the feminine of the partners) is the one who pries open the feelings of her partner and brings the family close and in touch. The feminine archetype is more capable of multitasking and has always got several things on the go, including the emotional management of herself, her partner, her family, and her friends as a priority.

They manage the calendar, just as they did in prehistoric times, and run the lives of those about them. They are the "family keepers," the backbone and skin of the social body. As a result, a man—or the masculine partner—often will go into a rapid decline after a grievous loss and not seek out a "talking cure" or a support network. If the wife had not died but only pretended to, he would have her doing all that for him. She would get him off to therapy, out with the men, and doing life-supportive things. But since she is not there, he won't do that.

JUPITER AND URANUS: TIME TO FLEE THE COOP

In this age frame, there are two main generic aspects. The first one to consider is the sixth Jupiter return combined with the sextile of transiting Uranus to natal Uranus.

Here we have two sky gods, both of whom are in "growth" and adaptation aspects (trine and sextile) thus supportive of a greater and more universal mental perspective. The increase in philosophical perspective (Jupiter) coupled with a natural detachment (Uranus) and the resulting liberation from the impatience of youth, urgency of the forties, the painful longings of midlife, and even the regrets of the sixties, brings this age into a golden one. As W. B. Yeats says, "let me die a foolish, passionate man."

Though we are creeping up on genuine "old age" at this time, the boost from Jupiter's return opens the door to a new twelve-year cycle of adventure. This adventurousness in a healthy body can bring a renewed interest in travel and exploration. Groups, tours, and cruises are full to capacity of individuals over the age of seventy! Especially now, with the advantages of better health—or at least better methods of dealing with

declining health—more people can take part in the activities and benefits that retirement brings.

There are many people who hop into their summer or winter vaca-
tion homes and drive them to destination spots where they can hang out
with other adventurous old folks and do it on a minimum budget. There
are many areas in the Southwest United States, for instance, that have
huge gatherings of retired people on a seasonal basis, getting together,
year in, year out, as a part-time lifestyle. They are called "snowbirds" or,
more irreverently, the gerontocracy of the Southwest! There are coastal
areas and mountain/lake areas around the world that are designed for retired people.

We look at all the new housing, especially in the most beautiful and
remote parts of the moderate and low latitudes, and cry because of their
relentless encroachment on nature. What we need to realize is that it is
due to demand, and that actually there are enough people who need and
will occupy these "blights on the landscape/seashore/mountaintop." My
own concept about the growth of civilization altered as I reached my
fifties and realized that—again—the huge Pluto in Leo generation is
now older, is not interested nor able to backpack or stay in hostels, carrying their croissants and lattes in bags, and who now has more free time
and disposable income as they reach their old age. They want retirement
homes and places to enjoy their latter years—even at the expense of nature and its uncluttered surrounds.

European destination spots are crowded. Asia, the Mediterranean,
the Caribbean—any place of beauty and isolation seems up for grabs.
For each generation, as it passes the torch of the future on to the next,
there is a wail of "It isn't like it used to be,"—and it isn't. However, it is
at this age, this phase of the seventies, that it is time to stop worrying
about the past, relinquish control over the future, and pass on the wisdom of one's years by acknowledging that there are things that are totally out of our hands. In other words, this is when it is time to let go of
hanging on to the past and enjoy the present.

The southeastern side of the American continent also offers travel,
adventure, and warmth to the elder populations, as it has since America
was populated by Europeans! A palm tree and a view of the Atlantic

Ocean from one's motel or mobile home is often the inexpensive luxury that prolongs a happy life. It is proven that people over the age of sixty-five who have friends, prolonged sunshine, relaxation in the form of games and physical exercise, and adventurous hearts live longer than people who don't make the effort or the time to play and are isolated from friends and/or family.

Since this age also is supported by the Uranus sextile, which is an aspect of innovative and radical change, especially in a social context, a form of healthy rebellion can arise. If one is mentally and physically still vigorous at this age, there is virtually nothing that cannot be achieved—within the context of one's actual age, of course.

The need for independence does not diminish until one truly feels it is time for increasing help. Assisted living communities are full of people who have simply decided that it was time for them to be respectfully attended to by professionals. And this is something that allows greater freedom of movement without jeopardizing friendships and family ties. Not every family is interested in housing their elders, and many elders do not want to live with their kids either. But in a reasonably healthy family, there is concern on all sides that all be "free" to live their lives in the way they want.

Often in this age frame one reconsiders one's lifestyle and one's friendships/acquaintances and begins to be more selective and think of the long term. Choices made within this supportive Uranus aspect that involve others or the society or groups are likely to be in the direction of greater freedom and less dependency upon others. Mind you, this could mean going into a retirement or health management home or center.

Freedom means a decrease in the need for "things" and a reduction of chores; fewer choices to be made; less stress in moving around; smaller spaces; time alone with the knowledge that it isn't a permanent aloneness—these are all very liberating ideas for a person who has the wisdom of years and the history of experience behind him or her, and an open road still in front.

The biggest single worry that aging people have expressed to me concerns what used to be called "senile dementia"—Alzheimer's disease. The fear of losing one's valuable marbles is acute. Since there has been such a positive focus on Alzheimer's and published personal stories, information, and literature—though no "cure" yet—society is approaching it with greater respect and understanding. This is no solace to an individual who may be symptomatic, but it is better than nothing, and certainly better than it was even in the mid-twentieth century.

In the case of small memory losses, and "spacing out," there are natural causes and thus natural purposes for it. In my discussion of ages seventy-five through ninety, I explore this natural phenomenon astrologically, neurologically, and spiritually.

Structuring life so that fewer surprises take place becomes important and essential, because one has reached the time in life in which a person deserves to have a ritual to count on and a safe life where more freedom is created. Things must be more planned, more in control, so that composure, dignity, and individuality are honored.

Time on one's own is essential, but not if the alone time is too extended or is not combined with company with others. At this time in life, one wants to have independence but not isolation. By the nature of aging, one's contemporaries thin out, and thus, family and/or community involvement needs to be part of the creation of one's own life. Planning, making calendars, and working in time for solitude and hanging out with one's own self are all important.

In *Solitude*, Anthony Storr says: "The happiest lives are probably those in which neither interpersonal relationships nor impersonal interests are idealized as the only way to salvation. The desire and pursuit of the whole must comprehend both aspects of human nature" (p. 202).

At this time in our lives, the building of character, the restoration of soul, and the continuum of individuation are the most productive acts in life. As I will show in the next chapter, preparation for life's natural course continues with energy and purpose. The intent of the soul to fulfill its sojourn in the body becomes increasingly more powerful.

CHAPTER 13

The Path Untrodden

Seventy-Five and Still Alive!

As I grow older and older,
And totter towards the tomb,
I find that I care less and less
Who goes to bed with whom.

—DOROTHY SAYERS

I want to begin this chapter with some feelings about aging from those who have reached seventy and beyond—clients, friends, and acquaintances. Not a single one of them thinks getting old is terrific. They don't all complain, but they have moved beyond a place where idealization of the aging process is possible. In the main, no one seems to like it much—especially not the body, as a less-than-ideal place—but most have come to terms with the inevitable process.

Those who are in good health and have maintained a lifestyle that includes physical, mental, and spiritual activity are not unhappy at all about getting older but are realistic and pragmatic about it.

FIGURE 10. THE PATH UNTRODDEN:
THE GENERIC ASPECTS FROM 75 TO 90

AGES 75–76   ♊ ♄

Fifth nodal return

Third Saturn opposition to its natal place (Saturn 180° Saturn)

AGE 80   ♄

Third Saturn square Saturn to its natal place

AGES 82–83   ☽

Third secondary progressed Lunar return

AGE 84   ♅ ♆ ♈ ♇

Uranus return

Neptune opposite Neptune (180°)

Seventh nodal inversion

Pluto in Leo generation receives Pluto in Aquarius opposite Pluto in Leo.

> *For the Pluto in Leo generation, the opposition of Pluto to Pluto occurs*
> *at age 85 within half a year or so of the Uranus return. This is the only*
> *Pluto sign to receive the opposition from itself before the age of 90*
> *(Pluto in Virgos receive the half-Pluto at 90)*

AGES 86–87   ♅ ♄

Uranus sextile Uranus (60°)

Saturn trine Saturn (120°)

AGES 89–90   ♄

Third Saturn return!

Though it is not a substantial part of my practice, I have several clients
who are past the age of seventy, and they are moving on toward their latter
years with lots to think about, many interests, and the time to pursue those
interests. The majority of them are enquiring not only about their health,
their long-term finances, their families, their home, and the timing for independent or even assisted living arrangements but also their spiritual lives.

Often their enquiry is about timing for elective surgeries such as hip or joint replacement and the like. They are also curious about the best timing for selling a no-longer-manageable large home, the best timing for a move to somewhere closer to their adult children, or even whether or not to move in with one of the children. They are seeking a continued conscious life, with as much comfort and self-awareness as possible.

People who are seeing an astrologer in latter years are still wedded to their individuation process, and are a minority in their own age group. Often they are artists, writers, or individuals deeply involved in their collective and community or in a spiritual practice that embraces life and death as a process. They often have a tribe or an affiliation with a group of people who are "on the same wavelength." These are the first to say that life continues to be challenging, interesting, deeply emotional, and full of realizations. Elders are even more aware that the threads that weave their tapestry of life are becoming increasingly significant—they say that it is more important to them that they live their truth than cooperate with the status quo.

Regrets are present—very much so—and there is an honesty that accompanies regrets told to me by elders. Often women regret not leaving a partner who was too controlling, who violated their truth and their reality, so as to maintain the status quo, and keep the home together for the children. Men will often regret their lack of full attention or involvement with their children, and their suppression of emotion and feelings.

I have an elder female client whose second husband died. She had had three children in her first marriage, none of whom were particularly close to her in spirit or geography; one daughter was in such a state of trauma about her mother that she was continually "mean" to her.

When her second husband died, she was seventy-three—so she had spent over fifty years as someone's wife and mother. The problem that arose after the loss of her second husband was realizing this very fact, and that she was now "free" for the first time in her life. Freedom at seventy is not freedom at twenty-one. Coming from a conventional place, her work had always been household oriented; maintaining a home and "doing" for her husband.

Suddenly, she was on her own, and the marital home was in a rural area, not close to amenities, clubs, hospitals, or senior places to attend meetings, lectures, films, and so on. The house had a large yard and much equipment—all toys of her late husband—and so on. Her shock was not only the loss of him but also the realization that she had very little of her own. This is a critical time, when a partner who has lost a long-term spouse "decides" to live on, or die soon afterward.

Since she felt her children to be either bossing her around or rejecting her for who she was, she fell into a very lonely place. She had contemporaries as friends, but they lived in the city—at least an hour's drive from her home.

After working through some of her guilt about putting the men in her life before her children, she came to some important realizations. She had been a man's woman, and now was on the brink of discovering who she was as an individual. It is never too late. I encouraged her to go into grief therapy, wherein she gained an ally and ongoing support to continue to unfold, and to discover her core self—who she was, what she wanted, and how she might go about fulfilling those needs.

Since our first consultation, and four consultations thereafter, she has sold the house, moved to a big city and condo near friends on the water, and begun attending photography courses, meeting people, and going to lectures. Her life has become an adventure and a learning experience. Her health, which is a problem as part of her aging body, has stabilized, and she can look forward—perhaps—to her Uranus return!

She has put her children in perspective; she has regrets, which she acknowledges, but she realizes that, like any other human being, she does not need to carry her children to the grave. Her kids are all over fifty, and thus really have to work on their own issues, and though she was not the perfect parent, I have yet to meet one. She was a "good enough" mother, but according to the kids, there remain problems. That is not really *her* problem now, as she walks toward the path that is only trod in the company of one's own self. It strikes me that it is even more important for the elder person to continue on the path of self-discovery, or there is not much else to do. Engaging in creative activity and giving out to others—if one is so inclined, that is good. I have discussed already the force and power of activity in aging.

The astrology of aging, if we stick by the generic transits from Saturn outward, becomes less active, and more time passes between aspects. If you look at the tables of midlife aspects between thirty-seven and sixty (figure 5) and then at the aspects between sixty and seventy-five (full adult maturity, figure 9), you see a decline of dynamic pressure.

Essentially, life is lived in sectors. There is a quick progression within the four seven-year cycles, from birth to the first Saturn return at twenty-nine, in which hundreds of aspects are taken into consideration.* From there we move on to the thirties, with rapid change and growth, and on to midlife, where there begins again a quickening of life-force, which is about twenty years long. From the astrology we have five major categorizations of life's transitional periods:

- *Birth to first Saturn return:* thirty years (four seven-and one-half-year cycles)
- *The thirties:* ten years
- *Midlife transition:* twenty years
- *Full maturity as an adult:* fifteen years
- *Elder status to Uranus return/Neptune opposition:* ten years

EIGHTY THROUGH EIGHTY-THREE: TO REMEMBER OR NOT REMEMBER

What is the worst of woes that wait on age?
What stamps the wrinkle deeper on the brow?
To view each loved one blotted from life's page,
And be alone on earth, as I am now.
      —LORD BYRON, *"Childe Harold's Pilgrimage"*
      canto stanza I, xcviii

At age eighty, a third square of Saturn to itself occurs. The first one was at twenty-one, the second at fifty-two, and now the final one brings increasing awareness of yet another threshold to be crossed.

*See Erin Sullivan, *Saturn in Transit: Boundaries of Mind, Body and Soul* (York Beach, ME: Weiser, 2000), pp. 33–67.

As Byron moans in his poem, there are fewer and fewer contemporaries around for the elder person, and more and more they are isolated by age, position, and lifestyle. The family becomes increasingly important to the eighty-plus individual, and though Byron was much younger than eighty when he penned these poignant lines, he felt the loss of his friends.

If we think of Saturn as the agency for structural change and acceptance of limitations and boundaries in our lives, then ideally this too is a period like the younger phases at twenty-one and fifty-two. The astrological similarities are about letting go of old friends and moving into a new realm of adulthood. At twenty-one, there is a distancing and separation from the friends of the teenage years, and a sudden growth spurt that challenges old companionable friends. Often at that age people complete schooling, enter the world as a fledgling adult, and broaden their horizons to include new and stimulating realms.

At fifty-two, people find themselves on another threshold of maturity where the friends and cronies of marriage and child-rearing often fade as one enters new areas—sometimes because of retirement, or relocation, or simply finding new ways of thinking and being.

At eighty, the options for choice in these matters are limited, and thus, the threshold that is crossed is almost purely based on family and circumstances. This is a time in one's life when one's beliefs and philosophies are firmly established, and it is essential for one's family and friends to accept this. It is highly unlikely that an elder is suddenly going to open his or her mind to a lot of new ways of thinking.

The formation of new relationships at this stage of life is largely dependent upon where and how one lives. I have a dear friend who at the age of sixty-nine began to develop Alzheimer's. She is a very sophisticated, well-traveled, and adventurous Sagittarius lady, and she comports herself with dignity even in the slow degeneration of her memory. She is accustomed to total freedom, and she has traveled the world many times over, and we had the most wonderful experiences when we traveled together. I was quite devastated by the discovery of her diagnosis and to realize that she would be in an assisted living condominium complex. I imagined her as she was, rather than how she is and will be.

One must not project one's own self onto any aging person. One must learn from aging friends and family members. We are often more miserable contemplating what we think their restrictions are than reality has it. The wonderful news I got from speaking with those "ordinary folks" over eighty was that they didn't really care much about it. I cared because I was "young," thinking how dreadful it must be—as most of us do. But it is not. It is only dreadful if pain, discomfort, or overextension of life has been such that one has passed one's "due date."

In these days of life-support systems, palliative drugs, and so on, it is essential that an old person have control over his or her life, and most especially after he or she really has lost control. I mentioned earlier the importance of making decisions about quality of life early on. One hopes that an eighty-plus person has made those decisions before modern medicine makes them for him or her.

One of our mutual friends met my lady Sagittarius friend at a large social event; she was holding hands with a distinguished-looking gentleman of similar age. Mildly concerned, but mostly excited, I emailed her daughter to ask about this, and yes, indeed, my friend has a gentleman friend who thinks she is beautiful (which she is) and exceptional (ditto) and loves her! They met at the complex, and have been in a loving and creative relationship ever since the first time they laid eyes on each other. Her daughter said wistfully that it was a shame they hadn't met years before—but isn't that a natural projection from a young, fruitful woman onto an old woman! As I am somewhere in between the two women's ages, I thought that this is the best time for her to have a lover enter her life.

There is an old joke about a couple in their late eighties who go to the justice of the peace to be married. The justice asks them how long they have been together, and they tell him twenty-six years. Astounded, the justice says, "Why have you waited so long to marry!?" They reply, "We were waiting for our children to die, because they didn't approve of our relationship."

In the case of artists, writers, and thinkers, this latter age is not their time of searching, exploring, or experimentation; it is the time of gathering a life work and establishing it for all time. This is the age to prepare and consolidate one's life work and goals so that a feeling of contentment and gratification comes from it.

For those who have a simple life, one of a more earthy type, where home and property and family are the central focus, then the satisfaction comes from seeing a life well lived, and receiving the rewards of it. Society's attitude and the general acceptance to old people is important, and this is where the advancing age of the Pluto in Leo generation (born 1937–1956) will have some influence for those who are born after that. Even if the government does not support its aging population, the re-gathering of the extended family will.

Fortunately, the longings and the needs we have at twenty, forty, and fifty-five are not at all what they are at seventy-five, eighty, and so on. Nature has a way for us to evolve, and thus, it is not with sadness and gloom that most people arrive at their later phases. Naturally, as with all rites of passage, there is a longing glance back, and a few regrets, but on the whole, acceptance is the mode of survival. There may be bouts of nostalgia, but nostalgia literally means the "pain of recall" (the Greek *nostos/algia*). For aged people, often, being forced to old remembrances is exceptionally painful, and they try to avoid talking about painful or re-gretful memories. Or nature softens her blows and the mind becomes in-creasingly selective about what it recalls! However, I have found that the older one actually is, the less pain is involved with the recollection of the past. Biology and neurology win out in the end.

EIGHTY-FOUR—IS THERE MORE?

To sleep, perchance to dream: ay, there's the rub;
For in that sleep of death what dreams may come
When we have shuffled off this mortal coil,
Must give us pause. There's the respect
That makes calamity of so long life.

—SHAKESPEARE, *Hamlet*, Act III, scene i

Ah, yes, the mortal coil. Our Western poets thrive on such things, but do we? By the time one has reached the hoary age of eighty-four, one is truly "stuck in one's ways." And, why not, I ask? One's ways have sus-tained one for a full circuit of the transit of Uranus, and if there is to be more innovation and ingeniousness beyond that, then it is a rare person who achieves it—and an even rarer person who truly cares.

The Uranus return is the "liftoff" aspect—at this life stage, there is little left of emotional attachment to things. There is a lot of history and wisdom in the heart, mind, and soul of an eighty-something person, but it lacks the lust, passion, and obsessive quality of the young spirit. There is little attachment to life itself—in a fearful fashion, that is. Yes, many elder people are afraid of dying, but the survey shows that they have arrived at a place of Uranian immorality. By age eighty-four, we come to a place of full individuation. The cycle of unfolding, reorganizing, and substantiating the ego is done by the time one completes the full cycle of Uranus.

If one is *compos mentis* and relatively at ease physically, then the capacity for wisdom is vast. The witness of Uranus has come full circle to give the individual the wisdom of the ages and the aged. Boring for some, the rambling interests of the aged can be compelling if one can restrain one's own desire to get a word in edgewise or offer up a comment—there is usually no need for a response or interchange. I have been seated between more retired judges and ministers at English dinner parties than I care to mention; they are a lot of fun. And the ladies of similar age are often very elegant, transcendent, and without gender issues, having come to terms either with their decorativeness or their naturalness. Certainly, if one is still struggling with the old problems of sexism, then one is still living in a past self-concept . . . a past that will never resolve.

When I was fifty-five, I went to a wedding of some young friends of mine, and was seated at a table with what some might have thought "boring old folks." It seemed that everyone else was sitting with the young and the cool, while I was seated between a dashing, elegant, conservative, seventy-five-year-old ex-ambassador, and an eighty-something ex–professor of literature, specializing in Shakespeare. Well, in the course of the dinner, on my right, I heard more about Shakespeare's metaphysics than I ever dreamed possible. This cute little man had spent an entire life pouring his wisdom into empty heads, all the while pursuing his passion of "occultism and Shakespeare," and it wasn't going to stop for some wedding party! Fortunately, I was quite content to hear all about it. I shall never again read King Lear with quite the same sensibility.

This book began with the half-cycle of Uranus and now, forty-two years later, ends the process of becoming, with the inauguration of the experience simply of being rather than doing. Uranus's transit "forces" conscious evaluation of one's self. The inner witness function contained in the psyche is symbolized in all Uranus traits. Since the Uranus return means that every possible psychic component in one's own unconscious and conscious mind has been shocked, awakened, observed, and transformed, then this next phase of life primarily involves detaching from mortal passions and longings and moving toward the immortal zone.

Not only does Uranus return at eighty-four but also there is the fifth nodal inversion. At this age, the nodal inversion has less to do with integrating isolated or segregated psychic components and more to do with moving closer to one's "home." Because we now are at an age when the concept of "accomplishment"—at its *most* ambitious—is about consolidating and collating one's life experiences and actions, rather than starting anew, this is a most satisfying astrology aspect; it puts longing and the pain of desire to rest.

Nodal inversions bring integration of one's inner opposing forces of life and death. At this stage, the psychological dance of Eros and Thanatos is a waltz, not a tango, and the interior life is much more attuned and harmonious than the external world around one. A more relaxed, or at least unattached, attitude becomes a sincere inner reality.

The planet Neptune opposes itself at this cycle too, along with a seventh return of Jupiter. These two spiritual agencies are meeting themselves in an interesting way. That Neptune is now in opposition to itself suggests a tunnel or passage from longing and desire toward spiritual fulfillment and illumination of spirit. In youth, Neptune filled us with imagination, longing, and fantasy about all possible things; midlife brought the square of Neptune to itself, dashing all hope of remaining forever young, replacing fantasy with real potential for spiritual growth; and by eighty-four, the longing for comfort, spiritual peace, and life's completion is the driving force that carries the soul to a place even more removed from the world of desire.

Jupiter's return symbolizes the growth spurt that occurs synchronously with the other two aspects—the Uranus return and Neptune opposition. Jupiter is the "god of religion" as well as the moral arbiter. The return of the concept of god, the divine, and the mythic relationship to human behavior becomes powerful. Regardless of one's religious training, many people in this age bracket do become "religious," in the sense that they are relating more to heavenly entities than earthly ones. God, the mystery of life, and the universal desire for unity with both transcends physical needs for accomplishment.

A RETURN TO THE ORAL TRADITION

There is more justification than just curiosity or quaintness for referring back to ancient myths and visions from traditions that are vastly older than the Euro-Western civilization. It is from these stories we gain insight into our contemporary psyche. The oral traditions from ancient through more modern times are valuable to us today as exemplars of archetypal experience. The loss of the oral traditions in contemporary cultures has been a great setback to modern culture but specifically has shunted the elders off to asylums, homes, and the basements of their families.

It was once the duty and the ceremony of the elders of tribes, colonies, and cultures to pass on the wisdom of the ages and the tales of human foibles and mortal nature and to transmit spiritual and earthly stories. To this day, the tales that the elders have in their minds are fascinating to younger people. There are many reasons for memory becoming increasingly selective in the elder years, not least of which is to remove the incidentals of everyday life so that the history and memory of the past is more acute and clear.

To restore the confidence and place of elders and aging people in our cultures, their stories need to be heard. Rather than writing off the ramblings of our neighbors or grandparents as the mutterings of old fools, we should be listening to them. For they have time that we do not—the time and the memory to relate stories that will have an impact, if we take the time to listen.

Not all elders are spokespersons for the gods, certainly, but they are the spokespersons of the origins of ideas, changes, and cultures for the younger generations. In your own family, for instance, they can recall the most intimate details of your own life; they have perception that has the distance of time and thus is not as egocentric or self-serving. So the next time Grandma hauls out the memorial "family album" and begins telling you a story about your infancy or childhood, or her memories of "how it used to be," take the time to hear her recollections, lest they are lost forever in the busyness of the teen, midlife, or even harassed late midlife years when "too much is going on."

Many communities have library or local projects that record—literally—an oral history. Especially if a cultural loss is evident, such as a native or other significant settlement society, then these oral-tradition recordings are paramount to the survival of these traditions.

RECOLLECTION, RETROSPECTION, AND THE RENEWAL OF THE GENERATIONS

The Uranus return passage gives the perspective of the heavens to what is left of the body on earth. An ancient Navajo metaphor for the Uranian witnessing I describe here is interesting. Since my own bloodline includes Native American ancestors, I am particularly attuned to lost cultures and subsumed civilizations.

The Navajo say that when we observe our lives from our earthly perspective, it is like looking at the underside of a woven rug where all the knots and ties show, and loose threads dangle, and the warp and woof are seen to be imperfectly interwoven. But when we look at our lives from a heavenly perspective, we are seeing the rug in all its divine perfection, from above, woven flawlessly, its pattern clear and crisp—the ideal patterns of our life.

Earlier I wrote about the agency and the character of Uranus, who is the heavens itself, and thus has a unique perspective from the upper aethers of our activities on earth. Witnessing, which is the Uranian agency for our capacity to "see from above" that which is below, becomes an exceptional advantage in old age. It replaces participation and subjectivity with long-range memory and historical perspective.

When Uranus returns at age eighty-four, the witness function is most powerful (though it begins to accelerate in the mid-seventies at the third

Saturn opposition), and it interacts with the oblivion of Neptune to bring a new type of consciousness to the aging mind. There are two important features to the dual interaction of Uranus and Neptune. Neptune removes the *details* of immediate actions, while Uranus recollects the gems from the past. Hence, the short-term-memory loss in old people was once the exaltation of the elders because of their capacity to recall history. And the long-term recall was the benefit, the legacy left to the younger generations.

As mentioned, the Neptune opposition obliterates much of short-term memory. This can be annoying to anyone, at any age, but when one is older, the fear that attends such memory blanks is compounded by the fear of developing senile dementia and Alzheimer's and so on.

However, the brain undergoes a periodic "pruning" process throughout its entire life, the first when it is developing in utero. The next major pruning occurs in adolescence, when the brain begins to civilize itself in the neo-cortex, lessening the limbic reaction of the pubescent and adolescent brain. There is always truth in nature, and the pruning of the aged brain has purpose and intent. The medical profession is wrong to call aging an illness that should be intervened and medically treated. Mind you, I am not disparaging good medicine, but pointing out something fascinating about the relationship between nature and culture. Nature has its own intelligent way of growth and decline—culture certainly improves on nature, but it can also suppress it.

For instance, by eighty-four, often one has had a series of minor blood clots or strokes—which are part of the pruning of the elder brain—that may have gone undetected. The collusion between the strokes I speak of and the old ways of the old tribes is profound. The natural strokes and clots of the aging brain do affect the short-term memory, but they can bypass and spare the long-term memory! Strangely, or should we say normally, there are certain tales and stories as well as abilities that a person affected by some forms of dementia can recall and relate perfectly!

As a Greek god, Neptune/Poseidon's realm was not only the sea but also underground freshwater streams and tributaries, earthquakes, and other "shape-shifting" earth traumas like earthquakes, floods, tsunamis, whirlpools, and the like.

There is an underworld river that, though it is not traditionally Neptune's domain, sounds suspiciously like it is affiliated with this planet/ god and its "oblivious" feature. In Plato's *Republic*, at the end of book 10, there is an allegorical tale about a man named Er, who was privileged enough to die and then return to his body with total recall of his soul's experience trekking through the realm of Hades, and the stages from death through reincarnation. Er tells the story:

After leaving the mortal body, and after many tests and selection processes, the immortal soul reached a vast, stifling plain that it had to cross. Upon crossing the blazing, parched terrain and reaching the edge, the soul came upon a river from which it was encouraged to drink to slake its thirst, before crossing over to the other side.

However, Plato says, "Those who were not saved by prudence drank more than their measure, and whoever drank more forgot everything."* Those, however, who drank only moderately were allowed a measure of recollection of all that their soul knew. The river was the River Lethe— the lethal river of oblivion or forgetfulness. Neptune sounds very much like the River Lethe, where we drink and forget, and individual recollection is lost to the soul incarnating in the womb.

The theory of recollection in Plato's ideal meant that we were born with all knowledge of everything right up to the minute of birth, and then "lost it," or "forgot it"—undoubtedly because of the amount or measure of Lethe's waters that was taken. The whole of incarnate life, then, was a process both of acquiring new knowledge and as well as the recollecting of all collective knowledge. Plato stresses the recollection of archetypal (*eidolon*) memories as the fundamental basis for life, and that only a fully recollected life was worth living. He has Socrates say "An unexamined life is not worth living," which after eighty years of life might seem extreme, but then the archetypes return to the elder mind in the form of paradigmatic tales!

Planets might be looked upon as places—compartments or *loci* that reserve memories or experiences. That we always associate the Moon with the womb as well as the mother is not incorrect, but it is incom-

---

*Plato, *The Republic, Great Dialogues of Plato*, W.H.D. Rouse, trans. (New York: Random House, 1956), p. 422 (book 10).

plete, because Neptune is the mythic Great Mother Womb, or the psychological collective unconscious. There are evolutionary theories about humanity swimming out from the primordial brine—which, hypothetical or not, is certainly true with respect to our births as individuals, considering that amniotic fluid is highly saline.

We emerge from the mother's body, the protective container (Moon) within which we were deeply guarded and sustained, suspended in the saline waters (a state of Neptune). That this moment of expulsion from the dark and timeless fortress is traumatic, both physically and psychologically, cannot be doubted. But how is it traumatic if we cannot recall it? In what way does this primal trauma affect one's consciousness in an everyday fashion? Trauma is any extreme experience, and as such, birth trauma is one shared by all. The separation from the all-giving life source and emergence into the limits and bounds of the world bequeaths a psychic longing to return to that place, where two hearts beat as one. The primordial fusion between body/soul and infant/mother is one that can never occur in normal states of living day to day, but comes closer as extreme age encroaches.

By the time Neptune has made transits to half the natal chart, the meeting of opposites—the Neptune opposition to itself—symbolizes the return to the Great Mother Womb, from which we all emerged, hence the infantile vulnerability of an old person.

Neptune guards the memory of the pain of separation from the mother-womb, never releasing it to full consciousness. It also acts as a repository for all subsequent births or losses, rejections and severings from secure, known places. Neptune anaesthetizes the pain of death-life, which is why so much credence lies in the traditional interpretations of Neptune being an escape from reality. However, reality may well be simply an accretion of the perceptions of all extant beings, all species and types, thus always morphing, and a highly subjective "interpretation" of the archetypal human experience.

And the Neptune opposition to itself in this age passage returns a person to the subjective realm of life, and to a kind of transcendent place of soulfulness. The river of oblivion flows through the subliminal mind, as does Lethe in the netherworld, offering the soul some earthly respite from the tedium and accomplishment that the body makes necessary.

When we say that extreme age is akin to infancy, that may only be true in the sense that one is closer to the unknown than in midlife—the unknown being before birth and after life. In astrological terms, the infant is not like the aged one, but they are linked by the spiral of life. The Neptune of the infant is not the Neptune of the aged. The Neptune of the infant is full of potential, whereas the Neptune of the elderly is full of experience. Thus, the dreams and the memories of the aged are enriched by the actual life lived, not by one that might be lived.

Transcendental aspects of Neptune can be activated through various forms of ritualized activity—be those psychotropic drugs or meditation practices, all are panaceas for *Weltschmertz* (global pain, world pain, or being-in-the-world pain). The astrological "residence" for that pain is Neptune, where it is absorbed, dissolved, and obliterated from consciousness.

The symbol of Neptune—the trident—depicts the tripartite mind/body/soul motif. Thus, the function of Neptune is toward a unity of disparate human conditions. And the emblematic life-journey from the boundless and all-encompassing place of the mother-womb ends ultimately as a return to the cosmic womb. So the Neptune opposition at eighty-four activates the soul's longing to return to that Elysian place, where it resides when not busily incorporated.

May the Force Be With You

I have mentioned Joseph Campbell as an exemplar of life and death timing. He was near the end of his life by no more than a few weeks when he undertook the filming of the now famous Bill Moyers series *The Power of Myth*. He did the filming when he was eighty-three, and only three months prior to his first Uranus transit to its natal place. His natal Uranus is 29° of Sagittarius in the third house, and closely opposed to Neptune. This interchange was apparent in his own life's end and was played out all through his life. (See figure 11 for his horoscope.)

Neptune is 3° of Cancer in his ninth house, and his reconnection of contemporary mentality back to the ancient gods of all time and all culture is his legacy to us. Indeed, his fascination with humankind's spirituality and the resulting religions of the world through all time is depicted with Neptune in the ninth house. In fact, religion itself derives from the Latin *religere*, meaning "to tie back, to bind back"—in the sense that religion is a way to link us to, bind us to, and tie us to something ineffable, to bring us back to something more profound than food and shelter.

His own religious leanings seemed to be without boundaries and more about circumambulating the core of religious experience. Campbell had natal Neptune in the ninth house. One could not even say he was polytheistic, as he was not a religious person but a spiritually alive person. In fact, to paraphrase a passage from one of his lectures that I attended in the early 1980s, he said that life was "not about seeking a meaning in life, but *seeking an experience of being alive*."

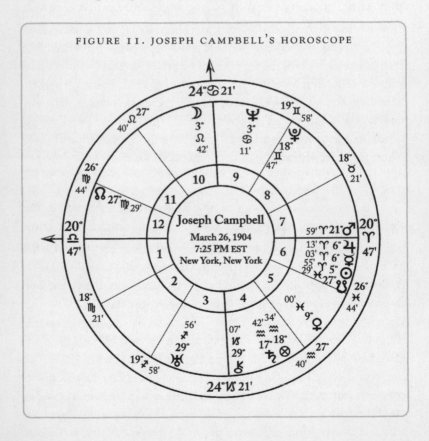

FIGURE 11. JOSEPH CAMPBELL'S HOROSCOPE

I will focus here on his Uranus return and the synchronous Neptune opposition. On October 30, 1987, the day he died, transiting Neptune was at 5° Cancer and had stationed direct in September at that degree, opposite to his natal Neptune, and exactly within minutes of the square to his 5° Aries Sun (which is conjunct Mercury at 6° Aries). This is a gentle aspect, slowly dissolving his life-force. Transiting Uranus was at 24° Sagittarius, within five degrees of his natal placement in the third.

So we had the Uranus return "liftoff" aspect, and Neptune opposite Neptune, the oblivion that cures. What a lovely and perfect aspect. His intellectual life was spent with books (Uranus third house) of cultural religions and myths (Neptune ninth house) and his life work was done—apparently. The interviews with Moyers were filmed at Lucas Ranch, George Lucas's home. George Lucas brought the power of the mythic hero's journey to the younger generation—actually, all generations—and he said in an interview that if he had never read *The Hero with a Thousand Faces* and met Joseph Campbell, he might still be writing *Star Wars* today and never have birthed it.

Brilliant legacy, isn't it? A man with an obsession and a passion, who never stopped exploring, and continued his mythic "rambles" into the last minutes of his life! And then, in the course of the year 1988, he became transasterized—that is, turned into a star at his actual Uranus return! Thank goodness for that!

As he himself said: "Full circle, from the tomb of the womb to the womb of the tomb we come: an ambiguous, enigmatical incursion into a world of solid matter that is soon to melt from us, like the substance of a dream."*

THIRD SATURN RETURN

The third Saturn return is a juncture many of us will not achieve, but for those who do, if their bodies are relatively comfortable, and their lives

---

*Joseph Campbell, *The Hero with a Thousand Faces* (Princeton, NJ: Princeton University Press, 1949), p. 12.

well managed, then they are an honor to the community and considered almost "holy" by people who know them and care for them.

Because of longer lives, this is a time not only when one might have grandchildren but also great-grandchildren to relate to, and with that see one's own future. The people I have spoken to who are in their nineties have openly, without emotion or sadness, talked about their death and their feelings about it as they come to meet their own authenticity at the third Saturn return and take another step beyond the family and toward the great unknown.

The first Saturn return at 29½ years of age was the "emergence from the family matrix," and a departure from the family as the primary point of reference. At their first Saturn return people are truly on the path to their individuation and adulthood. They undergo a reevaluation of their place in the family and in the world.

At the second Saturn return we saw that there was a recapitulation of the first one, wherein the family becomes again a focal point for identity, but in the sense of being the elder and thus having some *gravitas* in the family. Often by the second Saturn return, family issues that were problematic at forty are no longer problematic at sixty. This is due both to the maturation of any children of the sixty-plus person, as well as the mellowing and acceptance of one's sixty-year-old self.

At age sixty is the harmonious sextile of Solar Arc direction to the natal planets in the horoscope. At age ninety, the Solar Arced planets are *trine* to the natal horoscope planets. The entire chart is in harmonic agreement that the creative force of life—libido/eros—has reached a creative juncture. And since the trine that the Solar Arcs form to the natal planets is a "first/fifth house" trine, we are looking at a profound and creative return to Selfhood—to childhood, only in the sense that there are no projections upon life but meeting life as it arrives.

At ninety, the Self's impetus is toward the matrix of the cosmic family, the family of humanity where all are equal. The more consciously that one has arrived at this great age, the less fear surrounds one about the next stage in their journey. The primary concern is comfort, warmth, love, and freedom.

ACKNOWLEDGMENTS

All books have an inside story and a unique journey for the author—and any journey has its helpers and tricksters on the path. Both are necessary agents in all life's acomplishments.

To the many helpers—who far outnumber the triksters—I owe much, and to some of them I acknowledge their help in various ways and sundry guises:

To: Pythia Peay, author, who introduced me to Mitch Horowitz, the editor of Tarcher, I offer appreciation and thanks.

To: Mitch Horowitz. On December 15, 2003, he accepted the book. *Midlife and Aging* was contracted in January 2004 for publication in spring 2005. His belief in my work and the encouragement and effort he has brought to this book made all worthwhile. Mitch's recognition of astrology's place in the world of ideas and his passion for bringing the fires of antiquity to the contemporary thinker are both rare and inspired. Indeed, he said, "You know, one of the things that makes me bound out of bed each day is the certainty that we're really working with material that is kind of a surviving bonfire from antiquity; without serious attention to these ideas, they'd just die." Bravo.

To: Rebecca Martin and Nancy Booth—friends, colleagues, and soul mates. To Rebecca for her brilliance in programming and designing the unique and beautiful reports for Southwest Contemporary Astrology. To Nancy for her faith and forebearance and insight, as a co-creator of the *Solar Return Reports*. And to both of them for their unstinting support of my own work and their joint work within Southwest Contemporary Astrology!

To: David and Fei Cochrane and Ray Merriman—truth seekers and minions of justice all. Thanks!

To: My precious family: Yesca and Ralf and their son, Sascha, and daughter, Brooklynn; and to Spirit and Philip and their daughter, Sienna . . . without whom nothing is possible. And, finally, from the long past midlife juncture of my own, an overdue blessing to the classics department of the University of Victoria, who, almost twenty years ago, unwittingly offered succor and safety in a world of dead languages, myth, ancient philosophy, and the origins of Western civilization. Too, the wit and hilarity found there were a relief from the everyday contemporary world. I went there with a big question, and emerged with a renewed direction. The temenos of the university nurtured me through to my move to London and Penguin Books in 1989.

To three faculty especially:

Peter Smith, who introduced Greek, and made Latin worth getting up at 6:00 a.m. to get to class by 8:00 and was good for at least one belly laugh a class.

John Fitch, whose courses filled me with inspiration, thought, and who encouraged me to incorporate the classics into my already well-developed body of work—astrology and Jungian psychology.

And, to Gordon Shrimpton, who remains my friend and ally, and who, over many lunches at the Faculty Club, walks in the campus gardens, and intense discussions, fed my heart and soul.

Without them all, I might not have taken the midlife journey I chose. The depth and richness of that midlife threshold has made the "second half" of my life meaningful beyond imagination. The validation I received for living a contemplative life, a rich life of thought and exploration, I found there. All that now lies at the root of my work today. From them I learned to write good English well, and never to need a dictionary. To my many years of clients and students—thank you for your lives and stories . . . And, of course, always, to Howard Sasportas.

RECOMMENDED READING AND RESOURCE MATERIALS

Alpert, Richard. *Fierce Grace*. Film/video. Richard Alpert/Ram Dass in his seventies, after his stroke. A history and perspective on aging, with a powerful edict to Baby Boomers.

Beauvoir, Simone de. *The Coming of Age*. Translated by Patrick O'Brian. New York: Putnam, 1972.

Bly, Robert. *A Little Book on the Human Shadow*. San Francisco: Harper, 1988.

Borysenko, Joan. *A Woman's Book of Life: The Biology, Psychology, and Spirituality of the Feminine Life Cycle*. New York: Riverhead Books, 1996.

Bridges, William. *Transitions: Making Sense of Life's Changes*. Reading, MA: Addison-Wesley, 1980.

Campbell, Joseph. *The Hero with a Thousand Faces*. Princeton, NJ: Princeton University Press, 1949.

Campbell, Joseph. *Myths to Live By*. New York: Viking Press, 1972.

Dowrick, Stephanie. *Intimacy and Solitude*. London: Women's Press, 1992.

Eliade, Mircea. *The Sacred and the Profane: The Nature of Religion*. Translated by Willard Trask. London: Harcourt, Brace, Jovanovich, 1959.

Engelsman, Joan Chamberlain. *The Queen's Cloak: A Myth for Mid-life*. Wilmette, IL: Chiron, 1995.

Freudenberger, Herbert, and Gail North. *Women's Burnout*. New York: Penguin, 1986.

Gosden, Roger. *Cheating Time: Sex, Science and Aging*. London: Macmillan, 1996.

Hildebrand, Peter. *Beyond Midlife Crisis: A Psychodynamic Approach to Ageing*. London: Sheldon Press, 1995.

Hillman, James. *The Force of Character and the Lasting Life*. New York: Random House, 1999.

Hillman, James. *The Puer Papers*. Irving, TX: Spring, 1979.

Hogrefe, Jeffrey. *O'Keefe: Life of an American Legend*. New York: Bantam, 1992.

Homer. *The Odyssey*. Translated by Robert Fitzgerald. New York: Anchor Press, 1963.

Johnson, Robert. *Inner Work: Using Dreams and Active Imagination for Personal Growth*. San Francisco: Harper, 1986.

Jong, Erica. *Fear of Fifty*. San Francisco: Harper, 1994.

Jung, Carl Gustav. *Memories, Dreams, Reflections*. New York: Random House, 1965.

Lewis, Jim. *Peter Pan in Midlife: And the Midlife of America*. Edited by Erin Sullivan posthumously. Santa Fe/Silver City, NM: Southwest Contemporary Astrology, 2002.

O'Connor, Peter A. *Facing the Fifties: From Denial to Reflection*. Allen and Unwin, 2000.

O'Connor, Peter A. *Understanding the Mid-life Crisis*. New York: Paulist Press, 1981.

Roszak, Theodore. *America the Wise: The Longevity Revolution and the True Wealth of Nations*. New York: Houghton Mifflin, 1998.

Rubin, Lillian B. *Tangled Lives: Daughters, Mothers, and the Crucible of Aging*. Boston: Beacon Press, 2000.

Ruperti, Alexander. *Cycles of Becoming*. Davis, CA: CRCS, 1978.

Sasportas, Howard. *The Gods of Change: Pain, Crisis and the Transits of Uranus, Neptune and Pluto*. Contemporary Astrology Series. London and New York: Arkana, 1989.

Sasportas, Howard. *The Twelve Houses*. London: Aquarian Press, 1985.

Spiker, Stuart F., Kathleen M. Woodward, and David D. Van Tassel, eds. *Aging and the Elderly: Humanistic Perspectives in Gerontology*. Atlantic Highlands, NJ: Humanities Press, 1978.

Stein, Murray. *In Midlife: A Jungian Perspective*. Woodstock, CT: Spring, 1983.

Storr, Anthony. *Solitude*. London: HarperCollins, 1994.

Sullivan, Erin. *Saturn in Transit: Boundaries of Mind, Body and Soul*. York Beach, ME: Weiser, 2000.

Sullivan, Erin. *Your Personal Heroic Journey*. A personalized report by Erin Sullivan that describes the transit of Saturn from birth through age ninety. Santa Fe/Silver City, NM: Southwest Contemporary Astrology, 2002. For online purchase go to: www.ErinSullivan.com.

Von Franz, Marie-Louise. *Puer Aeternus*. Santa Monica, CA: Sigo Press, 1981.

Von Franz, Marie-Louise. *Creation Myths*. Dallas, TX: Spring, 1972.

Wickes, Frances. *The Inner World of Choice*. Santa Monica, CA: Sigo Press, 1988.

INDEX

About the Author

Erin Sullivan's thirty-something years of astrology practice and teaching, along with her background in classics and psychology, add a unique depth and breadth to her writing and practice. Her six major astrology books span the technical through the humanistic.

Erin's worldview always incorporates the big picture—long cycles—and contributes much to her understanding of the human condition. Her focus and skill lie in working with people in all stages of life.

Living and practicing in London from 1988 to 1989, she was also the series editor for Penguin Arkana's prestigious Contemporary Astrology Series.

Canadian born and world traveled, Erin now resides in Santa Fe, New Mexico, near her family. Go to her website for books, articles, personalized reports, and more: http://www.ErinSullivan.com.